D0055667

WHEN TEENAGERS WORK

WHEN
TEENAGERS
WORK

THE PSYCHOLOGICAL AND

SOCIAL COSTS OF

ADOLESCENT EMPLOYMENT

ELLEN GREENBERGER

LAURENCE STEINBERG

BASIC BOOKS, INC., PUBLISHERS

NEW YORK

Library of Congress Cataloging-in-Publication Data

Greenberger, Ellen.
  When teenagers work.

  Bibliography: p. 255.
  Includes index.
  1. Youth—Employment—United States.   2. Part-time
employment—United States.   3. Youth—Employment—
Psychological aspects—United States.   I. Steinberg,
Laurence D., 1952–   . II. Title.
HD6273.G74   1986   331.3'4'0973   85–73885
ISBN   0–465–09180–6

Copyright © 1986 by Basic Books, Inc.
Printed in the United States of America
Designed by Vincent Torre
86 87 88 89 RRD 9 8 7 6 5 4 3 2 1

HD
6273
.G74

To Mike, David, and Kari

and Wendy and Benjamin

DEXTER LIBRARY
NORTHLAND COLLEGE
ASHLAND, WI 54806

"[They go to work] with no plan and no training; their jobs usually anything they can get, having nothing to do with their interests and their capacities, only with business demand. . . . What would the average middle-class parent say to such an 'educational' program for his adolescent boys and girls?"

—Katharine DuPre Lumpkin
and Dorothy Wolff Douglas,
Child Workers in America (1937)

CONTENTS

ACKNOWLEDGMENTS

This book had its beginnings several years ago when we initiated a research project to study the effects of working on adolescent development. We acknowledge with gratitude the generous research support of the National Institute of Education and the Spencer Foundation. Throughout the project, we had the benefit of a highly talented and hard-working staff. We note especially the contributions of Mary Ruggiero, Alan Vaux, Laurie Garduque, and Sharon McAuliffe. A Ford Foundation grant enabled us to discuss youthwork with colleagues in Europe and to present the findings of our research to educators, psychologists, anthropologists, and policy makers. The grant also supported the early phases of our work on this book.

In the course of our own project on adolescent work, and in the ensuing years of researching and writing this book, we drew substantially on the resources of several friends and colleagues. It is a pleasure to acknowledge their contribution to this volume.

Urie Bronfenbrenner has been a thoughtful commentator on our research since its inception. His classic articles on the ecology of human development influenced the way we conceptualized a number of key issues. The 1973 report of the Panel on Youth of the President's Science Advisory Committee, chaired by James S. Coleman, presented an articulate advocacy of adolescent work. It sparked our interest in, and skepticism about, the value of youngsters' early labor-force experience under the conditions that prevail today. We are grateful as well to Jerald Bachman and his colleagues at the Institute for Social Research, the University of Michigan, who on several occasions provided us with information from their surveys of high-school seniors; to Jeylan Mortimer, for making research in progress available to us; and to Margaret M. Marini, for encouragement and valuable criticism of papers and chapters. Urie Bronfenbrenner and Jerald Bachman gave a close reading to a draft of the book and made excellent suggestions that helped us to improve the final manuscript. Our editor, Jo Ann Miller, raised good questions, gave good advice, and made sound judgments, all of which contributed to the final product. Jill Vidas processed and reprocessed substantial portions of the manuscript competently and cheerfully. To our families, we express our special gratitude. Over the course of a task that took us far longer than we anticipated, they gave us exceptional consideration and warm encouragement.

FOREWORD

by Urie Bronfenbrenner

The research presented in this volume documents the first systematic effort to explore a hitherto uncharted domain in the life of American adolescents. As the reader will discover, the findings confront social scientists and citizens alike with some disquieting facts and forebodings. The confrontation to researchers should be especially sobering, for it hoists them by their own petard. As the authors duly record, in the 1970s a series of blue-ribbon commissions, including the President's Scientific Advisory Committee, concerned by what they viewed as signs of increasing social deviance and lack of motivation among the young, recommended as a high policy priority the involvement of adolescents and youth in the world of work. Such involvement, the experts argued, would further the development of responsibility and, thereby, prepare the young to function more effectively in adult roles.

As revealed in the pages that follow, rarely have the recommendations of social scientists been so rapidly and fully transformed into reality (albeit by far more powerful forces than exist at the social scientist's command) And rarely have the consequences of a recommended reality proved so contrary to the original scientific predictions. Yet, as one of the "experts" whose prescience is contradicted by the science here reported, I hasten to add that rarely has a set of unexpected

findings had so much significance for future work in both
science and society.

This fruitful outcome is no accident. Although the authors'
findings are indeed unexpected from the general perspective
both of social science and popular wisdom, they are not seren-
dipitous, for the obtained results have emerged from a carefully
developed set of hypotheses based on a new and growing body
of theory and research on the forces that shape human development in the actual settings in which children live their lives.
The newer paradigms emphasize the importance of events and
processes taking place not only within and between these immediate settings, but also within the broader social, economic,
and historical contexts in which these settings are embedded.
Thus, in the chapters that follow, Greenberger and Steinberg
show that today's massive entry of teenagers into the labor
force while they are still attending school is a distinctively
American phenomenon arising from a convergence of at least
four sets of forces: (1) the comparatively recent yet profound
economic and occupational changes that have taken place in
all postindustrial societies; (2) a powerful ideology about the
psychological meaning of work deeply rooted in American history and culture; (3) the legacy of the 1960s in the encouragement of parental permissiveness and youthful self-gratification;
and (4) the increased emphasis on materialism and consumerism manifested in the society at large, and stimulated and
sustained on a massive scale by the mass media, with intensive
programming specifically directed at teenage—and what is
equally important—pre-teenage populations.

Having delved into the tangled roots of flourishing adolescent employment, the authors then proceed to trace the
growth of its bitter fruit. Once again, the emphasis is as much
on the ground as on the final figures. The investigators begin
with a careful description of the shallow soil and colorless
shadows of the settings in which "the average employed high-
school senior, working the average 20 hours per week at the

minimum wage, earns about \$275 per month." The motiva-
tion?—to be able to sustain the materialistic life-style to which
he or she has become accustomed. The unchallenging nature
of the paid work that the majority of today's adolescents do is
succinctly captured by the titles of the two job categories that
engulf almost half of all high-school seniors—store clerks and
food service workers. The pattern departs sharply from that of
a generation ago, when the mainstays of adolescent employment were skilled trades, farm work, and factory work. As the
authors document in their detailed descriptions, including the
apathetic comments of the adolescents themselves, the jobs of
today are dead-end and dull in contrast with the jobs of the
past. The patterns differ in yet another respect. Whereas not
so long ago it was the children of blue-collar families and of the
poor who predominated in the youth labor force, today the
earliest and most numerous entrants into the world of work are
the children of the well-to-do and well-educated. This is for two
reasons: first, they live in the economically thriving, typically
suburban areas where the service jobs abound; second, their
parents, moved by the same forces of materialism, now see
earning money as no less important an experience for their
children than gleaning knowledge.

But the most telling data provided in this revealing research
are those that emerge from the longitudinal and cross-sectional
comparisons assessing the impact, over time, of work experience on the young person's schoolwork, social behavior, attitudes, and aspirations. The dramatic disparity between expert
expectation and social reality is best conveyed in a brief summary by the authors themselves:

> Many of our findings will undoubtedly surprise those who advo-
> cate hefty doses of work experience for young people. Among the
> most striking of these findings are that extensive part-time employ-
> ment may have a deleterious impact on youngsters' schooling; that
> working appears to promote, rather than deter, some forms of
> delinquent behavior; that working, especially in the high-stress jobs

held by many teenagers, leads to higher rates of alcohol and drug use; and that, for many youngsters, working fosters the development of negative attitudes toward work itself.

In illuminating the context, causal chain, and consequences of adolescent employment, Greenberger and Steinberg exploit an impressive range of concepts and methods from a variety of disciplines. Thus, for the early chapters of the volume they draw heavily on the knowledge and skill of the historian, the demographer, and the sociologist. Their own training and experience in the study of human development, however, leads them to apply this contextual material in a manner and for a purpose seldom encountered in the discipline of origin— namely, analyzing how the broader context shapes the processes taking place in the immediate settings in which human beings live and grow, and how these processes in turn affect the competence and character of the next generation.

Herein lies the principal strength of this exciting work. In their marshaling of information and ideas from many disciplines to focus on processes of psychological growth at the individual level, the authors exemplify a major new direction in contemporary developmental science. The power of this approach is manifested not only in the new knowledge it provides, but also in the new vistas that it opens for future inquiry. Given the scope of the problems that their initial surveys revealed, the authors were wise in assigning top research priority to studying the disruptive effects of adolescent employment and the processes through which these effects come about. This proper emphasis, however, necessarily leaves unexplored the alternative—and apparently more psychologically rewarding—pathways followed by those youngsters who, for reasons still to be understood, take a different route. For example, what were the experiences of those teenagers who did not work extensively that enabled them to withstand the debilitating influences of job and peer group? The same question applies to those employed youngsters who were exceptions to the rule,

who worked in a boring or stressful setting but remained im-
mune to alienation.

The fact that such questions can now be raised is, in a very
real sense, no less a contribution of Greenberger and Steinberg's
seminal work than the provocative answers that have emerged
from their data. For it is the special strength of research on
development-in-context that the unanswered questions it raises
today become the key issues for the science and the society
of tomorrow.

WHEN TEENAGERS WORK

Introduction

THE NATURE of adolescence in American society has undergone a dramatic change over the past forty years. In increasing numbers, school-age adolescents have entered the workplace, holding part-time jobs after school that consume substantial portions of their afternoons, school nights, and weekends. The large teenage, part-time labor force that staffs the counters of fast-food establishments, waits on customers in retail stores, assembles parts in industrial settings, and cleans motel rooms and office buildings has become such a familiar part of our social landscape that we may fail to note its unique character or to ponder its larger social significance.

The burgeoning teenage labor force is unique in many respects. Although adolescents have worked in other eras, those who work today have different social origins and different motivations for employment than their earlier counterparts. The work they perform is also different, both in kind and in organization. And the student worker *per se* is a distinctly American phenomenon. In many countries of the western world, it is virtually unheard of for youngsters to participate intensively in the labor force while in school. The reasons why American teenagers are flocking to the workplace are embedded in events that have taken place in the school, the family, and the economy—and in the motives, values, and aspirations of young people themselves.

Until recently, the emergence of the world of work in the life of adolescents has gone largely unremarked and unstudied by psychologists and sociologists. In most classic studies of adolescence, the family, school, and peer group are identified as the major settings in which the socialization and development of youth take place (Coleman 1961; Douvan and Adelson 1966; Kandel and Lesser 1972). It is clear, however, that this vision needs to be corrected. The social ecology of adolescence has changed. The workplace, along with the more familiar settings in which children and youth come to maturity, now also gives shape and meaning to the lives of adolescents. Moreover, the addition of this "new" setting to the ecology of adolescence has reverberations in other parts of the social system. The significance of teenagers' immersion in the workplace, in other words, lies not only in the effects of working on young people themselves but in the effects of their employment on family life, the school environment, and peer relations.

Many people welcome the increased participation of the young in the world of work. Among these advocates of teenage work one finds youth policy experts, school critics, guidance counselors, representatives of industries and firms that depend on high-school students to fill part-time jobs, and parents of teenage workers. They think it is good for youngsters to get their feet wet in the real world. They speak of teenagers' learning to assume responsibility. They note that working youngsters can help their families financially, or underwrite their own luxury expenditures. Perhaps most important, they interpret job-holding as welcome evidence of a youngster's increasing maturity and believe that working during the high-school years will lead to a smoother transition to adulthood. This line of thought, which links working with maturity, rests on certain assumptions about how one goes about becoming an adult. Some advocates of youthwork believe that maturity involves the ability to perform roles typically filled by adults. And since one of the chief roles adults occupy is that of worker, job-holding by adolescents is viewed as an important step in the direction of growing up.

Other observers, who espouse a more internal definition of maturity, warn that a superficial ability to play adult roles can be achieved without commensurate development of self-understanding or clarification of social experience (Erikson 1959; Friedenberg 1959). Young people, they caution, may acquire the appearance but not the substance of maturity. What passes for maturity in fact may be *pseudomaturity*. In their view, true maturity requires the development of complex cognitive structures, including a stable sense of who one is; how one got to be that way; what the world is, and should be, like; and how one can "put it all together" in a coherent and meaningful way of life. These accomplishments come about over the course of adolescence and young adulthood, they believe, as a result of strenuous introspection, active engagement with others, experimentation in a variety of social roles, conflict, and often grievous (but nonetheless useful) mistakes. Heavy commitment to the role of worker may interfere with this time-consuming, unpaid, and vitally important work of adolescence.

The merits of these competing perspectives on adolescent work cannot be judged without recourse to empirical data. As we noted before, social scientists have been slow to turn their attention to the adolescent workplace and bring research to bear on issues arising from adolescents' increased labor-force activity. Deeply rooted convictions about the positive force that work exerts on people's lives—convictions that form part of a "dominant value configuration" in American culture (Williams 1970)—have made it difficult for us to look at youthwork with a critical eye. Over the past five years, however, a number of researchers have taken an interest in what adolescents do at work and what working does to them. Their studies focus on youngsters' employment during the school year in the kinds of ordinary, private-sector jobs that account for most adolescent work. We describe the findings of these studies in several of the ensuing chapters, in a way that we hope preserves their scientific integrity while maintaining the reader's interest. Unless otherwise noted, we discuss only those research findings that meet conventional standards of statistical significance. For the most part, we avoid technical language and extensive description of the methods of data analysis that were employed. However, some especially important methodological details are covered in notes at the end of the book and in the appendix. In addition, we provide citations to the original scientific publications for readers who are interested in pursuing a particular issue further.

The findings of recent research on youthwork constitute a challenge to popular wisdom and conventional belief. Some of the findings will surprise those who believe that hefty doses of work experience are a sure cure for an assortment of adolescent vagaries. Among the most striking of these discoveries are that extensive part-time employment during the school year may undermine youngsters' education; that working leads less often to the accumulation of savings or financial contributions to the family than to a higher level of luxury consumer spending; that working appears to promote, rather than deter, some forms of delinquent behavior; that working long hours under stressful conditions leads to increased alcohol and marijuana use; and— the *coup de grâce*—that teenage employment, instead of fostering respect for work, often leads to increased cynicism about the pleasures of productive labor. Findings such as these lead us to conclude that the benefits of working to the development of adolescents have been overestimated, while the costs have been underestimated.

We cannot be certain that youthwork had more positive consequences in the past. We believe, however, that insofar as working today may be unproductive for many youngsters, or have negative consequences for their development, the fault lies largely in the kinds of jobs we make available to youth and with the broader social context of their employment. Once both similar and relevant to adult work, adolescent work is now, for the most part, totally different from the type of work youngsters will do in the future. Once motivated by the economic needs of the family and the community, most adolescent work today represents "luxury" employment, of which adolescents themselves are the chief beneficiaries. And the workplace, once an arena where the generations were united in common tasks, is now an age-segregated adolescent stronghold. Under these conditions, we argue, involvement in a job may not advance the transition to adulthood so much as prolong youngsters' attachment to the peer culture.

Stated more broadly, extensive commitment to a job may interfere with the work of growing up. In a society where it is possible to make a quite different life from that of one's parents, and where the diversity of choices that lie before most youngsters is truly staggering, adolescents need time for identity clarification. From this perspective, psychoanalyst Erik Erikson (1968) has written of the adolescent's need for a "psychosocial moratorium"—a period of relative freedom from the kinds of roles and responsibilities that curtail identity exploration, a period in which there is time to ponder what sort of person one really is, try out different aspects of the self, and explore ways of fitting oneself into meaningful social roles. Excessive commitment to a job may pose an impediment to development, by causing adolescents to spend too much time and energy in a role that is too constraining and involves tasks that are too simple, unchallenging, and irrelevant to their future to promote development. Excessive involvement in work may promote instead what sociologist David Riesman, in a different context (see Friedenberg 1959), has called an "adjusted blandness" on the part of adolescents, at a time in life when curiosity, imagination, and combativeness may augur better for young people themselves and for the improvement of society. Too much time in the adolescent workplace is likely to mean too little time for exploration—including exploration of better, more adult jobs that do not offer pay; for discovering academic and extracurricular interests that are satisfying; for testing out changing conceptions of oneself; and for reflection that leads to the meaningful integration of one's experiences. Sheer lack of time or freedom, for the sake of getting on the payroll early, may interfere with the important psychosocial work of adolescence.

The crux of our argument is that undue emphasis has been placed on the value of work experience to adolescents—and unfounded hope pinned on its singular developmental benefits. Some readers may think to dismiss our argument as "middle class" in perspective: naive about the realities of life that many young people face, irrelevant to all but a privileged (or overprivileged) segment of the population, and unduly protectionist. We believe that such criticism misses the point.

Most youth who work, or work long hours, do not do so primarily out of dire economic need. In fact, youth from the lowest income strata are the least successful in obtaining school-year employment; and fewer than one in ten adolescents who hold a job during the school year contribute a substantial portion of their paycheck to the support of their families (Johnston, Bachman, and O'Malley 1982). Because youngsters from all social classes work after school and on weekends, our arguments pertain to youth from a broad social spectrum, who will pursue a variety of paths after high school. Insofar as we question the value of *extensive* employment during adolescence, moreover, it is not because we see adolescents as too fragile for the rigors of the workplace. Rather we feel that they may be bypassing the equally rigorous, but unpaid, work of growing up

—work that requires exploration, experimentation, and intro-spection. These activities, along with the concept "identity formation," have the ring of class and privilege. There is no intrinsic reason, however, that they should be the exclusive province of the well-to-do. Insofar as overcommitment to work stands in the way of these experiences, it is not good for adolescents, whatever their social circumstances.

Of course, we recognize that some adolescents desperately need their paycheck in order to assist an impoverished family; and some youth have such overwhelming intellectual or psy-chosocial handicaps that experimentation and introspection are impossible, and choice illusory. But for the majority of teenagers, the value of working needs to be weighed against the payoff from other activities. And for all adolescents who work —especially those who must work for economic reasons—we need to consider what makes for "better" work. Most youth can profit, presumably, from good work experience in suitable amounts. None will profit from an overdose of low-quality work experience that deprives them of their full measure of identity development.

Debate about whether working is "good" for adolescents, or better, under which conditions it may be "good," is not a trivial matter. The advent of the student worker has changed the nature of adolescence in our society, and the implications of this change are potentially vast. The experiences we offer adolescents and encourage them to master during the crucial preadult years help determine the assets and debits they will bring to adulthood.

CHAPTER

1

Teenage Work in America

WORK is a pervasive feature of human life. Teenagers in all eras have produced goods or services of socially recognized value. They have helped out in the household, lent a hand in family enterprises, toiled in a variety of newly mechanized jobs during the early phases of the industrial revolution, gone to the fields during the harvest season, and held occasional odd jobs outside the regular economy. Historically, however, working and going to school were, for the most part, mutually exclusive activities. In earlier periods of our history, children whose families needed their labor or the wages they could earn did not go to school after their work could make a significant contribution to the household; on the other hand, children whose families were affluent went to school and did not work.

During the last several decades, however, attending school and working have become firmly joined. One source estimates that 63 percent of high-school seniors and 42 percent of sophomores are working at any given time during the school year—figures that, when extrapolated to juniors and freshmen, indicate that well over a million high-school students between the ages of fourteen and eighteen are employed.[1] By the time they are seniors, over two-thirds of employed youth will spend fifteen hours or more per week in the workplace. And by the time of graduation, 80 percent of youngsters will have held a job during the school year at some point during their high-school career.

It is instructive to place the current situation in historical perspective. Social historians have noted that the demand for labor from children and adolescents is strongly tied to economic conditions and that adolescence itself may be considered an "invention" of prosperous societies. In many societies children acquired adult status as soon as they were able to do the work of adults. Only in societies that are sufficiently prosperous and productive has an interim period been introduced between childhood and adulthood that delays youngsters' transition to adulthood. In such societies youngsters typically are excused from full participation in the labor force and, in highly industrialized nations, provided with an extended period of education.

In colonial America, adolescence was the privilege of the few and the rich. Child labor was part of our English heritage and was valued as a source of cheap labor and as a means of inculcating the Puritan virtues of hard work and frugality. "By the time they reached maturity children were able to cover the costs of their rearing through their own labor"—typically as contributors to the work of the household, the family farm, or the family enterprise (Vulcan 1968, p. 76).

The rise of manufacturing in the nineteenth century rang up the curtain on a new era of child labor. The story is a familiar one. Machines displaced men, wages plummeted in response to the surplus of potential workers, and families became dependent on the additional earnings their youngsters could contribute to the household. Pressed by competition from the cheap labor of children, however, adult workingmen's organizations became the chief sponsors of statutory restraints on child labor. In addition, and in combination with other groups, they pushed for universal free and compulsory education. This interest in the expansion of educational opportunity was motivated by a classic blend of humanitarian and practical concerns. Only through education could fathers hope to better the life chances of their children, and only by making education both obligatory and free could they protect their own jobs and earnings. The first step in the invention of adolescence—the naming of a period distinct from childhood and adulthood—seems to have taken place in the third decade of the century. The political platforms of the workingmen's associations called for regulation of the employment of children and "youth" or "young persons," and legislative precedent was set for recognizing "youth" as a special period of the life cycle between thirteen and eighteen years of age.[2] Among those who fought for employment controls, however, the term child labor prevailed, "partly because of historic continuity, partly because early efforts mainly affected nine or ten year olds, and partly because the term was more likely to arouse public sentiment" (Vulcan 1968, p. 79).

In any case, actual reform of "child labor" did not take place overnight. Economic conditions during the remainder of the nineteenth century sustained the cycle, just described, in which the income of children often made an essential contribution to the family's well-being.[3]

The labor-force participation rates of children and youth declined steadily during the first half of the twentieth century

(Wrigley 1986). As a result of conditions less compatible with their employment, youngsters stayed in school. Lowered demand for cheap, unskilled labor—the sort that children and youth traditionally had provided—and expectations of future needs for more highly educated workers—workers capable of meeting the demands of more technologically sophisticated jobs—made it economically rational to delay youngsters' entry into the labor force and extend the period of their formal schooling. In this environment, the states enacted child labor legislation with broader coverage; and federal legislation, previously resisted on the grounds that it interfered with states' rights, was adopted in 1936 as part of the Fair Labor Standards Act.[4] At the same time, the period of compulsory schooling was extended. In 1900 the average minimum age for leaving school, in states that had passed compulsory schooling laws, was fourteen years five months; by the 1930s this figure had risen to sixteen years (Wrigley 1986).

The combined effect of the new laws regulating young people's work and prolonging their school attendance produced predictable social changes. Whereas in 1900 nearly 70 percent of fourteen- to nineteen-year-old males and about 35 percent of females of that age were working, by 1950 these figures had fallen to 40 percent and 25 percent, respectively. Flipping the coin, the size of the high-school population increased eightfold between 1900 and 1930, although the size of the high-school–age youth cohort actually had declined over this period (Vulcan 1968). And between 1900 and 1940 the percentage of teenagers who stayed on to complete high school—typically at about eighteen years of age—rose from less than 10 percent to over 50 percent.

Needless to say, the child labor laws often have been breached. The Great Depression, for example, changed national priorities from the protection of children and youth from premature work responsibilities to the shoring up of families against widespread economic distress. Manpower shortages during the two world wars also caused temporary increases in the employment of children and youth. Nonetheless, the ideal of "adolescence for all" was clearly in place in the United States by the middle of the twentieth century: society had mandated a protected period of life, one that was not dictated by biology. By 1940 about 70 percent of the fourteen- to seventeen-year-old population was enrolled in school; only 9 percent of this entire age group, whether enrolled in school or out of school, was identified by the U.S. Census as employed.[5] Still fewer—2.4 percent—were enrolled simultaneously in school and in the labor force.

The Emergence of the Student Worker

Until 1940 the U.S. Department of Labor did not record separately the labor-force activity of in-school and out-of-school youth—perhaps because the former group so seldom participated in the labor force. For example, in 1940 only 3 percent of fourteen- to fifteen-year-old male students and fewer than 1 percent of female students were employed, and older students' presence in the workplace was not substantially greater. Comparable figures for sixteen-year-old students were 4 percent and 1 percent for boys and girls, respectively; for seventeen-year-old students, 6 percent and 2 percent (U.S. Bureau of the Census 1940).[6] Over the next forty years, and continuing up to the present, however, a dramatic increase in student employment took place. In view of the fact that World War II introduced unusual labor-market conditions, we will trace the story from a postwar starting point.

Unfortunately, a clean story-line is not possible, due to asymmetries in data collection. Data collected by the Bureau of Labor Statistics (BLS) from the records of firms and establishments furnish possibly the best source of information, but the first year such information is available for sixteen- to seventeen-year-olds is 1947 and for fourteen- to fifteen-year-olds, 1953. The BLS did not track labor-force participation of youngsters by school enrollment status, sex, and age before these years.[7] The changing labor-force participation of students over the past thirty-five years is shown in figure 1.1.[8]

Between 1947 and 1980 the labor-force participation of enrolled students has increased substantially, due mainly to the increased rates of participation by sixteen- and seventeen-year-olds and, especially, to that of girls in this age group. In 1947 approximately 27 percent of school-going boys of this age were in the labor force; in 1980, 44 percent. Thus the increase in their labor-force participation, over a little more than three decades, was nearly 65 percent. At the same time, the labor-

Figure 1.1

Percentage of Enrolled Students in the Labor Force, 1947–1980.

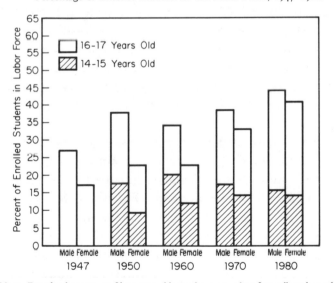

NOTE: Data for fourteen- to fifteen-year-olds are for 1953, when first collected, not for 1950.
SOURCE: Based on data from Office of the President, *Employment and Training Report of the President* (Washington, D.C.: U.S. Government Printing Office); and B. G. Reubens, J.A.C. Harrison, and K. Rupp, *The Youth Labor Force 1945–1995: A Cross-National Analysis* (Totowa, N.J.: Allanheld, Osmun, and Co., 1981), p. 221.

force participation of sixteen- and seventeen-year-old girls rose from 17 percent to 41 percent, for a gain of 240 percent.

The picture for younger students shows less dramatic change. Among fourteen- and fifteen-year-old boys, labor-force participation actually has declined slightly, from a bit over 17 percent in 1953 to just under 16 percent of enrolled students in 1980. For girls this age, however, labor-force participation has risen from a little over 9 percent to 14.5 percent—a gain of 57 percent.

Legal constraints imposed upon the work of youngsters under sixteen no doubt figure importantly in why the largest increase in rate of labor-force participation has occurred among older adolescents. Regulations concerning child labor typically prohibit employment of youngsters under sixteen years of age in retail and food service establishments. And, as we shall see, the retail and service sectors of the economy have spawned most of the new jobs over the past quarter century to which workers have flocked. At the same time, it seems likely that changing expectations about women and work, sparked by the women's movement and fueled by inflationary economic trends, have been responsible for the striking increase in labor-force participation of teenage girls. By 1970 the gender gap in high-school students' labor-force participation had closed substantially; by 1980 it was nearly gone.

Thus far we have centered our discussion on official labor-force statistics. Several recent surveys, however, suggest that "youthwork" today is greatly underestimated by government sources (Johnston, Bachman, and O'Malley 1982; Lewin-Epstein 1981).[9] These surveys go to adolescents themselves, rather than to employers or heads of households, to determine youngsters' involvement in the workplace. In the 1980 High School and Beyond survey (Lewin-Epstein 1981), based on a nationally representative sample of 60,000 high-school sophomores and seniors, 75 percent of sixteen- to seventeen-year-old boys and 68 percent of girls were projected to be in the labor force, compared to estimates of 44 percent and 41 percent for boys and girls this age, respectively, generated by the BLS in the same year (Office of the President, 1982). This discrepancy is shown graphically in figure 1.2. The survey of

Figure 1.2

Comparison of Two Sources of Data on the Percentage of Enrolled Students, Ages 16–17, in the Labor Force During 1981.

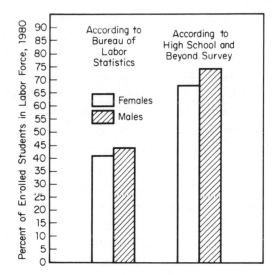

SOURCE: Based on data from Office of the President, *Employment and Training Report of the President* (Washington, D.C.: U.S. Government Printing Office); and N. Lewin-Epstein, *Youth Employment During High School* (Washington, D.C.: National Center for Education Statistics, 1981), table 2.1.

high-school students further showed that 59 percent of sophomores and 76 percent of seniors are likely to be in the labor force at any given point in the school year (Lewin-Epstein 1981). We will consider reasons for the discrepancy between governmental sources and youth themselves on labor-force participation by adolescents at a later point.

Adolescent Work Today

The picture we have just sketched shows the development of a historically novel trend. The customary decoupling of school and work has been undone, as youngsters enrolled in school have gone to work as well. Thus, despite a continuing decline in the overall proportion of teenagers in the labor force, due to the increasing numbers of youth who stay in school and the limits that school attendance places on employment, the proportion of adolescents enrolled in school and working part-time actually has grown. For reasons we shall detail presently, the student worker has emerged.

Along with change in the extent of students' employment has come change in the social origins of those who hold jobs. Teenage work in the past, we know, was the province of the lower classes. By the 1970s, however, it had become a cross-class phenomenon. A 1974 survey of a national sample of high-school students indicated that youngsters from all social backgrounds were equally likely to hold jobs (National Association of Secondary School Principals 1974). Findings from the High School and Beyond survey, conducted more recently, added an interesting twist to these earlier findings (Lewin-Epstein 1981). In this study seven family income levels were broken out, ranging from less than $7,000 annually to $38,000 or more. "In general," writes the report's author, sociologist Noah Lewin-Epstein, "both the labor force participation rate and the employment/population ratio actually increase slightly as income rises, until they peak in the range of $20,000 to $25,000 ($25,000 to $37,999 in the case of employment/ratio for seniors)" (Lewin-Epstein 1981, p. 24). Whereas labor-force participation rates vary no more than 4.7 percent between the several income groups, actual employment figures vary up to a maximum of 9.6 percent. Employment rates, moreover, are the *lowest* for the poorest youngsters. Table 1.1 shows the labor-

TABLE 1.1

Employment Status of Sophomore and Senior Students by Family Income:
Spring 1980

Family Income	Sophomores		Seniors	
	Labor-Force Participation Rate (%)	Employment/ Population Ratio	Labor-Force Participation Rate (%)	Employment/ Population Ratio
Less than $7,000	59.2	36.7	72.5	55.9
$7,000 to $11,999	58.0	39.4	75.3	60.5
$12,000 to $15,999	59.6	41.8	77.4	63.2
$16,000 to $19,999	57.7	43.1	77.9	64.9
$20,000 to $24,999	60.4	44.5	77.8	64.7
$25,000 to $37,999	58.6	43.9	76.6	65.5
$38,000 or more	55.1	41.5	73.6	62.7

SOURCE: Adapted from N. Lewin-Epstein, *Youth Employment During High School* (Washington, D.C.: National Center for Education Statistics, 1981), table 2.5.

force participation and employment rates for adolescents from varying economic backgrounds.

The argument that teenage work has shifted into the hands of more advantaged segments of society is strengthened by noting the racial distribution of student workers identified in the High School and Beyond survey. Among sophomores, 59 percent of "white and other" students had worked, or looked for work, in the week prior to the survey; figures for Hispanics and blacks were 56.6 percent and 53.8 percent, respectively. The same pattern prevails among seniors, although the magnitude of participation is greater: labor-force participation rates for the three groups, in the same order, were 76.7 percent, 75.1 percent, and 70.3 percent. Just as working has become a cross-class phenomenon, labor-force participation—holding a job or looking for one—has become a cross-racial fact of life.

Actual employment, however, is *not* equally a fact of life for youngsters of different ethnic backgrounds. The racial gap in *having* a job is far greater than the gap in *seeking* employment. Far more blacks and Hispanics seek than have, compared to their white counterparts. Among both sophomores and seniors, the largest discrepancy in actual employment is between black and white youngsters. Among sophomores, black males and white males show a twelve-point difference in actual employment (43.4 percent of whites are employed, in contrast to 33.1 percent of blacks). Among seniors, the gap between black and white males widens slightly but is exceeded in magnitude by the discrepancy between females. Whereas 63.1 percent of white girls are employed, only 44.8 percent of black girls have a job—a discrepancy of nearly nineteen points (Lewin-Epstein 1981).

Racial differences in students' employment, which mirror, in general outline, a well-known feature of the full-time, adult labor force, no doubt reflect the operation of several forces. Differences in where youngsters live—which region, and whether in a rural, urban, or suburban community—expose them to different labor-market opportunities. "The suburban community," Lewin-Epstein notes, "emerges as the most favorable for high school youth" (1981, p. 45). This is where the population centers are; and this is where the retail and service sectors of the economy, which have absorbed so many young workers, thrive. But even after region, residential location, and other factors are controlled statistically, ethnic differences in employment persist. Other things being equal, whites are the most likely, blacks the least likely, to have jobs. This fact leads us to underscore our assertion that the social origins of young workers are quite different today from what they were decades ago. Working while a teenager in school has become an option exercised most often by the white middle class.

In contrast to the dramatic change in the *proportion* of school-going youngsters who have joined the labor force over the past few decades, changes in the *intensity* of their participation have been less evident—and less systematic.[10] A good sense of the current situation can be gleaned from the High School and Beyond survey (Lewin-Epstein 1981).[11]

According to this report, the average sophomore boy with a job spends 14.8 hours working each week; the average sophomore girl, 10.5 hours. Comparable figures for senior boys and girls are 21.1 and 17.8 hours per week, respectively. A clearer picture of youngsters' involvement in work, however, emerges from "chunking" the data somewhat differently. Among sophomores, over 33 percent worked fifteen hours or more weekly; about 20 percent, twenty-two hours or more; and over 6 percent, thirty-five hours or more. Thus one in four sophomores were working at least the equivalent of a half-time job. Among seniors, the *average* worker was employed the equivalent of a half-time job; and nearly 10 percent worked the equivalent of a full-time job—thirty-five hours or more per week. Thus well over half of high-school seniors hold at least the equivalent of a half-time job. Consistent with our view that working has become a cross-class activity, the amount of time worked per week is not related to family income, parental education, or parental occupation.

What do these figures mean, in terms of their impact on a youngster's life? Let us see, by sketching the likely consequences of working twenty hours per week.

The average school day runs from eight in the morning until two or three in the afternoon. In order for a student to work twenty hours a week, he or she must have a work schedule that approximates the following: full-time employment on both weekend days, plus four additional hours on a school day or evening; or one full weekend day and an additional twelve hours distributed over two or more school days or evenings; or perhaps two weekday evening shifts, from 5 P.M. to 11 P.M., and two short shifts, from 5 to 9, on the remaining weekdays. If the youngster also participates in a time-intensive extracurricular activity, such as athletics, practice may occupy many or all weekday afternoons. In order to accommodate school and after-school interests, work is likely to be distributed over more, rather than fewer, days of the week and to include weeknights. In any case, this illustration suggests that the student with a half-time job is a very busy person, who commits, at the minimum, fifty hours to school and work; and if after-school activities are substantial, sixty hours or more.

An American Phenomenon

Although the employment of high-school students is not unique to the United States, it is nonetheless a distinctively American phenomenon. The proportion of the youth cohort who work, the extent of their commitment to jobs, and the social origins of youngsters who work are not duplicated elsewhere in the world today.

In most other countries, developing and industrialized alike, the worlds of school and work are still quite separate, as they once were in this country. Relatively few families in developing countries are economically fortunate enough to be able to keep their youngsters out of the labor force once they reach an age where their labor would make a significant contribution to the family's well-being: children in such families leave school at that time. Those few families who can afford to keep their youngster in school have no reason to encourage or allow their participation in the labor force. In countries whose degree of industrialization is comparable to that of the United States, many high-school students work during the summer months but relatively few work during the school year.[12] For example, at a time during the 1978–79 school year when over two-thirds of all American sixteen- and seventeen-year-old students were in the labor force, the comparable figure in Canada was about

37 percent; in Sweden, only about 20 percent; and in Japan, less than 2 percent (Reubens, Harrison, and Rupp 1981).

The more modest degree of labor-force participation in these and other highly industrialized countries of Europe and Asia is no doubt a reflection of their educational system, social priorities, and economic opportunities. Although these are not independent facets of life, it is useful to discuss each briefly in its own right.

The Europeans and Japanese place far greater emphasis than we do on educational achievement during, and before, adolescence. Students in these parts of the world encounter longer school days, more homework, and a more demanding curriculum. The average Japanese student knows more mathematics than ninety-nine out of one hundred comparable American high-school students (Savage 1983). Moreover, there are fewer openings in higher levels of the educational system, and they go to the top students—often identified by examination scores attained as early as age twelve or fourteen. Consequently, early school performance has serious and even irrevocable consequences for later life possibilities. In such a milieu, even if opportunities for intensive labor-force participation were to exist, one imagines that youngsters and their parents would consider very carefully the wisdom of embarking on an activity that might diminish school performance.

In contrast, the educational system in the United States is less demanding, more "spacious," and more forgiving. In 1980 the average high-school student spent less than one hour per week studying or doing homework (Lewin-Epstein 1981)—a fact that requires some cooperation from the school system, as we shall see later. Opportunities for postsecondary education of various kinds are more numerous in this country and are not limited to superior students. Also, mediocre or even poor early school performance does not disqualify youngsters from the possibility of obtaining a university education. Open-enrollment universities, such as the City University of New York, require only that students have a high-school diploma or its equivalent. Students are not denied entrance because of the quality of their earlier achievement. Under such conditions, youngsters who for any reason may have been late bloomers still may hope to become accountants, lawyers, and doctors.

Unlike the situation in the United States, in some countries where the government contributes to the cost of a student's education students are actually restricted, or entirely prohibited, from working. Norms concerning the responsibilities of parents, moreover, may dictate that they should provide for the needs of their children while the latter are still in school. As a Polish colleague of ours joked, "In Poland, a good father is one who takes care of his son until his son retires."

In addition to these forces, the structure of the economy in many countries also operates against the development of a large and highly committed teenage, part-time labor force. The most obvious of these structural factors is the opportunity for part-time work. Such opportunities are typically most abundant in the service sector of the economy; and countries with the earliest and greatest development of service-sector employment—namely, the United States and Canada—now have the largest proportion of student workers (Reubens, Harrison, and Rupp 1981). To give the issue a more concrete image, there are more McDonalds in Illinois than in Italy.

Still one more economic factor—this one, with political implications—figures in the lower labor-force activity of European and Japanese youth. In countries with high rates of unemployment, the top priority is to provide work for those who really need it. Political currents run strongly against practices that would permit or encourage students to hold jobs that are needed by out-of-work adults and youth who are no longer enrolled in school.

The Roots of Youthwork

The emergence of the student worker in this country is a

consequence of interlocking economic, social, and psychological changes that occurred over the past several decades. As we shall see, some of these changes resulted in the expansion of job opportunities for youngsters. Others resulted in producing a large proportion of youngsters who wanted employment. And still others served to remove or at least weaken the social, legal, and practical constraints on teenagers' employment that had existed previously.

In our discussion of cross-national trends, we indicated that school-going youngsters can work only where job opportunities of a special sort are available. The rapid growth of the service and retail sectors of the economy in this country created 15.8 million new jobs between 1940 and 1976—9.3 million in the service sector, 6.6 million in the retail sector (Ginzberg 1977). Put otherwise, the creation of jobs in these two areas of the economy helped to bring about a 63 percent increase in the size of the labor force over these years. A very large number of these jobs provided unique opportunities for students to work, as we shall see in a moment.

Although new jobs were added to the economy in record number, Ginzberg has pointed out that most of the new jobs were "bad" jobs. They are characterized by low wages, less than full-time hours of employment, irregular shifts, nighttime and weekend work, seasonality and other types of intermittency, low job security, minimal or nonexistent fringe benefits, and poor prospects for promotion. These "bad" jobs for adults, however, are in some crucial respects "good" jobs for youngsters—or if not "good," at least acceptable, and even attractive. Let us elaborate on this theme in some detail.

Obviously, part-time work is unacceptable to adults who must support themselves and often others as well. However, such jobs are virtually the only ones that are feasible for a school-going youngster. Similarly, irregular hours of employment, subject to change on short notice, are likely to interfere with other responsibilities of adults. In particular, the need to work at night, during the dinner hour, or on weekends cuts into an adult's time to spend with his or her family or with same-age peers who work "regular" hours. Yet many of the new jobs, especially those in the service and retail sectors, require irregular and off-hour (evening and weekend) work. The service and retail sectors thrive in the suburbs, and people are often best able or most likely to utilize services at exactly what we have referred to as "off-hours."

Irregular and off-hour work, however, coincides quite neatly with the availability of youngsters. And even the irregularity of their work shifts—two weekend days onc week, one the next, 5 to 8 P.M. on Tuesday, 7 to 10 P.M. on Thursday—may have virtues. Irregular hours less systematically deprive the young person of time to attend a school dance, go to a football game, or have dinner with the family. Moreover, although employers arrange work shifts primarily to suit their own needs, they often try to accommodate students' special needs (a night off before a big test). This flexibility is made possible by the existence of other irregular-shift workers who can be called in on short notice to take an absent worker's place.

The impact of low wages on adults' lives needs no description. Unlike adults, however, most school-going teenagers can afford to work at, or even below, the minimum wage, because they are subsidized by their parents. Most youngsters do not have to pay the rent or food bills. They do not work to support themselves and others but to earn spending money (and spend they do). In fact, research strongly suggests that the relatively low wages most teenagers earn are not a major source of discontent. The reservation wage of students—the lowest wage they *would* accept—is considerably below the current minimum. This finding has led some economists to propose a lower minimum wage for youth in order to create more job opportunities for teens (and, we note, to provide a larger pool of cheap labor for employers). The fact that the living expenses of student workers, unlike those of most adults who live in their own households, are subsidized also reduces the importance of job seasonality and job security to young workers.

Finally, adults who seek employment typically consider the quality and quantity of the fringe benefits they will receive and the likelihood of promotion and pay increases. Since most teenagers do not expect to continue in the jobs they hold part-time once they have finished their education, these future-oriented aspects of a job tend to be far less important. In short, the same jobs maligned by labor economists because they do not offer high-quality employment to adults meet many of the needs of teenagers.

We have sketched so far a number of ways in which the kinds of new jobs added to the employment scene since 1940 are acceptable, and even attractive, to school-going youngsters. Why are these young workers attractive to employers?

Some of the likely explanations already have surfaced. Youngsters, unlike many adults, will work part time, at low wages, and will accept irregular work schedules. In addition, they are likely to be relatively docile employees. With little or no prior job experience behind them, even a dull and poorly paid job may provide some stimulation, opportunity for self-testing, and satisfaction. With no expectations of staying forever, youngsters will tolerate jobs that adults, who are there for the long haul, would find intolerable. And youngsters are not so likely as adults to demand improvements in working conditions or pay, because they are typically naive about their legal rights and employers' legal responsibilities and because demanding workers usually can be replaced quite readily by dipping into the large pool of potential young employees. Especially when jobs require little skill or training—of which hamburger wrapping and bagging in the fast-food restaurant is perhaps the exemplar—replacement of a "difficult" worker with a new one entails little cost to the employer.

Why Teenagers Want to Work

Expanded opportunities for work have been a necessary, but not sufficient, cause of the influx of students to the workplace. Expansion of job opportunities, however, is not the only economic force that has prompted youngsters to seek jobs. Inflation has provided a major impetus as well.

The cost of being an adolescent has risen steeply in the last fifteen years—more steeply, in fact, than the rate of inflation overall. Consider, for example, some of the traditional "staples" of adolescent life in this country. In 1967 the national average for the cost of a movie was $1.29; for a gallon of gasoline, $0.33. By 1982 comparable costs had risen to $2.78 and $1.29 for movie going and gasoline buying, respectively (Dorfman 1982). In a story on "kidflation," the *Wall Street Journal* reported that a market basket of fifteen items frequently purchased by children (and still likely purchases for adolescents) cost 38 percent more in 1980 than in 1975, a period during which the Consumer Price Index rose "only" 26 percent (Rothbart 1981). It was also observed that despite "kidflation," allowances had stayed more or less flat over periods of several years. Parents tend to give their fourteen-year-old daughter the same allowance her older sister received when *she* was fourteen, three years earlier. Moreover, wages associated with the informal, casual jobs typically held by youngsters, such as baby-sitting and newspaper delivery, have not kept pace with inflation. Inflation, in combination with the prospects of a "fixed income," clearly have fueled adolescents' interest in entering the labor force.

Along with inflation of the costs of the "staples" of adolescent life, young people appear to have developed an inflated interest in the acquisition of luxury goods. An increase in materialism, over time, is hard to document but easy to believe on the evidence of one's eyes and ears.

Looking back ten years, we recall the emergence of designer clothing, not just in the closets of adults but on the backs of the nation's high-school students as well. (Why the alligator should have become a status symbol is beyond the scope of our inquiry.) At some point, too, the high-school parking lot underwent a change. Few old jalopies remain as sputtering testimony to a youngster's first affordable "wheels"; many are the up-to-date models of automobiles that look just like—or better than—our own. The list of other high-priced consumables introduced in the 1960s and 1970s, and aimed at the youth market, is a long one: electronic games, ten-speed and then twelve-speed racing bicycles, mopeds, portable tape recorders, and elaborate stereophonic equipment for the home, the car, and the runner are but a few of the more popular objects of teenage consumption.

New and expensive tastes are likely to have motivated youngsters to earn more spending money of their own. There is a limit to what parents will, or can be expected to, provide. In interviews we conducted with the parents of working adolescents, as part of an extensive program of research in Orange County, California, we heard stories similar to the following:

INTERVIEWER: Why do you think Chuck wanted to work?
MOTHER: Money.
FATHER: He has always been motivated by money.
MOTHER: He wanted a car. . . .
FATHER: He had an allowance, but you can't buy a car or buy the stereo system he has with no job.

INTERVIEWER: Do you know why Bill was looking for a job?
FATHER: He wanted spending money, more than we gave him. . . . He wanted to buy his own clothes . . . expensive clothes, and we told him, "We buy clothes from Sears," and he wanted better.

Another very concrete fact supports the notion that teenagers have become more interested in the acquisition of material goods or, more simply, have become bigger consumers. Teenagers spent about $40 billion in 1981 from their own earnings and money given to them. This figure is 50 percent higher than five years before, despite a 70 percent decline in the size of the teen population (Yovovich 1982). Certain industries, moreover, depend mainly on youth for their sales—among them the movie and record industries. The sizable discretionary income of adolescents, much of it due to their employment, has not gone unnoticed by the advertising industry, which directs a substantial amount of effort to reaching the youth market.

It is difficult to say whether the increased consumer spending of young people preceded or followed their increased participation in the part-time labor force, but the two forces obviously fed one another. As more teenagers developed expensive tastes and a hunger for luxury goods, they found it necessary to go to work; and as more youngsters entered the labor force and began earning money that they could spend as they wished, more money was spent on developing and expanding the youth market. In our study of employed high-school students, the majority indicated that they worked chiefly for money rather than to gain experience or skills. Asked to indicate the chief reason for being employed, 38 percent endorsed the statement "in order to earn money for things I really needed"; 36 percent replied, "I didn't really have to work, but I wanted to have money for 'extras.'" The fact that youngsters' employment enables them to increase their level of consumption seems obvious—parents are not supporting all of the expensive habits of their children. Indeed, a national survey of more than 18,000 high-school seniors in 1981 indicates that most spend between half and all of their earnings on their "own needs and activities" (Johnston, Bachman, and O'Malley 1982). A high-school teacher's survey in six Connecticut high schools led him to conclude that most youngsters' earnings go to "gratify . . . sophisticated materialistic tastes . . . to buy gasoline for the numerous gas guzzlers that fill the parking lots of every high school, to buy tickets for an endless assortment of rock concerts and sporting events, to buy expensive jeans and exotic footwear" (Manning 1980).

The amount of money earned by youngsters and potentially available for spending is worth noting. The average employed high-school senior, working the average twenty hours per week at the minimum wage, earns about $275 per month.

Spending patterns are a direct indication of interest in material goods, but that interest no doubt has many roots: imitation of the parent generation, aspirations for social acceptance, and vulnerability to age-targeted advertising, among them. One wonders whether teenagers' more general shift toward materialistic values also may have contributed to their increased participation in the workplace, where money for spending can be acquired. Let us explore this possibility in some detail.

National opinion surveys have tracked young people's attitudes toward money over the last decade and a half. They yield an interesting record, but an imperfect one, for two reasons. First, as is typically the case in ongoing surveys, the survey questions undergo some change over time. Items that are used in one survey year are sometimes eliminated, or significantly reworded, in another; and items not incorporated in earlier years are added in later ones, as new issues for research emerge. Both these features tend to frustrate attempts to trace the history of an attitude or opinion over a significant span of years. Second, direct questions about the value an individual places on money are likely, we believe, to underestimate the "true" extent of money-mindedness. This is so because, in many quarters, it is not considered socially acceptable to admit to strong interests in having a great deal of money or an abundance of material goods (especially when this goal is pitted against other goals that place one in a more socially favorable light). Although this problem is a constant factor that probably does not distort trends over time—at least, not if the social desirability of admitting materialistic values remains relatively stable—it does lead to an inaccurate representation of the *level* of importance respondents attach to money.

With this caution in mind, we turn to survey findings that illuminate the recent history of young people's interest in material well-being. Some of these surveys include high-school students; most focus on older youth. However, even value surveys of young adults—those in the eighteen-to-twenty-five group—are likely to tell us a good deal about values that are in process of formation among their younger brothers and sisters. High-school and post–high-school youth, after all, are likely to have grown up in quite similar social and economic circumstances and thus to have developed considerable similarity in their basic orientations. And the values of the next-older cadre of young people are likely to trickle down to, and influence, the views of their juniors.

Studies of youth in the 1960s revealed a widespread devaluation of the importance of money and what it could buy. Many social analysts have discussed the social and political realities that led young people to turn their backs on a materialistic orientation they attributed to an adult generation that they felt had let them down. The hippie provided an appealing counterculture image for youth of that era—especially for college youth. The image was that of a young man (or woman), with few worldly possessions, who shared his resources, such as they were, with his friends. No one, however, claimed that materialism was dead. In 1969—toward the end of this era—a national survey showed that 83 percent of college youth rated money as important in some degree (Yankelovich 1973).

Pollster Daniel Yankelovich (1973), reporting on national surveys of college youth, shows that money was rated "important" or "fairly important" by *fewer* persons in 1971 (77 percent) than in 1969. Between 1974 and 1978, however, an item with similar content but more stringent response options was administered to a national sample of fourteen- to twenty-five-year-olds. It drew a *higher* rate of support over successive years although it yielded lower overall rates of endorsement. Thus 35 percent of respondents said that money was the "most important" or a "very important" facet of life in 1974, whereas in 1978 the comparable figure had climbed to 46 percent, the highest percentage since the survey was first conducted eight years earlier. Between 1974 and 1978 a greater proportion of young people also agreed that it made sense to enjoy now and pay later (American Council of Life Insurance 1978).[13]

Alexander Astin (1982) provides the most consistent over-time data on the importance of money to young people. In annual surveys of some 300,000 college freshmen attending a representative sample of two-year and four-year institutions, he has queried respondents about a variety of life goals. He finds a consistent and strong upward trend in the importance of "being very well off financially." In 1969, 40 percent of college freshmen rated this an "essential" or "very important" life goal; in 1982, nearly 70 percent. Astin also notes another consistent but contrasting trend—a decline in the value of "developing a meaningful philosophy of life." Over a sixteen-year period, the number of young people who considered this an "essential" or "very important" goal fell precipitously, from 83 percent to 49 percent. Commenting on this pattern of findings, Astin suggests that "some students may view the making of money as a kind of 'philosophy of life' in itself" (1982, p. 31).

Data from a smaller, less representative data set that we collected from high-school students in 1978 are consistent with Astin's view. Of the 531 sophomores and juniors queried, 51 percent agreed with the following statement: "My goal in life is to make a lot of money and buy a lot of things." Sixty-four percent reported of themselves, "Adults who have acquired a lot of wealth really have my respect and admiration." And 75 percent said, ". . . The more money I have, the more things I want to buy."[14]

In view of the apparent increase in students' materialism, it is not surprising that their orientations toward education and career expectations have shifted. The shift involves a declining commitment to the idea that knowledge is valuable for its own sake and an increasing adherence to the idea that education is useful as a means of obtaining *other* valued goals: above all, a good (read "high-paying") job. In 1968, for example, 41 percent of a national sample of sixteen- to twenty-five-year-olds agreed that the amount of money one could earn was, in fact, an important or very important criterion in choosing a career; by 1973, 61 percent endorsed this view (Yankelovich 1974). And in 1978 the American Council of Life Insurance survey revealed that money was the second most important criterion of adolescents and youth in making a choice about a job or career—following four percentage points behind job security, the top-ranked criterion; and six and seventeen points, respectively, *ahead* of doing "stimulating and creative work" or work that allowed one to make a "meaningful contribution." The author of this report concludes, in what appears to be an understatement of the findings, "Material needs . . . take precedence over other work values" (p. 42).

During the same period college freshmen expressed declining interest in the arts, humanities, and social sciences and increased interest in majors such as engineering, computer science, and business that are likely to lead to more lucrative careers. (The number of students entering college who expected to major in business increased by 80 percent between 1966 and 1981.) In this cultural milieu, it is not surprising that high-school students have flocked to the workplace: in the absence of a strongly competing ethic, such as commitment to learning for its own sake or to careers involving service to others, the lure of the paycheck must be very powerful.

Thus far we have linked young people's increased interest in working during their high-school years to economic factors and changing youth values. Changes in family functioning also appear relevant to understanding why teenagers work. Between 1940 and 1980 not only teenagers but also women entered the labor force in unprecedented numbers. Whereas 28.2 percent of women were in the labor force in 1940, by 1980 the figure stood at 51.5 percent (*Economic Report of the President,* 1981). Moreover, the decade from 1970 to 1980 was marked by the largest rate of increase in women's labor-force participation over this entire time period (Grossman 1981; Johnson and Waldman 1981). The labor-force behavior of women with children may be of special significance in understanding the dynamics of teenagers' employment.

In 1940 only 10.5 percent of women with children under eighteen were in the labor force. By 1980 the labor-force participation of women with minor children had grown by nearly a factor of five, to 55.5 percent (U.S. Census). The meaning of these figures is conveyed more vividly in terms of the proportion of children affected. In March 1981, 30.7 million youngsters under eighteen (or 53 percent of all minor children) had mothers in the labor force. The proportion of mothers working, or looking for work, is highest, as one might expect, among those with older children. In short, teenagers are the most likely group to have employed mothers.

Economists have attributed the increased labor-force participation of women to forces that parallel those that, we have argued, prompted the emergence of the student worker: expanded job opportunities, inflation, and increased materialism and consumerism. Labor economist Eli Ginzberg (1977), for example, maintains that the rapid expansion of job opportunities "unquestionably facilitated the increased participation of women in the labor force" (p. 47). One consequence of this increased female participation was an increased demand for part-time work (presumably because it is more consistent with women's family responsibilities); and, as we have demonstrated already, many of the "new" jobs in the retail and service sector could adapt to, or even thrive on, the needs of individuals seeking part-time work. Like teenagers, women became good candidates for bad jobs.

And like teenagers, women's increased labor-force participation seems to have been a response to inflationary processes and to changing social values. Sar A. Levitan and Richard S. Belous (1981) comment:

> Since World War II, American households have shown a strong propensity to increase their consumption of goods and services. Many wives joined the work force to finance these upward consumption patterns. Like the mechanical rabbit leading the greyhounds around the race track, these aspirations have consistently stayed ahead of rising productivity, often requiring another paycheck in the search for the "good life." (P. 26)

By 1980, they note, three out of five families had at least two household members in the labor force—generally the husband and wife. One wonders about the proportion of households where not two but three or four members are in the labor force—one or more school-going teenagers as well as their parents. Unfortunately, there are no data concerning this question.

Our digression into women's labor-force participation is based on the speculation that their increased presence in the workplace has not simply paralleled but encouraged youngsters to seek jobs. First, insofar as improving the family's standard of living is an important motive for women's employment, their entry into the labor force served as a model for teenage children. Prompted by their own view of what constitutes the "good life," teenagers have trodden the same path to acquiring what they want—the path that leads to a paycheck. This mechanism, we propose, operates at both the individual and the community level. That is, the employment of individual mothers may serve as a model for the employment of her own children; and the employment of women in the larger social milieu may affect youngsters' own labor-force participation, independent of their own mother's work status and motives for employment. The "modeling" hypothesis is consistent with the fact that the labor-force participation of girls has increased more dramatically than that of boys during peak periods of growth in maternal employment.[15]

Second, women's increased involvement in the labor force has changed the daytime ecology of the household. With the average number of children per family now at only a fraction more than two, many teenagers are likely to come home to an empty house; others, to a home where they have the responsibility for looking after a younger sibling and doing household chores. Getting a paid job may seem more attractive to adolescents than either of their options at home.

Popular Thinking About Youthwork

The emergence of the student worker, we have seen, was a response by youngsters to complex and interlocking economic and social changes: among them, expanding opportunities for part-time work, rising inflation and "kidflation," increasing materialism and heartier consumer appetites, and changing educational values. For the most part, adults have applauded youngsters' interest in working, although the forces prompting them to give youthwork their blessing generally are quite different from the motives that propel youngsters themselves to seek jobs.

Perhaps the two most common themes in popular thinking about youthwork are the belief that work builds character and teaches youngsters what "real life" is about—life outside the protected and protecting environment of the family and the school (Stephens 1979). Working is expected to have a positive influence on character by inducing youngsters to become more responsible and self-disciplined. Working is supposed to enlarge youngsters' understanding of life by opening their eyes to the expectations that prevail, and the kind of accommodations that must be made, in this arena. In the "real" world of work, furthermore, youngsters learn the value of money—namely, that it takes a lot of work to make it, little work to spend it, and much skill to manage it well.

These themes are amply evident in the book *Our Children Should Be Working* (Stephens 1979). In this volume sociologist qua minister William Stephens sings the praises of farm work, baby-sitting, and paid odd jobs to defend his argument. Menial labor for pay, Stephens argues, fosters responsibility, discipline, and "seasoning"; farm work, he suggests, produces self-reliance, responsibility, and diligence:

> The strongest and simplest arguments in favor of farm work . . . have to do with hardening, work habits, and mechanical skills. Conditioning to some of the hardships one encounters on farms, and to the very high and arduous work standards, should prepare a youth to cope with, and be comfortable in, a wider range of situations in later life. . . . Many of us have been sheltered from the realities of these sorts. Now it seems prudent that youth be better prepared, than we were, to take care of themselves. (P. 44)

And further:

> There is the simple equation: a dollar equals so many minutes of boredom, monotony, privation, and hot-dusty-sweaty-heavy work on the job. This seems to inspire youth to conserve their money. . . . The menial summer jobs are a yearly reminder: "I don't want to be stuck in a life like this, like these other people I am working with." The jobs are further inspiration to work hard at school. They provide seasoning to tough employment conditions. (Pp. 176–77)

Both the notion that work builds character and that it acquaints youngsters with important truths about the real world surfaced frequently in interviews with parents whom we interviewed in our Orange County, California, study. Asked whether they thought it was a good idea for youngsters of their children's age to work, most said yes. The character-building theme was evident in many references to the notion that work makes youngsters more responsible—although not all parents found it easy to explain exactly what they meant by this term. Most, however, made reference to some aspect of dependability: thus working taught youngsters to be punctual, to put work commitments ahead of personal preferences ("They know they have to go to work even if they don't want to"), and to live up to the trust that had been placed in them, noted especially of youngsters who had jobs that involved handling large amounts of money.

The kinds of real-life lessons that parents believed were taught in the workplace are suggested by the following interview excerpts:

FATHER OF FOOD SERVICE WORKER: Let's face it . . . some time in life, someone is going to tell you what to do. . . . I think work is the only place to learn to deal with it. . . . Parents can give you a little discipline, but it isn't accepted. . . . You can't learn that in school, because there is another so-called tyrant, the teacher. But then they get . . . a boss, and you get out there and learn it.

FATHER OF CRAFT SHOP ASSISTANT: Even though it is more relaxed there than some places, he does have to satisfy the customer. He does have to be accurate. . . . When he makes a mistake, he pays for it. Once . . . someone had come in and purchased a lot of things, and it was when he was first working over the counter, and he wrote up most of the things, but not all. Jack [the boss] took it out of his pay. It was a good lesson.

MOTHER OF FOOD SERVICE WORKER: They actually learn the value of money. They ask for this and that, but when they are spending their own, it's different. . . . Like she realizes how much things cost and how many hours she worked to earn the money.

Of the two notions—that work builds character and that it educates youngsters about the realities and demands of adult life—the former has especially deep roots in American culture. The early Protestant church endowed work with positive moral connotations and hard work with an especially bright moral glow. On the premise that work expresses obedience to God's design for man, a life spent in hard work was viewed, in Calvinist and Puritan theology, as the best assurance of salvation. And perhaps because, other things being equal, hard work "pays off," money making was not condemned. On the contrary, money making was viewed as "willed by God . . . a mark of his favor and a proof of success in one's calling" (Fullerton 1959, p. 18). The only stipulation was that money should not be spent on frivolous consumption or self-aggrandizing display. In addition to its intrinsic worth, the Puritans considered work "the best prophylactic against . . . the 'unclean life' " (Fullerton 1959, p. 16). In this religious climate, children and youth were not spared exposure to the rigors of work. Indeed, training that was intended to foster the habit of hard work became part of a young person's religious preparation.

The pervasiveness of an American value configuration marked by esteem for hard work and for financial success based on it hardly needs documentation (Williams 1970). Tales of the frontier indicate that extraordinary diligence and perseverance were required to bring a recalcitrant environment under control. And the adventures of Horatio Alger and Andy Hardy are paeans to the accomplishments of hard-working young men, who started with nothing and ended with much—the fruits of ingenuity and a taste for work. In support of the potential payoff of work, R. T. Crane, inventor of the construction hoist that bears his name, told college students in a 1911 address:

> My advice to you, boys, is stop where you are, hustle for a job; make good. The men who have succeeded are the men who began

their life-work early. I admire these parcel boys on their bicycles, alert, energetic and attentive to business. They are the kind of boys that every business man has his eyes open for, and if they have brains combined with energy and loyalty they are going to get along. (P. 15)

What do the Protestant work ethic and its secular derivatives have to do with attitudes toward youthwork today? They may explain, in part, why many adults are so convinced that working is good for youngsters. Insofar as we imbue work with moral overtones, for example, we are likely to see youngsters who hold jobs as good and decent kids—a construction of events that is especially likely when we know that they do not, in fact, "have to" work. And insofar as we believe that work makes us better people, we may create self-fulfilling prophecies, attributing improvements in youngsters' attitudes and behavior to the salutory effects of labor. The fact that youngsters use their earnings for what the early Protestants surely would consider frivolous purposes seems to escape notice or, at least, condemnation. Although frugality still has its advocates, so does spending.

The Politics of Youthwork

More recently, social and political events that shook this country in the 1960s also helped to shape attitudes toward youthwork. The 1960s were years of open and often flagrant conflict between the younger generation and their elders with respect to a host of issues: Vietnam; sexual mores; drug use; and the importance of power, money, and other conventional trappings of success. The schools became aware that they contained (in both senses of the word) a growing number of bored, restless, and alienated students, who, for a variety of reasons, did not find attending school rewarding or relevant. Middle-class parents worried about when—and whether—their "flower children" would grow up and get a job. Parents whose children had dropped out of high school or learned little while there worried about how their youngsters were going to get along in the years ahead.

In this troubled era, government agencies and private foundations commissioned a number of panels to study the situation of youth and the health of the social institutions designed to guide their development.[16] The reports written by these distinguished panels, composed of educators, social scientists, manpower experts, and youth policy specialists, claimed that young people needed better preparation for the adult roles and responsibilities they would be expected to fulfill—or for what came to be called the "transition to adulthood." At present, the panels argued, there was too much reliance on the schools to prepare youth for the varied tasks of adulthood. It was time, they claimed, to call on other institutions to share the responsibility for overseeing young people's development. One of their key proposals was that earlier and more extensive participation in the world of work would facilitate the transition to adult life. Their brief in behalf of work rested on the premise that the workplace would offer experiences that the school and family could not—an expanded version of the view that working teaches youngsters needed lessons about life in the larger world —and on the assumption that work experience would lead youngsters to become more responsible, cooperative, and participatory members of society—an expanded and secularized version of the view that work builds character. It is instructive to examine the arguments developed in these reports, because they are important in their own right and because they coincide in several respects with beliefs that many adults hold about the value of work experience to youth.

The primary concern of several panels was that the structure and duration of schooling in the United States have produced a highly age-graded society. Children and adolescents are isolated from meaningful contact with older persons and spend their time almost exclusively in the company of their agemates (National Commission on Youth, 1980; National Panel on High Schools and Adolescent Education, 1976; President's Science Advisory Committee, 1973). This social arrangement, the panelists argued, keeps youth young rather than encouraging them to adopt more adult perspectives. Specifically, the commissions claimed that age segregation had deprived adolescents of opportunities to learn more about the roles adults fill; acquire work habits, job skills, and worldly wisdom from adults in the workplace; learn about the roles that prevail in the adult community and the kinds of deviations from norms that are tolerated; and build up a supportive network of elders to whom they could turn for advice and help. Consequently, the reports called for the earlier integration of adolescents into the labor force—while they were still students. This, they felt, would help repair some of the debits in young people's social accounts. Although their motivation was clearly social, not religious, in nature, the spirit of the Protestant ethic is nonetheless apparent in their formulations. Restated, a central argument of the panels was that expanded contact with the older generation would bring straying youth into the fold.

A second, closely related theme emerged in the reports: the inability of the schools to prepare youth for the range of responsibilities they will face as adults. On the one hand, the reports argued, the structure of authority in the school limits youngsters' opportunities for self-management, initiative, and decision making. On the other hand, the structure of tasks in the school and the criteria by which rewards are allocated fail to nourish cooperation and a sense of responsibility for others. The capacities for both individual and social responsibility need to be exercised and expanded during adolescence, the panels argued, if a youngster is to be ready for adult roles.

From the panelists' perspective, the workplace seemed likely to enhance these capabilities because of critical distinctions between going to school and going to work. For most teenagers, for example, going to work and taking a particular job, unlike going to school, are matters of personal choice. Thus if youngsters go to work, report to the job on time, carry out assigned duties, and perform competently, it follows that they are developing and drawing on internal sources of motivation and self-regulation. At work, the panels felt, initiative and decision making would be required and rewarded. Holding a job in adolescence also would allow youngsters to acquire experience in a role that would occupy a central place in their adult lives. Finally, the reports proposed that youngsters would get in the workplace an antidote to the individualistic achievement orientation promoted by the schools. At work, they suggested, youngsters would learn that some tasks cannot be accomplished independently but require mutual cooperation. A restaurant will not function smoothly, for example, just because the cook is in the kitchen. The manager must do his or her job, and the waiters, cashier, and other staff, theirs, in concert with each other. The panels also hoped that working would inspire feelings of usefulness and a sense of participation in the larger society.

A third argument of the panels for encouraging work experience during high school centered on the notion that there is much to learn, in an information-rich society, from people and activities located outside the school. If the school is to concentrate on what it is best at—improving youngsters' academic skills—other settings must be relied on more heavily to teach job skills and practical skills of living that are beyond its proper scope. The workplace is one example of such a setting. In that arena, they hoped youngsters would learn job skills not taught in school and have opportunities to practice and apply the academic skills they had acquired in the classroom. As wage earners, furthermore, they would learn valuable lessons about money and how to manage it.

A fourth argument for earlier integration of youth into the world of work stemmed from concerns about high unemployment in the out-of-school youth cohort. Ethonographic studies in simpler societies typically reveal a more continuous, less abrupt passage from youth to adulthood, with youngsters participating from a very early age in the work of the community, in the kinds of work activities that they will be expected to carry out as adults. With a handful of exceptions, this pattern has virtually disappeared from life in our society. The exceptions are children who grow up on farms or in families with small, nonfarming, business enterprises—and even they are dwindling in number. Thus, the panels concluded, many youngsters fail to acquire work skills that might bridge the path to adulthood. Insofar as lack of work experience and work skills are two factors that contribute to youth unemployment, the panels suggested that earlier integration into the labor force would improve young people's chances of being employed as young adults.

One final argument in favor of increased exposure of youth to the world of work deserves note. The Carnegie Commission report (1980) urged more extensive work experience for youth on the grounds that working would reduce crime and delinquency. Although this was the only report to make the argument, such a notion is not only part of a widely shared belief system in our culture, as we indicated earlier, but the source of many government-mandated job programs for youth and rehabilitative programs for young offenders.

Questioning the Value of Youthwork

It is possible, as we have seen, to make an intuitively appealing case for youthwork. Although the Protestant ethic has lost some of its earlier dominance in our lives, we nonetheless smile approvingly at young entrepreneurs who sell lemonade on hot summer days and at their older sisters and brothers who march off to staff the fast-food emporia. And if distinguished commentators on the needs of youth smile with us, surely the emergence of widespread and spontaneous youthwork is a good thing. Before agreeing to this proposition, however, it is worth examining the phenomenon in a closer light.

The assumption of the school critics that youngsters have lost contact, over the years, with the world of work—an assumption that is central to their case for encouraging more extensive labor-force participation by youth—is faulty in one important respect. As we have mentioned, *school-going* youngsters are actually more likely now than forty years ago to participate simultaneously in the world of work.[17] The more important question, in any case, is whether working produces the positive consequences for which it has been touted. Do youngsters who work develop substantial relationships with their elders in the workplace? Or is the workplace that youngsters encounter typically one populated by peers? Do youngsters who work learn lessons about the real world that will help them to handle adult roles and responsibilities more competently? Or do the conditions that motivate youthwork today—work not prompted by economic need or by concern for developing an adult career—shield youngsters from reality? Does working, as assumed, "build character"? Or is it possible that the kind of work we make available to youth does little to stimulate initiative and cooperation? Does working improve prospects for post–high-school employment? Or does it interfere with schooling and take a toll on later-life success? Does working keep young people out of trouble? It is conceivable, on the contrary, that experiences on the job, and the substantial earnings that many youngsters have at their disposal as a consequence of working, create new opportunities for deviance.[18]

The questions we have just raised are often condensed into one: Is working good for adolescents? In the next several chapters we shall examine the evidence.

The Adolescent
Workplace, Old and New

I N the 1946 Frank Capra film, *It's a Wonderful Life,* protagonist George Bailey—an adolescent when the story begins—is employed during his youth at a neighborhood drugstore. Each weekday afternoon George diligently reports to the store, where he sweeps the floor, mans the soda fountain, and delivers prescriptions to the pharmacist's customers. He is the only assistant to the store's owner, a gruff but kind older man with a drinking problem. Their relationship is similar to that between a nephew and crotchety uncle: they bicker and get on each other's nerves, but there is a good deal of unspoken affection between the two.

Because George is the pharmacist's only assistant, he is also usually the only other worker in the store, and he is given a good deal of responsibility for managing the store's daily affairs and handling the store's clientele. On more than one occasion, we learn, George has done far more than was expected of him. He often corrects the owner's mistakes. Indeed, at a critical turning point in the film, George discovers that the owner, drunk, has accidentally filled a customer's prescription with a household poison. George intercepts the prescription before it reaches the customer, saving her life and, of course, the pharmacist's neck.

During the course of his work shift, George chats amiably with a variety of family friends and acquaintances about local goings-on, his family's health and activities, and his own plans for the future. Because the drugstore serves as a neighborhood meeting place, George often serves as a link in the town's informal communication network. He keeps up a friendly conversational pace without taking time away from his job responsibilities. Concentrating on the work at hand—scooping ice cream into a frappe glass, wiping down the counter, ringing up a sale—his work activity is peppered with snatches of informative dialogue: Yes, he is planning on attending the state university in the fall. No, as far as he knows, Mrs. Johnson has not recovered from the flu. The pep rally starts at seven that evening.

On payday, George turns his paycheck over to his parents. The money is to be saved for his and his younger brother's college tuition. A small portion is returned to George, for dating and incidental expenses. But although his pocket money comes in part from his weekly paycheck, there is no question that it is given to him by his parents in the same fashion that parents might give their child an allowance. His earnings, like those of his father, belong to the family.

This is the stuff that movies are made of, to be sure. Yet the picture of George Bailey's adolescent employment presented in

It's a Wonderful Life is the archetypal portrayal of a responsible American teenager on the job. Comparable illustrations could be drawn from any of a number of stories of American youth. Working at the corner drugstore, baby-sitting for the next-door neighbor, working on the family farm, apprenticing with a skilled tradesman are highly valued activities in American culture. And these activities form the bases for the images of adolescents at work which suggest that having a job is character building, that youngsters learn self-reliance and social responsibility from work, and that employment teaches adolescents important lessons about frugality, self-denial, and altruism.

For George Bailey and teenagers who work under similar circumstances, work may serve all of its putative virtuous purposes. It is not difficult to imagine that the adolescent who is given responsibility for overseeing a store's operations will become more responsible as a result of the experience, or that a youngster who must make small talk with customers in order to keep the store's clientele happy will learn something about how to interact with adults. Nor is it hard to believe that an adolescent who works in order to help stock the family larder, or put a sibling through college, or pay for his or her own future schooling will come away with new and more mature attitudes toward money and its uses. For young people whose work conditions allow it, early employment can be an important bridge between childhood and adulthood—a means of learning skills, acquiring knowledge, and developing values that have significant future payoffs.

But not all young people have jobs that demand responsibility or permit informal interaction with adults, and not all working young people use their earnings to help their families or save for their future education. In fact, the type of adolescent work idealized in stories such as *It's a Wonderful Life* is becoming increasingly rare in contemporary American society. Put simply, the conditions that once made early employment an important and valuable component of youngsters' preparation for adulthood are fast disappearing.

The Changing Adolescent Workplace

In order to understand the impact of work on adolescents' development, it is necessary to look closely at the nature of the work they do and at the circumstances surrounding their employment. Under which circumstances is working likely to benefit youngsters, and under which circumstances is it likely to interfere with their healthy growth and development? In our view, three dimensions are crucial: whether the work experience imparts skills or knowledge valuable for adult work life (the educational context of the experience); whether the work is performed in order to fill a financial need of the youngster's family or the community, or out of a sense of the youngster's future financial needs (its economic context); and whether the work brings young people into contact with adults who have a stake in preparing them for adulthood (its social context).

It is important to bear in mind that the aforementioned dimensions are used to describe the overall context of the work experience, rather than specific aspects of certain jobs. The quality of work experience is shaped not only by the nature of the work performed but by the motivation for working, the purposes to which the earnings are put, the way in which the young person defines his or her role as a worker, and the broader social environment in which the work is performed, to name just a few. We use the term work experience in its broadest sense—to refer to the sum total of all factors, considered together, that influence youngsters' experience at work.

Each of the three dimensions can be thought of as a continuum along which adolescents' work experiences vary and can be evaluated (see table 2.1). Some adolescents' experiences in the workplace provide clear and strong links to adult work roles; others teach little that will be valuable later on; still others impart habits or attitudes that actually may interfere with the successful assumption or performance of adult work responsibilities. Similarly, some adolescents work because the survival of their family or community depends on and requires their labor; other adolescents' work may not be required by those around them but may benefit their families and community nonetheless; still others work exclusively to satisfy their own financial needs and use their earnings purely for the consumption of nonessential goods and services. Finally, some jobs facilitate meaningful contact between adolescents and their elders; other jobs neither foster such interaction nor impede it; still others further age-segregation and intergenerational distance. This conceptual framework provides an interesting way to contrast adolescent work today with that in previous eras.

Over the last century, the conditions surrounding work for American adolescents have moved steadily away from the positive pole of each of these three dimensions. Whereas work at one time served a valuable educational purpose for young people, performed an essential economic service to the family and community, and facilitated the development of relationships between young people and nonfamilial adults, during the past one hundred years early work experience has declined in its educational value, in its economic significance, and in the degree to which it fosters meaningful intergenerational contact. Moreover, during the last quarter century, we believe, much of the work available for young people has shifted from neutral positions on each of these dimensions to negative ones. And for this reason, over the course of the last century, the impact of early work on young people's development has become less positive.

TABLE 2.1

Dimensions of Adolescent Work Experiences

| | Context | | |
	Educational	*Economic*	*Social*
Positive	Imparts skills, knowledge, habits, or attitudes that are valuable for successful assumption or performance of adult work roles	Serves some economic necessity to family and/or community (work is necessary for family's or community's well-being)	Brings youth into contact with adults and fosters meaningful intergenerational relationships
Neutral	Does not affect the acquisition of work-relevant skills, knowledge, habits, or attitudes	Work is not required by family or community but may benefit either financially	Neither facilitates nor impedes intergenerational ties
Negative	Fosters habits or attitudes or teaches skills that may be undesirable for future work roles	Work serves financial needs of individual youth exclusively and earnings are used chiefly for immediate consumption of nonessentials	Furthers separation of young people from adults; strengthens peer culture and accentuates intergenerational differences

The Changing Educational Context of Adolescent Work: The Erosion of Continuity

In so-called traditional, or nonindustrialized, societies, youngsters typically are included in the work activities of the community from an early age. They accompany their parents, members of their extended family, or other workers in the community during much of the work day. The worlds of work and education are merged. Working side by side with adults, young people learn the tasks that they will be expected to perform on their own—and pass on to a new generation of youngsters—when they themselves attain adult status. Although the tasks delegated to children may differ from those reserved for adults, the nature of the work is essentially the same. More important, the work tasks themselves form a foundation upon which are built the capabilities necessary for adult work in the community. Thus, while youngsters may learn how to collect building materials before learning how to build, how to track animals before learning how to use weapons or kill them, or how to prepare food for cooking before actually learning how to cook, the skills and knowledge they acquire through these early work activities are part of enduring sequences that will be drawn upon throughout adulthood.

This sort of continuity between the knowledge and skills acquired through early work and those needed for adulthood has not been limited to life in traditional societies. Prior to industrialization, it also was common for young people's early work experience to be directly linked to the work they eventually would perform as adults. In the United States and in much of western Europe—at least up until the end of the nineteenth century—many young people were socialized into adult work roles through apprenticeships, both formal and informal, in which they were paired with adult workers in order to learn a specific craft or trade. In many cases, especially in those where the apprentice boarded with his or her employer, the relationship between the two was expected to serve a social as well as an economic function: the adult was charged with the socialization and education of the youngster; the youngster was expected to treat the mentor dutifully and respectfully. Indeed, as historian John Gillis (1981) points out, the householder—the employer of the young person—was called *pater familias,* "because he should have fatherly care over his servants, as if they were his children" (p. 8).

Some apprenticeships were between family members; some were extrafamilial. But in either case it was assumed that the apprentice would continue on in the same line of work as the mentor after having acquired the necessary skills. Often boys learned their fathers' work in preparation for joining, and eventually succeeding, them in the business or on the farm. Like the early work experience characteristic of life in nonindustrialized society, the adolescent apprenticeship provided for a continuous transition into adult work roles—the work performed during adolescence was essentially the same as the work performed during adulthood. And as a consequence, the learning that occurred on the job for the apprentice was clearly and directly relevant to the work that individual would perform as an adult.

Often apprenticeships were arranged for youngsters by their families; this was especially the case among youth whose families were involved in manufacturing. For example, historian Joseph Kett (1977), in his history of adolescence in America, recounts, as fairly typical for males living in urban environments, the youth of Baxter D. Whitney, who was born in Massachusetts in 1817:

> At the age of 6, Whitney began to work at piecing rolls in his father's [woolen] mill, a task which occupied him full-time until he was 11, except for two weeks spent each summer and winter in school. At 11 he was sent to work on carding, at 12 on repairs. A year later his father sent him to Worcester to assist a firm of machinists in constructing looms for the senior Whitney's mill. Four years later, Whitney, now 17, entered Fitchberg Academy for a term before returning to Winchendon as a repair foreman for a company which had bought his father's mill. (P. 25)

During the last quarter of the nineteenth century, increased industrialization, the erosion of opportunities within the skilled trades, and the rise of secondary education together led to the disappearance of apprenticeships. Shrinking opportunities for adult craftspersons led to the zealous guarding of opportunities in the skilled and semiskilled trades by unions (Kett 1977). According to one study of British youth, by the turn of the century only about 15 percent of out-of-school employed teenagers were working in the skilled trades (Gillis 1981). Similar conditions existed in the United States. According to Kett (1977): "The Massachusetts data indicate that skilled crafts virtually excluded teenagers is the 1870s. In carpentry, cabinet making, brick making, blacksmithing, and masonry . . . young people aged 16 to 20 comprised less than 20 percent of the workforce 16 and over" (pp. 146–47).

The declining number of apprenticeship opportunities during the closing decades of the nineteenth century led to quite different outcomes for youngsters from different social and economic backgrounds. Adolescents from affluent families— who in the past might have had desirable apprenticeships arranged through family connections—instead were enrolled in school. These teenagers did not seek employment until their schooling was completed, often after a prolonged professional education.

Youngsters from poorer families reaped no such benefits of industrialization. Adolescents whose families were dependent on their children's earnings could not afford to continue in school. Rather they were forced to work in whatever jobs were available, typically, in dead-end, "boy labor" jobs created by industrialization, such as errand runners or street vendors— jobs that were unlikely to provide opportunities for advancement.

The gradual disappearance of apprenticeships in America over the course of the nineteenth century marked the end of naturally occurring work experience that was structured with the specific intent of preparing young people for the careers they would have as adults. It also marked the beginning of a very important, class-differentiated change in the route individuals would take in order to travel from adolescence to adulthood. "Prior to the late 19th century," writes Kett, "class differences had not been reflected primarily in the early and middle teens" (that is, the activities of youngsters, before their late teens, were not sharply differentiated by their family's social position). "Youth of different classes had worked side by side on farms and in small machine shops, even though their ultimate destinations differed" (p. 152). And these early jobs more often than not led to career employment in related fields, although at different statuses for the affluent and the poor.

By the beginning of the twentieth century, however, early experience in the labor force had come to have little educational relevance for adult employment. No longer did adolescent work form an educational bridge to adulthood. For middle-class youngsters, preparation for future work roles was to take place primarily in the classroom. And for the less fortunate, adolescent work was to come to mean dead-end, menial, errand-running. As one writer described the situation in turn-of-the-century England, "Boys are kept to boys' work, men to men's work; there is no natural passage from one to the other" (Bray 1913, cited in Gillis 1981, pp. 126–27).

As discontinuous as adolescent work experience had become by the turn of the century, however, it has become even more so over the last eighty years. This is hardly surprising, for continuity in work experience can exist only when the nature of working life changes very little from generation to generation and when the successful performance of adult work requires relatively little formal schooling. In the highly technological, highly specialized, and rapidly changing job market of contemporary America, however, adolescent work has become, for many, irrelevant to adult careers.

One reason for the erosion of continuity in work experience is that in a hotly competitive job market, beginning job opportunities are determined more by labor market conditions at the time an individual decides to enter the work force than by individual interests and capabilities. Gaining early work experience as a means of breaking into a career later on is of limited usefulness in today's job market. A sixteen-year-old, for instance, may take on a job at the local gas station with the intent of becoming an auto mechanic after completing high school. But two years later, diploma and work experience in hand, he may find that there are simply no openings for auto mechanics in the community—for him or anybody else. This sort of structural mismatch—between individuals' prior training and labor market opportunities—is a common problem in contemporary society. (It also is one of the primary reasons for the poor track record of vocational education programs, which often prepare students for jobs that do not exist.) Our rapidly changing labor market no longer permits individuals to anticipate with certainty job openings two or more years in the future. In many fields, much of the training youngsters conceivably might receive during adolescence will be outdated by the time they enter into adult occupations. (Indeed, the nature of jobs themselves changes so quickly that many young adults find themselves entering occupations that did not even exist when they were teenagers.) It is for this reason that employers increasingly have come to rely on internal, employer-specific, on-the-job training programs rather than hire individuals who ostensibly have received their training through adolescent work experience. Today, in direct contrast with previous eras, the best preparation a young employee can bring to a new position is not job-specific training in that field—this the employer can best provide—but a strong educational background and an ability to learn new skills. The work experience one accrues as a teenager—even in jobs that in the past may have given the individual a leg up on a career ladder—is unlikely to link up directly to a similar adult career.

With the continued expansion of white-collar and professional opportunities and the concomitant shrinkage of openings in blue-collar segments of the labor force, the nature of career routes—and in particular, the point at which the individual makes a transition from adolescence into adult work roles—has changed dramatically. Once upon a time, an apprentice carpenter might have worked his way up to being a master carpenter. A supermarket boxboy who stayed with the same company might have moved up through the ranks gradually and eventually become a regional sales manager. A clerk at a neighborhood pharmacy one day might have taken over the store. Today, however, wrapping hamburgers at the local fast-food franchise is less likely to lead to a management position in the food service industry than is a master's degree in business administration. Because the continuity that once existed between adolescent and adult work is no longer found in the jobs of contemporary youth, adolescent employment no longer provides the education or training that lays the groundwork for adult occupational success.

Three occupations historically have provided continuity in young people's passage from adolescent to adult employment: the skilled trades and crafts, factory work, and farm work. Adolescent jobs in each of these occupations have clear adult counterparts: adolescent apprentices resemble adult craftsworkers; young factory workers perform tasks similar to those performed by older ones; farm hands work alongside farmers. Youngsters who have worked in these occupational categories in the past often have continued in these trades as adults, suggesting that bridges between adolescent and adult employment have existed in these sectors of the labor force. But over the past one hundred years, adolescent work in these occupational groups has diminished significantly and has been replaced by employment in occupations that have little connection to adult employment.

That the nature of adolescent work has become more discontinuous can be seen by examining census data concerning the occupations of employed youngsters at different points in time. We noted earlier that the employment of young people in skilled trades and crafts positions declined dramatically at the turn of the century with the disappearance of apprenticeships. Indeed, by 1940, when the Bureau of the Census first began providing detailed information on the employment of adolescents, only 1 percent of all employed sixteen- and seventeen-year-olds—in school as well as out of school—and less than one-half of 1 percent of employed fourteen- and fifteen-year-olds were working as craftspeople.

A similar decline in adolescent factory work took place several decades later (see figure 2.1). Thus, whereas during the first part of the twentieth century many adolescents were employed as factory workers—largely in cotton mills and canneries—these jobs gradually disappeared as the child protection movement gained momentum, more stringent child labor laws were enacted, and compulsory schooling became more widespread. Child labor legislation was so effective that by 1940, only 13 percent of all working sixteen- and seventeen-year-olds (students and nonstudents) and less than 5 percent of fourteen- and fifteen-year-olds were employed as operatives in factories, and even fewer as nonfarm laborers. Last to decline historically was adolescent farm work. In 1940 farm work accounted for nearly half of all employed sixteen- and seventeen-year-olds and over two-thirds of all employed fourteen- and fifteen-year-olds. By 1950 only about one-third of employed teenagers worked on farms; by 1960, this figure had dropped to about 10 percent; and by 1970, to about 5 percent. The percentage has remained at this level since that time.

Figure 2.1

Percentage of Sixteen- and Seventeen-year-old Workers (Students and Nonstudents Combined) Employed as Skilled Laborers (Crafts and Trades), Factory Workers, and Farm Workers, 1940–1980.

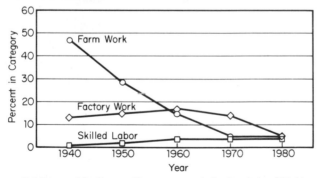

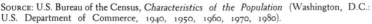

SOURCE: U.S. Bureau of the Census, *Characteristics of the Population* (Washington, D.C.: U.S. Department of Commerce, 1940, 1950, 1960, 1970, 1980).

In contrast to the decline of crafts, factory, and farm work during this period, the employment of young people in retail and service positions expanded rapidly. In 1940 service workers (excluding private household workers) accounted for only 3 percent of employed fourteen- and fifteen-year-olds and only 6 percent of employed sixteen- and seventeen-year-olds. Sales workers accounted for approximately 9 percent and 7 percent, respectively. Thus in 1940 between 10 percent and 15 percent of young workers were employed in retail or service positions. By 1970 retail and service positions accounted for nearly half of all employed fourteen- and fifteen-year-olds and over one-third of all employed sixteen- and seventeen-year-olds (see figure 2.2).

The flow of adolescent workers into sales and service work —perhaps more a tidal wave than a flow—was especially strong among student workers, for whom the part-time, flexibly scheduled positions in restaurants and shops appeared tailor-made. By 1980 teenagers were employed in a substantially "new" adolescent workplace. Together, jobs in the retail and service sectors accounted for 56 percent of all employed sixteen- and

Figure 2.2

Percentage of Sixteen- and Seventeen-year-old Workers (Students and Nonstudents Combined) Employed as Service Workers (Excluding Private Household Workers) and Sales Workers, 1940–1980.

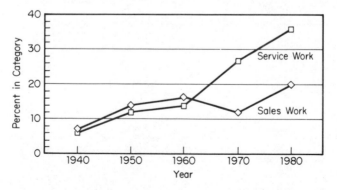

SOURCE: U.S. Bureau of the Census, *Characteristics of the Population* (Washington, D.C.: U.S. Department of Commerce, 1940, 1950, 1960, 1970, 1980).

Figure 2.3

Percentage of Sixteen- and Seventeen-year-old Workers (Students and Nonstudents Combined) Employed in the "New" (Service and Sales) Versus the "Old" (Crafts, Factory, and Farm) Adolescent Workplace, 1940–1980.

SOURCE: U.S. Bureau of the Census, *Characteristics of the Population* (Washington, D.C.: U.S. Department of Commerce, 1940, 1950, 1960, 1970, 1980).

seventeen-year-olds—nearly half of all male sixteen- and seventeen-year-old workers and over two-thirds of all female workers of this age (see figure 2.3). The "old" adolescent workplace of crafts, factory, and farm positions, today accounts for only 14 percent of sixteen- and seventeen-year-old workers.

Although the entire American work force had been moving in this direction, the shift from farm, factory, and crafts work to retail and service work was far more rapid among teenagers than among adult workers (see figure 2.4). Between 1960 and 1980, the proportion of adult workers employed in skilled crafts positions remained constant, at 13 percent, and the proportion employed as operatives—that is, in factory and related positions—dropped only slightly, from 18 percent to 14 percent. Only farm work fell off sharply during this period, from 9 percent of the adult labor force in 1960 to about 3 percent in 1980. Thus these three occupational categories accounted for about 40 percent of the adult labor force in 1960, and 30 percent of all adults were still employed in factory, farm, or skilled trades positions as of 1980.

During this same period, however, the proportion of teenag-

Figure 2.4

Percentage of Sixteen- and Seventeen-year-old Workers (Students and Nonstudents Combined) Versus Adults Employed in Service and Sales Work, Crafts, Factory, Farm Work, and Other Work in 1960 and 1980.

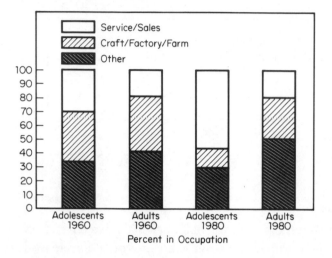

Percent in Occupation

SOURCE: U.S. Bureau of the Census, *Characteristics of the Population* (Washington, D.C.: U.S. Department of Commerce, 1960, 1980).

ers employed in these three categories fell precipitously—from about 36 percent to approximately 14 percent. (Skilled crafts positions remained constant over the twenty-year period, at about 4 percent; farm workers dropped from 15 percent to 5 percent; and factory workers fell from 17 percent to 5 percent.) And while the proportion of working sixteen- and seventeen-year-olds employed in sales and service work increased markedly during the period from 1960 to 1980—from 30 percent to 56 percent—the proportion of adults employed in these sectors increased barely at all—from 18 percent to 19 percent. Compared to the changes affecting the nature of adult occupations, those occurring in the adolescent workplace were enormous.

Perhaps more interesting is that even within the relatively broad occupational categories that now dominate the teenage labor force—in government terminology, the occupational group labeled "service" workers includes a diverse array of occupations—employment opportunities for adolescents are extraordinarily narrow today. Indeed, according to the High School and Beyond survey (Lewin-Epstein 1981), just two specific job categories account for nearly half of all employed high-school seniors: store clerks (27 percent) and food service workers (21 percent). (This survey, of course, does not include out-of-school youngsters.) These two jobs constitute the core of the new adolescent workplace. Jobs in the skilled trades, farm work, and factory work—the three mainstays of adolescent employment in past eras—together accounted for only about 13 percent of the total number of high-school seniors who held jobs (6 percent, 4 percent, and 3 percent, respectively).

The emergence over the past few decades of food service work and store clerking as the prototypical adolescent jobs has changed the nature of adolescent employment drastically. The discontinuity is apparent when teenagers are asked if they plan to continue as adults in the occupations in which they work during adolescence. Not surprisingly, teenagers who work in today's prototypical adolescent jobs are, compared with their peers, less likely to plan to continue in the same sort of work following graduation. This discontinuity is probably a blessing in some parents' eyes. As the parent of a food service worker put it in an interview with our research staff: "I don't want her to get into any [job] that she would get locked into. I think the type of job that she has now is not what I want her to do for the rest of her life." In contrast, youngsters who work in occupations that, although once important, today have become uncommon in the adolescent workplace are among the most likely to plan to remain in the same field later on. This difference, by the way, is true for both noncollege-bound and college-bound youngsters.

According to the High School and Beyond survey, for example, among high-school seniors not planning on going to college, 31 percent of adolescents employed in food service work plan to continue with the same job after graduation; among youngsters employed in the skilled trades, more than 60 percent report that they will stay with their "adolescent" job after graduating; similarly, more than half of all noncollege-bound seniors working in factories plan to continue with their job. Among college-bound youngsters, the percentage of seniors working in the food service industry who plan to continue in their job after high school is also relatively low: only about one-fifth expect to stay with the same job following graduation. In contrast, for college-bound adolescents working in the skilled trades, nearly one-third plan to continue in their "adolescent" job after graduation; among college-bound adolescent factory workers, the figure is 29 percent. In short, adolescents who are employed in the new adolescent workplace—a workplace consisting primarily of food service workers and store clerks—are less likely than their peers who work in the "old" adolescent workplace to have jobs that provide bridges to adult employment.

There are those who would argue, we suspect, that the value of early work experience in a rapidly changing society is not diminished by the fact that jobs no longer teach young people specific job skills that they will call upon in adult occupations. Rather it might be argued that early employment remains a valuable steppingstone to adult employment even today because it helps young people develop positive work habits, such as dependability, punctuality, and diligence—habits that will be just as valuable in adulthood as they are during adolescence. One could suggest, for example, that even though the job skills demanded of an adolescent fast-food worker differ markedly from those of an adult computer programmer, both jobs require workers to care about the quality of their work, to report to the job each workday, and to give an hour's work for an hour's pay. In other words, a case could be made for the role that early work experience plays in preparing young people for adult work by socializing them into the general work habits, values, and attitudes that will be expected of them in their adult occupations. In order to investigate this possibility—that what is learned from early work experience is not occupation-specific but rather applicable across a range of job types—it is necessary to look beyond the occupational categories of young people and examine what takes place on the typical young person's job.

What Teenagers Learn on the Job

As part of our own research program on teenagers' jobs, described more fully in the following chapter, we collected information on youngsters' work activities through detailed observations of adolescents in the workplace. Nearly one hundred workers were observed, selected to provide a cross-section of adolescent employees in six different job types: food service workers, retail store clerks, clerical workers, manual laborers, skilled laborers, and cleaners. During an average of nearly two hours spent observing each worker, a continuous record of each youngster's work and nonwork activities was made by a trained observer.

One of the questions we were interested in concerned differences among job types in the degree to which adolescent workers were given opportunities to learn or practice skills that might have some long-term payoff for future employment. We looked at this question by examining the extent to which youngsters were asked to call on the skills they had been taught in school, since one potentially valuable outcome of early employment could be that working provides opportunities for youngsters to see in a concrete way the usefulness of skills that schools present only in the abstract.

When we examined the amount of time youngsters spent reading, writing, performing arithmetic computations, or creating new information or materials for use in the worksite, we found that very few jobs in any category provide substantial opportunities for young people to use skills they have been taught in school. Overall, the picture looks rather dismal in this regard. The average youngster spends less than 10 percent of his or her time on the job—only about five minutes of every hour—in activities such as reading, writing, and arithmetic. More than one-fourth of the typical teenager's time on the job is spent in one of two activities: cleaning things or carrying things. Most jobs are characterized by little task variety, highly routinized activity, and the constant repetition of fairly uninteresting tasks.

But perhaps more important than this broad generalization is that the jobs prototypical of the new adolescent workplace are the least likely of all to be environments for general learning. Indeed, the fact that most adolescents spend so little time in cognitively demanding activity while at work—at least in the new adolescent workplace—makes it extremely difficult to argue that adolescent work experience continues to play an important role in preparing young people for the jobs they will encounter as adults. The average adolescent food service worker, for example, spends only about one minute of every hour on the job using school-taught skills. The youngster who is employed as a skilled laborer, in contrast, spends about 15 percent of his or her time in these activities. Clerical workers spend more than one-fourth of their time reading, writing, or performing arithmetic computations; store clerks spend only about one-tenth. Although we do not take issue with those who point out that the jobs of many adults are unstimulating, we find the argument that youngsters ought to gain experience in uninteresting adolescent jobs in order to ready themselves for similarly uninteresting adult ones quite fatuous.

Whether early work experience actually facilitates the growth of self-reliance, fosters healthy work habits, or engenders positive work-related attitudes and values are some of the questions that we examine in the following chapter. At this point, however, it is interesting to consider whether the sorts of work environments found in the new adolescent workplace even provide *opportunities* for individuals to develop these traits and behaviors. Using observational and interview data, we contrasted typical adolescent work environments along several different measures related to this issue.

In general, paralleling our findings concerning opportunities for learning, the overall picture of opportunities for developing self-reliance in the adolescent workplace is not impressive. Most adolescents' jobs hardly resemble those depicted in films like *It's a Wonderful Life*. Instead, the majority of teenagers have few chances to make major decisions and have little influence over the actions of others. Most work under a great deal of time pressure and are expected to repeat a limited number of highly routinized tasks quickly, efficiently, and without having to think very much about what they are doing. To put it concretely, wrapping fast-food items in paper containers as fast as one can is unlikely to teach a worker very much about self-reliance or decision making.

More important, perhaps, the findings again point to the limitations of employment in the new adolescent workplace. Specifically, food service workers are most likely to describe themselves as "goofing off" on the job, are least likely to report having opportunities to work alone (and consequently, we suspect, to develop self-management skills), are among the most likely workers to report having only few opportunities to make decisions (they are surpassed only by clerical workers on this dimension), and work under the greatest degree of time pressure (suggesting, in all likelihood, limited opportunities for autonomy). In contrast, skilled laborers and operatives—youngsters working in the "old" adolescent workplace—are least likely to report "goofing off," among the most likely to report having opportunities to make decisions, and generally work under less time pressure than their peers.

It appears, then, that jobs in the new adolescent workplace are not likely to provide extensive preparation for future work roles. Over the last one hundred years the educational value of early work experience has diminished steadily. Once a necessary part of preparation for adult careers, adolescent work experience has become virtually irrelevant to future work roles. Once a direct bridge between adolescence and adulthood, teenagers' jobs now constitute a secondary labor market that is largely disconnected from career employment. Once contexts for the socialization of responsible and productive adult activity, today jobs in the adolescent workplace provide few opportunities for young people to practice or acquire work habits that will serve them well in the future.

The Changing Economic Context of Adolescent Work: The Rise of Luxury Youth Employment

In the United States the economic context of adolescent work has passed through several stages. In preindustrial America, as in other preindustrialized countries, the labor of young people was necessary for familial and community survival. Prior to the introduction of compulsory secondary education, adolescents were expected to contribute to the economic good of their families and communities, and once youngsters had attained the requisite level of strength, size, capability, or expertise, they were put to work alongside adults. Adolescents usually were employed in the work activities of their parents or of nearby families—typically in farming. Indeed, one reason for the generally larger size of families in preindustrial America than in the twentieth century is that the labor of children was needed in order to keep family enterprises running smoothly. Whether youngsters worked for their own family or for another depended on that family's level of affluence, the number of children living in the household, and the relative value to the family of additional laboring hands versus cash payments or payments in kind that their youngster's labor could produce.

As industrialization spread and factories grew, young people's work shifted from the shops where skilled crafts were practiced and from farms into textile mills, coal mines, and canneries (Markham, Lindsey, and Creel 1914). During this period, which lasted roughly from the late-nineteenth century through the first decade of the twentieth century, the labor of adolescents remained economically important for families. Their wages were essential to maintain their parents' households. But the industries in which adolescents worked were marked by increased mechanization, and productivity became less and less a function of the sheer number of available workers. Society's economic dependence on the labor of adolescents began to wane. Over a period of about twenty years, adolescents lost their collective foothold in the labor force and their critical role in contributing to the economic well-being of society.

While it is clear that some segment of the working population was going to have to bear the consequences of automation at the turn of the century, it is not obvious why this burden necessarily had to fall so hard on the shoulders of young people. Several tenable explanations have been advanced. One is that the changing nature of work required a new type of worker—stronger, more experienced, and more capable of operating the machinery developed during the early stages of automation. Employers may have turned away from hiring adolescents out of concerns that young people could not work as efficiently or capably as adults (Bakan 1972). A second hypothesis links the decline in adolescent employment to the growth of trade unions: because automation resulted initially in greater competition for a declining number of job opportunities, organized labor fought hard to limit the use of young workers where adults might earn a living (Mnookin 1978). Yet a third possibility concerns the growth of the child welfare movement. During the early part of the twentieth century, child protectionists were crying out for stricter laws designed to protect young people from dangerous conditions and exploitation in the workplace. Some writers (Markham, Lindsey, and Creel 1914) linked the use of child labor to crime, illiteracy, poverty, and moral degeneracy.

In all likelihood, each of these three factors was important. But whatever the driving forces, the disappearance of young people from the labor force and their movement into schools could not have been achieved had it not been for the growth of the middle class during the second half of the nineteenth century and, specifically, the rise of middle-class values. As Gillis (1981) has noted, because of the trend toward smaller families in the middle classes, parents could afford a lengthier period of dependence on the part of their children and could make a more planful investment in their children's growth and development. This investment typically included extended schooling. Whereas the working classes needed to have large families so as to have as many children as possible in the labor force and earning money, the middle classes could afford to delay their children's employment and invest in the long-term payoff of education. Inasmuch as entering the labor force cut short schooling, exposed youngsters to dangerous conditions, and most likely led to a blue-collar occupation, it was viewed by middle-class parents as potentially interfering with their children's futures. Writes Gillis:

> [The] careers of boys were . . . carefully supervised by the parents, who, recognizing the decline in traditional kinds of apprenticeship, were taking a much greater interest in secondary education. Even businessmen, for whom classical education had

previously held little attraction, were increasingly concerned to gain for their sons the benefits of schooling to 16 or 17. (P. 100)

As for girls:

> Girls of the middle classes were kept at home until marriage, tightly supervised by their parents until they passed safely into the bosom of another family. An interest in female education was growing in the second half of the nineteenth century, partly as a result of surplus young women for whom marriage did not beckon. (P. 99)

Behind these social changes was an important change in the economic context of adolescent employment. Schooling—particularly when it lasts beyond the early years—is a very expensive proposition. Secondary education is essentially a luxury that can be afforded only by societies that can forego the labor of young people. And although one might reasonably attribute the withdrawal of youngsters from the labor force to the changing nature of work, the expanding power of trade unions, the growth of the child protection movement, the rise of the middle class, or the spread of compulsory schooling, the transformation of adolescents from workers into students would not have occurred had society not been able to afford it. By 1930 the United States had developed a level of affluence, and a type of economy, that enabled the nation to offer secondary education to a large segment of the population. In this respect, then, the rise of compulsory education during the first quarter of the twentieth century reflected the decline of the economic necessity of adolescents' work to society.

It is equally important to bear in mind, however, that in 1930 half of all fourteen- to seventeen-year-olds were not enrolled in school, mainly because a large number of families still depended on the fruits of their youngsters' employment. As a consequence, the withdrawal of youngsters from the labor force and their concomitant movement into secondary school began with the middle classes and only with time trickled down the socioeconomic ladder. Kett (1977) explains:

> The closing decades of the 19th century saw the emergence of a sharp difference between the opportunities available to middle-class and working-class youth. . . . The most attractive new jobs were opening up in the white-collar sector of the economy; the least attractive new positions were in factories. The prerequisite for access to white-collar jobs was the possession of formal education to age 14 and preferably to 16 or 18. Parents sufficiently wealthy to forgo the labor of their children during early and middle adolescence guided their offspring through a more prolonged period of schooling and thus qualified them for desirable jobs. Poor parents, on the other hand, had to rely on the labor of their children for support, and could not afford the opportunity cost of even slightly prolonged education. (Pp. 151–52)

Such socioeconomic differences in patterns of schooling and working were apparent on the aggregate as well as the individual level. Compulsory school attendance laws, for example, were enacted last in the more impoverished states—typically in the deep South—and those that were enacted usually granted exemptions to families who claimed poverty (Markham, Lindsey, and Creel 1914).

Accordingly, it was not until the middle and late 1930s that the ability of families to do without the labor of their youngsters became a cross-class phenomenon. (Although the increased wealth of the population certainly was not the only factor contributing to the spread of school enrollment, it undoubtedly played an important role; the child protection movement, concerns about the education of immigrant children, and changes in educational philosophy were also important.) That an increasingly broader segment of the population could afford to do without their children's earnings is reflected very clearly in changes in school enrollment patterns during the first four decades of this century. The proportion of American high-school–aged youngsters enrolled in school rose from about 10 percent at the turn of the century, to 33 percent in 1920, to 50 percent in 1930, and to more than 70 percent by 1940 (Tanner 1972). Over the course of the fifteen-year period between 1930 and 1945, increasingly more families reached a level of economic comfort sufficient to keep their children out of the labor force for most of adolescence and to allow their children to remain in high school. With few part-time jobs available during the school year, most youngsters' employment was limited to summer work. Indeed, in 1940 only 2 percent of fourteen- and fifteen-year-old students, fewer than 3 percent of enrolled sixteen-year-olds, and fewer than 5 percent of enrolled seventeen-year-olds held jobs during the school year.

By 1945 adolescent employment was clearly something that all but the very poor could do—and did do—without. However, during the postwar years, the economic context of adolescent work changed sharply. The American economy moved in new directions. As the service and retail sectors of the economy expanded, part-time employment opportunities grew, thus permitting—for the first time in American history—students to enter the labor force in large numbers. Writes labor force expert Beatrice Reubens: "It is true that a tradition has long existed in the United States that it was respectable, even praiseworthy to work one's way through school, but [before 1940] the numbers [of students who worked] were not large. Prior to World War II, attending school and holding a . . . job were almost exclusive activities" (Reubens, Harrison, and Rupp 1981, p. 296).

More interesting, perhaps, than simply the increased postwar popularity of working while attending school is the fact that the students who entered the labor force now came from among the nation's more affluent families.

Consider the following statistics, some of which were noted in chapter 1. In the 1980 High School and Beyond survey of high-school sophomores and seniors discussed earlier (Lewin-

Epstein 1981), information was gathered on the relationship between student employment and family income. The lowest rate of employment was among youngsters from families with annual incomes below $7,000. The highest rate of employment among sophomores was among those from families with incomes exceeding $20,000 annually. And among seniors, the highest rate of employment was found among those from families with annual incomes exceeding $25,000. The net result of the socioeconomic imbalance in teenage employment has been the rise of a condition that one might term luxury youth employment—namely, the widespread employment of youngsters who work not because of individual or familial financial need but because of a desire to accumulate discretionary income.

A direct illustration of the prevalence of luxury youth employment can be seen in an examination of spending patterns of employed youngsters. Although these spending patterns are influenced by a variety of factors—of which economic need is but one—understanding what youngsters do with their earnings gives some indication of how economically superfluous their work is. Youngsters who turn all or part of their earnings over to the family are probably living under more pressing financial circumstances than are adolescents who are saving for higher education or some other similar long-range purpose (such as establishing a separate residence after high-school graduation). And youngsters who save most of their earnings for higher education or some other long-term goal are probably living under more pressing conditions than are those who are free to spend all of their earnings on immediate personal needs and activities.

Data derived from the 1980 survey, Monitoring the Future —an annual national study of high-school seniors, directed by Lloyd Johnston, Jerald Bachman, and Patrick O'Malley (1982) —indicate that few youngsters spend their part-time employment earnings in a manner that suggests they work out of financial need. As we noted in chapter 1, only a very small minority of the survey sample reported using "most" or "all" of their earnings to help pay family living expenses (groceries, housing, and so on) or saving most of their earnings for future education. In contrast, a far larger number of males in the sample used most of their earnings for car payments or other car expenses, and, most telling of all, many youngsters reported spending most of their earnings on immediate personal needs and activities: clothing, stereo equipment, records, movies, recreation, and hobbies. If we view car expenses as falling into the category of immediate personal needs, we find that more than half of all working teenagers use the bulk of their earnings for discretionary spending. More than half of all working teenagers spend *none* of their income at all on family living expenses, and nearly this proportion report that they do not save any income at all for future education or other long-term anticipated expenses. In short, whereas working during adolescence was associated with familial financial need during the first half of the twentieth century, by 1980 it had become a distinctively individualistic, self-motivated phenomenon.

To what can we attribute the influx of well-to-do youngsters into the labor force? Why should working during adolescence, once a practice limited to the needy, have become such an absorbing activity among middle-class youth? At least three explanations are plausible. First, it is clear that the expansion of part-time job opportunities with schedules consonant with the school day permitted an adolescent population already eager to work to fulfill their desires for employment. One factor that certainly must have limited youngsters' labor-force participation in previous eras—particularly middle-class youngsters, whose parents certainly would not permit their children's schooling to be compromised by work—was the inherent scheduling conflict that existed between school and full-time employment. With the advent of part-time retail and service jobs, however, middle-class youngsters could now compete with their poorer peers for available employment opportunities.

A second explanation concerns the location of job opportunities in the service and retail sectors. As mentioned, data from the High School and Beyond survey indicate that employment rates are higher for suburban than for urban or rural youngsters. One reason for this difference is that service and retail job opportunities are relatively more plentiful in suburban areas. As teenage employment moved away from skilled crafts, manufacturing, and agriculture, it also moved away from inner cities and outlying rural areas. And since middle-class youngsters are likely to compose a relatively higher proportion of the adolescent population in suburban areas, they are also likely to compose a relatively higher proportion of the teenage labor force.

Although both of these accounts are plausible, neither really sheds light on whether, or why, middle-class youngsters' *interest* in working may have increased over the years. An examination of the changing place of adolescents as consumers in the national market economy suggests that the influx of middle-class youngsters into the part-time labor force may have been fueled by the deliberate and highly successful attempts of the advertising industry to cultivate consumption among these youngsters. "Prior to World War II, youth advertising was limited and generally aimed at college students or young married couples. During and after the war, however, leading American corporations and retail merchants began to recognize the extent of the youth market" (Gilbert 1984, p. 13).

One reason for the timing of this realization was that the concept of the American teenager was not really "invented" until World War II. (Although the term adolescent first appeared in the *Reader's Guide to Periodical Literature* in 1919, "teenager" was not listed until 1943. The magazine *Seventeen*, whose birth marked the commercial recognition of the "teenager," was first published in 1944.) The "adolescent" may well have been a product of the industrial revolution, as historians generally point out (Bakan 1972), but the label carried with it a different meaning and referent from those connoted by "teenager." "Adolescence" referred to a transitional stage of the lifespan, during which young people were recognized as being in a period of preparation for adulthood; it was "invented" during the industrial revolution insofar as industrialization both necessitated and permitted a lengthier transitional period than had previously been the case. Yet although adolescence prior to 1940 may have been a time of transition, it was neither a time of irresponsibility nor a time of autonomy. Young people were firmly under the control of their parents and of society's institutions.

But all of this was to change during the immediate postwar years. Spawned in part by the increased popularity of relatively more permissive patterns of child rearing—based largely on misinterpretations of John Dewey and Freud—and in part by the postwar rise in maternal employment, the "teenager" was born. The term referred to more than simply an individual whose age placed him or her somewhere between childhood and adulthood. It carried with it a sense of freedom, autonomy, and frivolousness; it connoted an individual who was not old enough to function as an adult member of society but who nonetheless was no longer under stringent parental control.

During the late 1940s, when this concept of "teenager" came into usage, the size of the population aged thirteen to nineteen years old was less than 15 million. By 1955 it had grown only slightly, to about 16 million. But between 1955 and 1965 it swelled by 60 percent, to 24 million, and by 1975 it had reached nearly 30 million—double the size of the teenage population just two decades earlier. The economic implications of this growth were enormous.

One of the first to promote the understanding that teenagers represented a large—and growing—consumer market was Eugene Gilbert, who founded the Gilbert Youth Marketing Company in 1945. Gilbert well understood that the changing nature of family life—and the transformation of adolescents (persons of a certain age) into teenagers (persons with a great deal of freedom, few responsibilities, and ample leisure time) —was a marketing dream-come-true. The decline in parental authority over all sorts of teenagers' behavior—including, potentially, their spending patterns—coupled with the increased affluence of their parents would produce a huge market of young consumers with a sizable amount of disposable income (Macdonald 1958). "Free money" was what Gilbert called it. He saw early on that many teenagers, their pockets stuffed with allowances but their consumption unburdened by financial obligations, actually had more disposable income than did their parents. "The adult market is a depression-conscious market," wrote Gilbert in his 1957 book, *Advertising and Marketing to Young People:* "Even those who have never suffered financially are nevertheless acutely aware of what they term 'extravagant' purchases. . . . Young people, on the other hand, have never known a nonprosperous world. What the adult considers a luxury, young people consider a necessity to keep pace with today's living" (Gilbert, cited in Macdonald 1958, p. 74).

Gilbert realized that the expansion of mass media would help lead to the spread of a national, homogenous youth culture with extraordinary commercial potential. Once this potential was realized, it was relatively simple for marketing firms to shape the tastes and nurture the acquisitive desires of young consumers.

It is not entirely clear to what extent youngsters' interest in working sparked their interest in spending and to what extent their interest in spending kindled their interest in working. But the two motives undoubtedly played off each other in an increasingly powerful cycle of luxury work and luxury consumption. The growing number of working middle-class youngsters with money in their pockets stimulated manufacturers and retailers to exert stronger efforts to capture their share of, and further cultivate, teenagers' discretionary spending. And at the same time, the deliberate campaigns of advertisers to sell the

luxury goods that were increasingly portrayed as necessary components of the middle-class teenager's social life impelled more
and more youngsters to take on jobs.

The Changing Social Context of Adolescent Employment:
The Rise of the Age-Segregated Adolescent Workplace

Over the course of the twentieth century, the workplace in
which young people are employed has become increasingly
age-segregated. Rather than working side by side with adults
—adults who might serve not only as on-the-job instructors but
as confidants and mentors—today's young people are more
likely than not to work side by side with other adolescents. As
a consequence, one of the most important functions that early
work experience may have served in the past, namely, the
integration of young people into adult society, has been considerably eroded. Rather than mingling the generations and providing a context for the informal interaction of young people
with their elders, today's adolescent workplace has become a
bastion for the adolescent peer group.

The decline of intergenerational contact in the workplace
over the last one hundred years is attributable to several factors.
The disappearance of apprenticeships during the latter part of
the nineteenth century, discussed earlier, marked an important
turning point in this regard. It began a movement away from
one-to-one work relationships—one adult working in close
company with one youngster—and toward the more economically profitable, but less educationally valuable, situation in
which one adult supervised a large group of young charges.
Ultimately this trend continued, with the ratio of adolescents

to adults present in the typical work setting growing to the point where today adolescents work essentially unsupervised by adults in many work settings.

This change took place for many reasons. Apprenticeships in the trades and crafts, of course, were built around close supervisory relationships, partly because they served a variety of non-work as well as economic purposes. Moreover, training a youngster in craftswork required one-on-one supervision, or something close to it, largely because of the highly skilled nature of the work involved. But as adolescent work moved away from positions in the crafts and skilled trades and into unskilled jobs in factories, the need for close supervision and training was obviated. The more unskilled jobs for adolescents became, the less there was a need for close adult supervision.

The discovery of more efficient means of managing inexperienced workers helped further the trend toward lower levels of adult supervision. Although the factories operating at the turn of the century undoubtedly had higher ratios of adolescents to adults than did smaller enterprises of previous eras, it was still necessary for employers to provide adult supervision to ensure that quality control did not slip. But with the advent of more scientific management strategies and the increasingly widespread use of automated machinery, the need for close supervision or intensive training of inexperienced workers by adults diminished. In many jobs, youngsters can now be "oriented" to their duties in groups, and in a minimal amount of time, thus saving the employer the expense of having to pay an experienced adult worker to train new employees. Indeed, as fast-food restaurant owners realized during the 1950s, for example, the implementation of finely tuned and carefully tested work procedures—having preweighed and preformed hamburger patties shipped frozen to individual restaurant franchises, or using machines that dispensed preset amounts of soft drinks automatically—allowed owners to replace adult supervisors entirely in many cases. The operation can be run as effectively and far less expensively without adults present. In many fast-food restaurants today, for instance, sixteen-year-old employees are supervised by eighteen- or nineteen-year-old "managers." The industry's 300 percent annual turnover rate may perhaps result in part from this management strategy, but the strategy has proven to be cost effective.

Changes in the nature of the adolescent-employer relationship—or, more precisely, changes in the extent to which forging and maintaining such a relationship was desirable—also played a major role in reshaping the age mix in the workplace. The craftsman was forced to develop a personal relationship with his apprentice because the apprentice was likely to continue on in the same line of work, perhaps as a partner in the craftsman's business. The growing discontinuity in youngsters' jobs, however, lessened the likelihood that adolescent employees would find themselves positioned on a career ladder and, consequently, diminished employers' need to make personal investments in their charges. Moreover, the rise of large corporations during the early twentieth century, and the resulting rise of middle management, meant that the individuals who were charged with supervising adolescents' work were no longer the same individuals who had a strong economic stake in the company's future success. As opposed to a self-employed craftsman, for example, who had to invest a great deal of his own time (and, consequently, money) in the training and socialization of a young apprentice—and who could not afford to have an apprentice leave before his personal investment was repaid—a middle manager in one of today's large corporate employers of young people can afford a calculated degree of job turnover among his or her employees. In many cases it is cheaper for an employer to let young workers make a certain number of mistakes, or let a certain number of them quit, than to invest in more adults to train them and oversee their work.

Changes in the nature of the workplace took place alongside these changes in the nature of work. The work conditions typical of the early-twentieth-century sweatshops were appalling, and the environments in which youngsters work today are in most respects vastly superior to those of earlier times. But at the same time it is important to point out that as a social context, the adolescent workplace of seventy-five years ago had an important advantage over its counterpart today: turn-of-the-century factories, farms, shops, and mills put young people in touch with adult members of the community, adults from whom they learned about work, about the expectations of the community with respect to being an adult, about their strengths and foibles. Consider, for example, this adult's recollection of his early work in rural Illinois during the latter part of the nineteenth century:

> On arrival in Geff our mother . . . hired me out to [Mrs. Rapp] as a chore boy about the store; it was the capsheaf of my ambition. I was to have four dollars the first month and then, in the winter, my board during the school months. I was 12 then and have never been out of a job since. Actually my pay was raised to five dollars a month the next spring and I stayed on there through three full years. My experience with [the] yard was almost a duplicate of that related by Booker T. Washington in his *Working With the Hands.* I, too, had an uncompromising overseer; I, too, had to work with a blunt-edged sickle; I, too, had to hack away hour after hour at the long, tough grass to get it even. . . . When I finished it the first time, Mrs. Rapp came out for inspection. She made no criticism or suggestion but praised me mildly. And, to quote the words of Booker T. Washington, "When I saw that all this change and improvement was a creation of my own hands, my whole nature began to change. I felt a self-respect, an encouragement and a satisfaction that I had never before enjoyed or thought possible." (Cited in Coleman 1972, p. 74)

With the growth of compulsory secondary education and the rise of the child protection movement, the valuable social context of adolescent work began to break down. Youngsters became separated from the world of adult work—so separated, in fact, that by 1940 few teenagers were employed on a regular basis. The workplace had ceased to be a context in which young people could be socialized by elders outside their own families.

Although youngsters rediscovered the world of work after World War II, the workplace they found was very different from the one their predecessors had occupied. The nature of the workplace had changed. Adolescents, who had worked alongside adults at the turn of the century, had become a part of a distinctly adolescent labor market, where they worked apart from their elders, in the minimum-wage, part-time, retail and service positions that only teenagers could afford to hold.

The erosion of intergenerational contact in the workplace during the first half of this century was mirrored by changes in family life or, more specifically, by changes in the family as an economic and work institution. One of the most important work settings in which adolescents had had contact with elders was the home. During the mid-nineteenth century, when a large percentage of the population was engaged in agricultural work, the daily work tasks of the family provided opportunities for young people to receive a good deal of informal socialization from parents and older siblings, since adolescents often accompanied family members on chores and errands. Thus, because children and their parents often were employed in the same work setting, work provided additional opportunities for parents to instruct and socialize their children.

As the population became more urban, however, and work life and family life became more and more separate, such opportunities became increasingly scarce. The disappearance of the household as a workplace moved many adults who had been employed in family enterprises out of the home during the day and into work settings that were physically separated from residential neighborhoods. Moreover, with industrialization and the growth of large factories, urban areas became centers of employment where thousands of workers could be dispersed over numerous work settings. Thus when children worked in factories and shops at the beginning of the industrial era, it was no longer necessarily the case that they worked for the same employer or in the same work setting as their parents.

During the second half of the twentieth century, improvements in public and private transportation made it possible for more and more adults to leave home each day—mothers as well as fathers—and travel long distances to work. Eventually it became possible even for youngsters to travel to jobs beyond the boundaries of their home neighborhoods. This increased mobility had two important implications for the growing age segregation of the adolescent workplace. First, it continued the trend, established during the earlier part of the century, for parents and children to be able to work for different employers in different locales. This limited the amount of contact children and their parents might have during the course of a work day and contributed to the decline in authority that parents had over their teenagers' behavior.

Second, the separation of children's work from that of their parents made it less likely that children would be working for an employer who was familiar with the family. Smelser (1959), for example, notes that at one point in history, parents tried to ensure that their children were apprenticed to suitable masters. Judgments of suitability were possible, of course, because the apprentice's parents and potential mentors lived in the same or neighboring communities and were known to each other—if not personally, then by reputation. But with youngsters today working in communities far from home, and with both parents and youngsters often working outside the neighborhood where they live, such social connections are difficult to forge and to maintain. Our own surveys of young workers indicate that, in contrast to what must have been the case in earlier eras, surprisingly few adolescents today report having found their job through a social tie of their family. Actually, nearly as many teenagers report obtaining their jobs through friends (24 percent) or on their own (23 percent) as through a family connection (26 percent). Thus not only have adolescents become increasingly segregated from adults in the workplace, but the few adults that they are likely to encounter at work are more often than not strangers to their family. Consequently, these adults are far less likely than their earlier counterparts to perceive themselves as having a legitimate stake in the young person's socialization and development. The age segregation that has developed in the new adolescent workplace is psychological as well as social.

By 1970, although the majority of teenagers had returned to the world of work, most were employed in jobs that isolated them from, rather than connected them with, their elders. In our studies of employed teenagers we saw repeatedly—via questionnaires, interviews, and observation—that the workplace adolescents encounter is no longer a source of extensive interaction with adults. By our observations, the average worker spends 78 percent of his or her time outside the immediate vicinity of an adult and only 12 percent of it near a supervisor. ("Adult," incidentally, was generously defined as someone at least two years older than the youth.) Indeed, in some types of jobs, such as food service work, adolescents interact with other teenagers just as often as with their "elders."

Given that teenage workers spend so little time in the company of adults and specifically in the company of adult supervisors, it is not surprising to learn that youngsters receive little formal instruction from adults at work. We observed just over one instance per hour, on the average, of an adult giving instructions or explanations to youngsters about their work. This undoubtedly is because little instruction is necessary to prepare youngsters for the job tasks that they are assigned. (What most young people do at work for pay is an extension of activities they have already learned and performed in other settings.) Youngsters and their elders, on the average, do not even talk about work a great deal while on the job. Moreover, although instruction is generally infrequent on all teenagers' jobs, it is far less plentiful in the new adolescent workplace than in other work environments. Clerical workers and skilled laborers, for example, receive more than eight times the amount of on-the-job training as do food service workers, and about twice the amount as store clerks.

The observational data, we must stress, pertain to events that are visible and audible. It is certainly possible that youngsters learn job skills, and more general work-related skills and attitudes, without direct attempts by adults to impart this knowledge. As we noted in chapter 1, many of the blue-ribbon commissions advocating more extensive participation of young people in the world of work based their argument in part on the hope that youngsters would encounter on their jobs adults who might serve as mentors or confidants. The low proportion of time youngsters spend near adults, however, suggests that these commissions may have been overly optimistic, and sounds a cautionary note: Adolescents cannot learn from adults by observation and inference, if adults are not in fact observable in the workplace.

These findings foreshadow what we learned about the incidence of adults in the workplace who serve as sources of advice and comfort for adolescent workers or, in the language of the day, as sources of "social support." For not only are teenagers today less likely to be employed in the company of elders, to receive extensive supervision on the job, or to discuss work with adults very often, they are also unlikely to be employed by or with adults with whom they are able to form relationships that transcend—physically or psychologically—the boundaries of the work setting itself. There may have been a time during which work settings provided opportunities for youngsters to encounter adults who transmitted "skills, culture, ideas, and information" and served as "personal resources" to whom youngsters could turn "in times of stress" (President's Science Advisory Committee 1973, pp. 132–48), but that time appears to have long since passed. Our observations indicate that when interaction between adolescents and adults does occur, it is likely to be limited to the immediate work tasks at hand, suggesting that even in situations where adults are present, they are not functioning as confidants or guides to the mores of the community. Indeed, youngsters spend only about 2 percent of their time on the job—about one minute per hour —engaged in discussion with adults of topics other than work.

To buttress our observational data, we also asked our samples of workers a series of questions designed specifically to assess the extent to which they felt close to, or formed relationships with, adults at work who might serve as sources of guidance or support. Only about one-third reported feeling "close" to their supervisors. It is instructive to place this figure in context. More youngsters reported feeling close or very close to their mother, father, favorite sibling, best friend of the same sex, and best friend of the opposite sex than to their favorite adult at work. (The only individual they said they felt less close to than their best-liked adult at work was their best-liked teacher at school.) Fewer than 10 percent reported that they would "definitely" discuss a personal problem with an "adult or supervisor" at work. (For contrast, the figures for "mother" and "best friend of the same sex" are 39 percent and 55 percent, respectively.)

One final piece of evidence helps to characterize relations between adolescents and the adults they encounter at work. Between 90 percent and 97 percent of young workers—figures from our interview and questionnaire studies, respectively— indicate that they interact with their adult supervisor exclusively in the work setting. They do not see these workplace "elders" anywhere else. Four out of five youngsters reported that their interactions with adult coworkers other than supervisors also are confined to the workplace.

Our evidence clearly challenges the claim of workplace advocates that working will enrich youngsters' supply of interested, caring, supportive adults. By all indications, the adolescent workplace today most certainly does not function for most teenagers as a context in which meaningful personal relationships are formed between young and old. It would not be exaggerating to say that the new adolescent workplace has been just as effective as the schools in segregating youth from adults.

The New Adolescent Workplace

The conviction that work experience benefits adolescents is based on an image of the world of work as it existed in previous eras, when youngsters were engaged in work activities that readied them for adulthood and contributed to the economic well-being of their communities. Many young people worked in jobs that were similar to the jobs they would eventually hold as adults. Many worked side by side with their parents, or with other adults, from whom they learned important lessons about what it meant to have adult roles and responsibilities. Most, if not all, worked because their family needed their labor or their earnings.

These conditions that once made early employment an important and valuable component of youngsters' preparation for adulthood, however, are fast disappearing in contemporary America. The new adolescent workplace is an "adolescent" workplace in the sense that young people perform tasks and use skills there that few will perform or use again in work settings after they cease to be adolescents. It is an "adolescent" workplace in the sense that young people have little meaningful contact with adults who have a stake in their socialization for the future; much of the social contact in the new adolescent workplace is between agemates, or near agemates, rather than between young and old. And it is a *teenage* workplace in that the economic rewards it generates typically are used for the accoutrements of a period of life characterized by much freedom and little responsibility—records, movies, designer clothing, fast food, alcohol, drugs—and not for long-term "adult" investments, such as college, or for increasing the adolescent's ability to establish an independent household.

In short, the educational, economic, and social contexts of adolescent work have changed dramatically. For this reason, the view that early work experience is an inherently valuable activity, with clear and predictable positive psychosocial consequences for young people, may no longer be true.

CHAPTER

3

Working and Adolescent Development: The Research Evidence

U NTIL recently there has been little empirical research on the effects of working on adolescents. Advocates of work generally have recommended specially designed jobs for youth, but most adolescents work in "naturally occurring" jobs that were not designed specifically to advance their educational or psychosocial interests. It is important to ask: Are the consequences of working about which social analysts have speculated in fact occurring under prevailing workplace conditions? Are there effects of working that these experts had not anticipated? In this chapter we examine what is known about the benefits and costs to adolescents of part-time employment during the school year. Our discussion focuses on the effects of working on youngsters' responsibility, schooling, rates of crime and delinquency, health and well-being, and future employment prospects. The studies on which we draw for answers include surveys of nationally representative samples and more intensive investigations of smaller samples of suburban youth. Further detailed information on these studies is summarized in the appendix.

Developing Responsibility

One of the most often stated and least critically evaluated beliefs about working is that it teaches youngsters to be "responsible." This is the impassioned message behind *Our Children Should Be Working* (Stephens 1979), and this is the conviction of many people about what youngsters get out of holding a job. The President's Science Advisory Committee (1973), concerned about deficiencies in the socialization of youth for adult roles, also looked to work experience to stimulate growth in responsibility. The committee's Panel on Youth, it will be recalled, argued that the schools, because of their hierarchical organization and their need to focus on the development of youngsters' cognitive skills, provide a deficient environment for adolescents to learn self-management, independence, and initiative. Moreover, because of the schools' emphasis on individual achievement, youngsters have too few opportunities to work jointly with others on tasks that affect the well-being of others. The former set of skills—self-management, autonomy, and initiative—reflects the ability to take

DEXTER LIBRARY
NORTHLAND COLLEGE
ASHLAND, WI 54806

personal responsibility; knowing how to cooperate with others and perform reliably work that matters to others reflects the capacity for *social responsibility*—and both kinds of skills are needed for successful performance of adult roles. Finally, the panel noted, the demands of attending school interfere with young people's gaining job experience and thus with their acquiring the competencies of a good worker. The panel and other school critics proposed, therefore, that adolescents should get more exposure to the workplace, where they believed youngsters would have more opportunities to plan and monitor their own activities, work with others, and perform economically productive tasks.

Expectations that holding a job will teach youngsters to be "more responsible" seem reasonable enough. Whether these expectations can be confirmed empirically is another matter. Most of the information we have about the responsibility-inducing effects of working comes from a study we conducted. In the course of this project, we explored opportunities for responsibility-taking at work in interviews and on-site observations of employed adolescents. We also compared questionnaire responses of workers holding their first steady part-time jobs with those of youngsters who had never worked regarding aspects of responsibility that could be evaluated outside the work context. In one component of our research comparing workers and nonworkers, we assessed workers only *after* they had begun working (Greenberger and Steinberg 1981). In "cross-sectional" research of this kind, it is difficult to attribute any differences between individuals—here, workers and non-workers—to the experience that most obviously differentiates them—in this case, being employed. It is possible, for example, that any differences in responsibility between the groups *pre-dated* the workers' taking a job.[1] In another component of our comparative research, therefore, we followed up our sample of nonworkers and reevaluated them on various dimensions of responsibility a year later (Steinberg et al. 1982). By that time, some had become workers, while others remained nonworkers. In "longitudinal," or over-time, research of this kind, it is logically more defensible to attribute any differences in responsibility between workers and nonworkers to the experience that distinguishes them—employment—as long as their scores on the same measures of responsibility at the time of initial assessment are held constant.

We took a broad perspective when assessing "responsibility," in view of the multitude of virtues the term covers. In the domain of personal responsibility, we assessed opportunities for self-management and decision making, workers' perceptions of their dependability and initiative, and evidence for changes in self-reliance and work habits, among others. In the domain of social responsibility, we evaluated the extent of cooperation in the workplace and workers' sense that their efforts are meaningful and have consequences for others.

PERSONAL RESPONSIBILITY

The amount of time youngsters work alone is one indicator of opportunities for self-management in the workplace. We found that such opportunities vary across job types. Approximately 13 percent of youngsters in our study in Orange County, California, reported that they typically work by themselves, in the absence of any coworker or supervisor. Even when youngsters' typically work with others, however, coworkers and supervisors are not omnipresent. Observation of youngsters on the job suggests that the average worker spends nearly half of his or her time not in the immediate company of others and only 12 percent of his or her time in the presence of a supervisor.[2]

Although these figures suggest that many young workers have ample opportunity to exercise self-management, we need other information to tell us to what extent they do so. A supervisor, for example, need not be in the immediate microenvironment of the youngster—at his or her work station—in order to call the shots. A series of items on our survey questionnaire attempted to ascertain youngsters' role in making decisions and exercising authority. As we indicated in chapter 2, opportunities for decision making and initiative taking are infrequent on most jobs in the "new" adolescent workplace.

Not surprisingly, only a small proportion of our novice workers report that they act in a supervisory role toward anyone. Nearly half our sample, on the other hand, felt that they had some say in deciding what they themselves did at work; and three-quarters felt they had some say about how they went about doing their work, even though they had not played a role in deciding which tasks should be done. The extremes offer an interesting picture. About one-quarter agreed with the statement "My supervisor decides what I do and how I do it" and the same proportion of youngsters described themselves as "pretty much my own boss." These figures are similar to those found in a national survey of high-school males, in which 39 percent said they "almost always" or "often" had a chance to plan work with a supervisor (Mortimer and Finch, in press). Summarizing these data requires care. Perhaps it would be fair to say that while many adolescents work without direct surveillance by others, including supervisors, the majority do not take part in planning their work. Nonetheless, most youngsters feel that they have the leeway to decide how to go about getting their work done.

It may come as a surprise, then, to learn that when asked to rate the extent of opportunities to "make their own decisions" at work and in school, youngsters perceive no difference in the two settings (Greenberger, Steinberg, and Vaux 1981). In retrospect, it seems plausible that youngsters have a range of choices at school, among them: whether to go to school on a given day; whether to attend a particular class; how much effort to put into an assignment; in some cases, which of several alternatives to select when doing an assignment; whether to go along with the crowd at a particular moment; and, of course, whether to give the classroom teacher cooperation or grief. In any case, our finding challenges a major claim—or should we say dream—of critics who have argued that working youngsters would have opportunities to make decisions and take responsibility for them to a degree that is not possible in school. Perhaps adolescent jobs are as infantilizing as critics of our educational system believe high school to be.

Participants in our program of research also took a paper-and-pencil test of self-reliance, focused on the tendency to take the initiative in situations, to view themselves as being in control of events, and to make decisions independently, without excessive approval-seeking. Sample items from the self-reliance scale, assessed on a four-point continuum from "strongly disagree" to "strongly agree," included "luck decides most things that happen to me" and "someone often has to tell me what to do." As may be obvious, disagreement with these items reflects greater self-reliance. In the initial cross-sectional study, workers of both sexes scored higher than nonworkers. Further analysis of the nonworkers showed that self-reliance was no higher to start with among youngsters who were seeking jobs than among those uninterested in employment, leading us to the tentative conclusion that working might actually *cause* growth in self-reliance (Steinberg et al. 1981). In the longitudinal study, however, we uncovered a curious variant of this finding. We again found evidence to suggest that working leads to increased self-reliance—but only for girls. Although the gains for girls were quite small, they were statistically significant. Girls who had spent more time in the workplace, furthermore, showed greater growth in self-reliance. Boys' self-reliance scores, in contrast, actually declined slightly but significantly after taking a job (Steinberg et al. 1982).[3]

Why should working affect the development of self-reliance differently for boys and girls? One possibility that we examined and subsequently dismissed is that sex differences in the consequences of work for self-reliance might be due to differences in the job environments that boys and girls typically encountered. This, however, does not appear to be the case, since boys and girls describe a similar degree of opportunity for self-management and decision making at work. An alternative explanation is that the meaning of, and instigations to, work are different for the two sexes. For boys, taking on a job is consistent with social expectations for what they must do in the future. For girls, in contrast, entering the labor force is less firmly tied to future role expectations; and they may view working, more than boys, as an act of self-assertion. More intensive work experience may serve to reinforce girls' sense of themselves as able to "take care of business" without direction or affirmation by others.

Apart from its effects on self-reliance, what evidence is there that working youngsters develop the habits of a good worker? We found that youngsters who work make small but significant gains on a self-report measure of dependability, persistence, and motivation to perform work well. Both the cross-sectional and longitudinal portions of our study point in this direction. More intensive employment, furthermore, is associated with greater gains in work orientation, as was the case with self-reliance among girls (but not boys) who work (Steinberg et al. 1981; Steinberg et al. 1982). Sample items on the work-orientation scale, responded to on a four-point continuum from "strongly disagree," to "strongly agree," included "I often don't finish work I start" and "very often I forget work I am supposed to do."[4]

Interviews with working teens, however, prompted us to wonder whether the measure of work orientation might be susceptible to distortion by a self-fulfilling prophecy—that is, the belief that having a job will make one a more dependable, hard-working person may lead youngsters who work to rate themselves more favorably than do their peers on these traits. In the interviews, conducted for us by a group of university undergraduates and graduate students, we did not question youngsters directly about "good work habits." Instead we asked more general questions about what working was like, whether youngsters thought they had learned anything from working, and whether they thought they were good at their job. All questions were open-ended; youngsters were at liberty to answer in their own words rather than to select among predesigned response options. Subsequently, we coded interview transcripts for content that was relevant to personal responsibility. We tried to distinguish among different levels of responsibility and work orientation, beginning with bottom-line behaviors such as showing up regularly and punctually, proceeding to a level characterized by dependable performance of assigned tasks, and topping out with job performance that clearly went beyond the call of duty. Because the figures we will present do not result from asking questions uniformly of all respondents, they may underestimate the true extent of responsible/work-oriented behavior (Greenberger and Steinberg 1981). Nonetheless, we believe that these figures are noteworthy, because they reflect more spontaneous self-descriptions than are prompted by our questionnaire measures.

One-third of the interviewees spontaneously talked about the fact that they were punctual and seldom absent: "I only called in sick when I was really sick"; "I've been there all the days they asked me to come in." Approximately one in ten, on the other hand, told about frequent absence and tardiness. (Based on our questionnaire survey, however, working youngsters seem to miss work less often than they miss school.) Moving up a notch in our coding scheme for responsibility, we noted that a little over one-half of our interviewees spoke of doing assigned tasks dependably. However, just under one-half talked about neglecting such tasks or "goofing off." We heard, on the one hand, "I learn all the specifications about a plant, like how it grows, how to water it," from a nursery worker; and on the other hand, from a food service worker, "People go in the back room and have Windex fights. . . . We had a hot fudge fight one time. . . . The manager got real mad." Often the same youngsters described themselves as both dependable and a "goof-off." Presumably, dependability is not a completely stable trait in adolescent workers (nor indeed, perhaps, among their adult counterparts), but varies as a function of the nature of the task and other, changing features of the worker and his or her job situation.

We were especially interested in instances of doing more than one's assigned tasks, or what we have referred to as going beyond the call of duty. In a national survey of high-school males, where respondents were asked directly how often they were interested enough to do more than the job requires, a minority of 30 percent answered either "often" or "almost always" (Mortimer and Finch, in press). This is a question, however, to which people may be tempted to respond with a rosier picture of themselves than others would recognize. In our interview sample, only 4 of 103 youngsters spontaneously described behavior at the top end of our responsibility/work orientation dimension.

> BABY-SITTER: Well, they got a divorce and it was really hard on the kids. She used to go out every night. The kids used to have TV dinners every night, and so I started cooking for them and stuff, 'cause I felt really bad for them.

> BICYCLE REPAIR WORKER: The thing that makes me feel best is . . . when I do something for one of the customers that actually helps them. Like I'll sit down . . . and I'll tell them, "Okay, this piece goes here," and I'll draw them a little picture . . . and I'll show them how to put the bicycle back together and . . . they come back later and say, "Oh hey, I put it back together the way you said!"

The fact that most youngsters do not seem to extend themselves on the job does not necessarily imply a fault in their character. The jobs typically available to youth do little to inspire a high degree of commitment and concern. Would we really expect a young janitor, who cleans office buildings at night, to give the floor a treatment that isn't called for on the work order—for an office staff he will never see? Jobs that are impersonal, temporary, offer few opportunities for advancement, and do not lead to desirable future employment may elicit, at best, dependable but not extraordinary performance from employees.

We have left until last one of the major means by which working may affect youngsters' exercise of personal responsibility: money. As we noted at the outset, students who work during high school bring in a sizable monthly paycheck: $143 is the national average for sophomores; $272, for seniors. Funds of this magnitude provide opportunities for learning self-management and for exercising decision making. Indeed, more working youth than nonworkers have their own savings account and enjoy the use of a credit card—usually on their parents' line of credit but with purchases paid for out of their own earnings (Greenberger, Steinberg, Vaux, and McAuliffe 1980). Although workers and nonworkers both have considerable freedom to decide what to do with their money, workers are more likely to have complete autonomy than nonworkers. Their greater degree of control over financial decisions seems to arise from parents' belief that youngsters have the right to do what they want with money they earn themselves—in contrast, for example, to money they are given in the form of a weekly allowance or gift. Such money is more likely to be earmarked for specific purposes or its proposed uses subjected to parental scrutiny. The belief that youngsters should be able to use money they have worked for as they wish emerged time after time in interviews with the parents of working youth and was expressed with a sense of rightness bordering on religious conviction.

In any case, youngsters exercise a high level of discretion

(and indiscretion) over the use of their earnings. And the fact that over half of high-school seniors, as documented in chapter 1, *spend* between half and all of their earnings on their "own needs and activities" gives them plenty of practice in making consumer decisions and taking responsibility for their choices. In view, however, of what the phrase "needs and activities" covers, it is debatable whether being responsible for how one uses one's money is the same thing as learning to use money responsibly.

Two different processes seem to underlie working teens' expenditure of earnings. First, they assume responsibility for buying some of the things, such as clothing, that their parents previously had provided for them; and second, they buy things that they did not own before and that their parents likely would *not* provide—for example, an automobile, which is still the quintessential grand purchase of teenagers. On balance, then, working youngsters pay for more of their expenses of living than nonworkers (Greenberger, Steinberg, Vaux, and McAuliffe 1980). Moreover, workers' reduced financial dependency on their parents is not just a matter of parental expectations. It is equally, or more, a matter of youngsters' own choice. Many youngsters seem to assume new financial responsibilities without explicit discussion or coercion—especially in relation to satisfying their taste for "extras." If the voluntary assumption of greater financial burdens is not economically rational, we suspect that it is, nonetheless, *psychologically* rational. The value of feeling less dependent on one's parents, and of experiencing less surveillance over and criticism of one's purchases, must be considerable for a teenager.

SOCIAL RESPONSIBILITY

Thus far we have looked at a variety of ways in which working could provide opportunities for growth in personal responsibility. There is less research concerning the impact of work experience on the development of social responsibility. The few relevant studies address the extent to which working youth are drawn into activities that require and reward cooperative effort, the degree to which they feel that their work has meaning and utility in the larger scheme of things, and the use of earnings to benefit the family.

Surveyed by questionnaire about opportunities for "helping people" at work and at school, working youngsters in our study gave higher marks to the workplace; however, we saw little evidence of close or sustained cooperation in our jobsite observations.[5] Instances of asking for, offering, giving, or receiving help occurred, on the average, fewer than three times per hour. Youngsters holding different types of jobs did not differ in the extent of cooperation, although differences might have reached statistical significance with a larger sample of individuals. Manual laborers, for example, appear to cooperate with each other somewhat more frequently than other workers, for reasons that seem obvious: lifting and carrying are often multiperson tasks.

Regardless of whether workers cooperate directly, they nonetheless may feel that they are part of a joint effort and that they bring something important, as individuals, to the role they fill. We coded the interview protocols of 103 workers for evidence of such sentiments and found a variable sense of belonging or contributing to a larger social enterprise. Nearly one in five youngsters felt virtually no sense of interdependence with other workers and/or no sense of having any personal significance to the organization.

INTERVIEWER: What would happen—what would it be like at work—if you didn't come in one day?
MANUAL LABORER: They'd just call someone else to work for me. . . .

A little over one-half spoke of their job in ways that suggested a moderate level of interdependence among workers, typically qualifying their answer in terms of how busy things were on a given day. Only about one in four youngsters perceived themselves as very much part of a team effort and as an important member of that team:

> FOOD SERVICE WORKER: . . . they'd be furious [if I didn't come to work]. Then they couldn't go home, because if I'm not there, who's going to count the money? Who's going to do this and that? Even if a lower girl doesn't come in, the head girl is swamped! They do a lot of business.

This youngster experienced a level of interdependence that workplace advocates hoped would be common, but that is in fact quite rare.

Two studies cast some light on whether adolescents feel that their work is meaningful and useful. In our study a majority of adolescents stated that the product or service they helped to provide was up to the standards that the public deserves: 55 percent agreed slightly with this statement; 33 percent, strongly. We also asked youngsters to indicate the extent to which they endorsed an extremely negative statement about their jobs. The statement "I feel that most of the things I do on my job are meaningless" drew support from only 2 percent of respondents. A more neutral but related question elicited a higher rate of agreement from a nationally representative sample of high-school boys. Asked to rate how often they felt that the work they performed was meaningful and important, these youngsters were sharply divided in their views: while half felt that the work they did was "almost always" or "often" meaningful, the other half felt it was so only "occasionally" or "seldom" (Mortimer and Finch, in press).

We come, finally, to the question of whether working youngsters, by earning additional income, are able to increase their family's well-being. This is perhaps the most concrete and convincing manifestation of how the work of adolescents might promote growth in social responsibility—at least, for those adolescents whose families actually could benefit from an infusion of extra dollars.

According to a national survey of high-school youth (Johnston, Bachman, and O'Malley 1982), by far the majority of working youngsters do not contribute much of their earnings to their families: 82 percent allocate none or "only a little" to help defray the costs of housing, groceries, and other expenses of living. Youth from less economically advantaged circumstances probably contribute more than others. For example, only 58 percent of black youth in this survey reported that they did not give any of their earnings, or gave only a little of their paycheck, to their family, compared to 87 percent of white youth. Nonetheless, the proportion of earnings going to youngsters' families certainly is not staggering. For the sample as a whole, only 8.4 percent reported allocating half or more of their paycheck to helping the family (5.5 percent of whites, 21.5 percent of blacks); and only 1.1 percent reported turning over their entire paycheck for this purpose (0.7 percent of whites, 3.2 percent of blacks). Without information on their family's economic needs, it is impossible to say whether adolescents who work are gaining substantial experience in taking responsibility for others.

DOES WORKING PROMOTE RESPONSIBILITY?

It is difficult to draw together the many strands of evidence we have laid out and speak definitively to the question of whether working encourages the development of responsibility. In general, working, along with managing the money that accrues from working, provides adolescents some opportunities to exercise more responsibility. But adolescents who work are more likely to learn or practice personal responsibility than to learn, practice, or experience a high level of cooperation and interdependence—the more "social" aspects of responsibility. In order to put these conclusions in context, two issues need to be considered. The first concerns the degree to which working actually *promotes* in adolescents increased responsibility and competence to fulfill the role of worker; the second concerns deficiencies in the kind of responsibility young workers seem to be developing.

School critics have argued in favor of increased labor-force participation for adolescents in part because they allege that the schools are unable to prepare youngsters to function adequately in the workplace. This assumption, which we have not yet questioned, has been challenged by others. In a radical critique of the schools entitled "School Is Bad; Work Is Worse," the writers claim that there is no evidence to support the argument that schools fail to socialize youth for work and considerable evidence that they do so very well (Behn, Carnoy, Carter, Crain, and Levin 1974). In support of their argument that schools do socialize youth to the attitudes, traits, and values required in the workplace, the authors point to a study showing that teachers' evaluations of students' "conduct" are better predictors of supervisors' ratings of young people's proficiency as workers than are their academic records (Brenner 1968). They also draw attention to several studies that suggest that the number of years one spends in school are related statistically to earnings and occupational success, independent of measures of cognitive attainment. In other words, something about going to school, over and above learning the three R's, seems to fit youngsters for the world of work. Political economist Herbert Gintis (1971) has proposed that schooling prepares youth for working in modern bureaucracies by providing practice in such skills as adopting the proper level of subordination vis-à-vis higher-ups, controlling emotions, adapting one's behavior in accordance with external rewards, and accepting discipline and routine.

It is possible, therefore, that for many youngsters—especially the middle-class youngsters who dominate the part-time job scene today—the workplace is not so much an arena for the acquisition of new habits of work as a new setting in which to practice habits already acquired elsewhere. As the father of one working youngster said, "I think all the basic things were there before she worked." Although this may seem to be an unnecessarily fine distinction, we think it is an important one. It is conceivable, for example, that other activities in which young-sters engage or might engage, such as after-school sports, un-paid community service, or extensive involvement in home chores, might offer a similar level of opportunity to practice being a responsible person. The major difference between behaving "responsibly" at school and at work—or in other settings—may lie in the forces that motivate such behavior and the kinds of rewards that are available.

In any case, most of the research we have reviewed does not address changes in responsibility that accompany working but rather reveals the extent to which the workplace offers opportunities for exercising responsibility and the frequency with which youngsters take advantage of these opportunities. Evidence that working actually causes *change* in adolescents' level of responsibility is limited to three domains. First, girls who work, and who work more intensively, gain greater feelings of self-reliance. (Among boys, on the other hand, working may produce the opposite effect.) Second, working enhances young-sters' view of themselves as having good work habits—a finding we have interpreted with some caution. Finally, working leads to increased financial autonomy, and this, in our view, repre-sents the most dramatic and unambiguous effect of working on adolescents' lives. Whether autonomy should be equated with responsibility is another matter.

Money, of course, is not only a ticket to independence but a vehicle for investing in one's future and contributing to the welfare of others. Statistics on giving and saving, however, are not impressive, as we have noted here and in earlier chapters.

Although it is true that the assumption of some of their costs of living by working youngsters amounts to an indirect transfer of income within the family, the value of this income transfer is quite a bit lower than it might seem. This is so because parents, if they alone were underwriting their children's needs and activities, would not buy them all the things they purchase for themselves. Over 80 percent of high-school seniors who work, moreover, save "none" or only "a little" of their earnings. Money earned and saved during the later years of high school could be used, of course, to offset the costs of further education and to help establish an independent household. The failure of youngsters to save, therefore, can be viewed as a loss of assets for making the transition to adulthood.

Overall, the kind of responsibility that working adolescents seem to be developing has a somewhat egocentric flavor. They obtain jobs more to earn spending money than to gain experience or to explore an area of work that might interest them in the future. They view themselves as good workers, and they get to work dependably (at least, those who remain employed) and do what is required of them—but seldom do more. They control a substantial amount of money, but they spend it largely on themselves to support a higher level of consumption than their parents would, or could, provide. Adolescents, however, did not create this situation. The nature of the jobs available to adolescents and the laissez-faire attitude of parents about their children's use of their earnings set limits on how much youngsters can grow in personal and social responsibility.

Working and Schooling

Observers of the American high school often have commented that it is burdened by an excess of responsibilities. Originally founded to impart advanced skills in academic subjects, the high school now is expected to accomplish a wide range of vocational and social objectives. Panels that were convened over the past ten years to examine the needs of youth have argued that other institutions must share the burden of education for young people approaching the transition to adulthood by providing environments that supplement, and extend the boundaries of, school-based education (President's Science Advisory Committee 1973).

According to the panels whose recommendations we reviewed in chapter 1, adolescents especially need more opportunities to work. The workplace, they speculated, would offer a real-life setting in which to practice cognitive skills acquired (but not necessarily well learned) in school; and would provide training, both formal and informal, in areas that are not the prime concern of schools: job skills, practical skills of living, and the wisdom that comes with experience in living. It is important to test these expectations against the reality of today's naturally occurring adolescent jobs and to examine a fundamental assumption that underlies advocacy of more extensive labor-force participation for youth. This assumption, seldom stated explicitly, is that work experience can reinforce and expand the curriculum of the school without detracting from learning in that setting.

LEARNING IN THE WORKPLACE

In the observational component of our study, we examined in detail the activities of ninety-one youngsters while they were working. They were employed in six prototypical adolescent jobs. As we indicated in chapter 2, most youngsters at work do not spend much time practicing the basic academic skills of reading, writing, or computation. Food service workers, manual laborers, and cleaners spend an average of 2 percent or less of their time at work reading, writing, or doing arithmetic.

Clerical workers, machine operatives and skilled laborers, and retail sales clerks spend more time applying the three R's to the task at hand: on the average, 29 percent, 15 percent, and 11 percent, respectively. Except perhaps for clerical work, these figures do not suggest that the workplace is a practice field for improving school-taught skills.

We also attempted to gauge the extent to which student workers receive training in job skills. We defined "training" as instruction in how to do a task or explanation of why something should be done, or done in a certain way. In a retail store, for example, a supervisor or coworker might show a youngster how goods are supposed to be displayed, tell the youngster how to fill out paperwork for a given transaction, or tell the young worker why he or she should have handled an interaction with a customer differently. For the six different job types, observers recorded an average of between 0.43 and four acts of job training per hour. Food service workers, who constitute a large proportion of adolescent workers, received the least job training, followed by cleaners and manual laborers. Machine operators and skilled laborers, taken together, received the most training.

As we noted in chapter 2, deliberate job training by other persons is, of course, not the only means by which youngsters may acquire job-related skills. People also learn by observation, when not specifically instructed to do so, and initiate their own learning. Thus it is likely that our figures, based on what we could see, underestimate the extent to which adolescents may be learning job-related skills while they work.

Nonetheless, the low incidence of deliberate job training deserves some thought. In most cases we were observing youngsters who had held their job for several months. Perhaps most job training takes place early in the course of employment, and we simply missed it. If this is true, it follows that most adolescent jobs can be mastered within a very short time, and that many youngsters who work, rather than learning new skills, draw on skills that are already in place. Most sixteen-year-olds would require little instruction in sweeping floors, washing dishes, wrapping sandwiches, unloading boxes, or stacking objects on shelves—although they might perform these skills better in the workplace than at home or elsewhere. Even among skilled workers, it is likely that a considerable level of competence at the task was acquired *before* employment—for example, in vocational courses—and was, in fact, a prerequisite for being hired.

Other data from this study support our sense that the adolescent workplace does not teem with opportunities for learning. The activities that together take up much of young workers' time, virtually regardless of what kind of job they hold, often are very simple indeed. For example, cleaning, carrying, and moving objects from one place to another take up between 14 percent and 55 percent of the time of the average adolescent who holds a cleaning job (no surprise!), or a job as a manual laborer, or a retail sales job, or a job as a food service worker. Cross-cultural research provides an interesting perspective on such work. In preliterate societies, fetch-and-carry tasks are the type of work most commonly assigned to two- and three-year-olds (Whiting 1984). Adolescents in our sample had few illusions about the degree of expertise their work called for. Nearly half felt that a grade-school education or less would suffice to enable them to perform their jobs.

Although adolescents do not typically get much job-related training, exposure to the world of commerce and the opportunity to bank and spend substantial amounts of earnings may yield a return in practical knowledge. Accordingly, we administered a test to working and nonworking youngsters that tapped their knowledge of selected business operations, money and banking concepts, consumer-oriented arithmetic, and rational consumer practices.[6] Items on this multiple-choice test included, among others, what is meant by a particular store's "market" and by the term overhead; how net income differs from gross income; which of several sources of information would provide the best data about which stereo is the best buy; and how much money an item would cost if bought on a particular installment plan. Results of our analyses, unfortunately, create doubts about the effect of working on practical knowledge.

In the cross-sectional study of workers and youngsters who had never worked, where no prior assessment of "practical knowledge" was available, workers scored higher than nonworkers. In doing this analysis, we statistically controlled for the possible effects of students' grade-point averages (GPAs), on the premise that youngsters who perform better in school subjects also might perform better on a test of practical knowledge. (As in all analyses, we also controlled for students' grade level, sex, and social class.) We found that once GPA and employment status had been entered into the statistical analysis, we gained no further explanation of why youngsters varied in practical knowledge by considering the intensity of their employment. Whether an individual works is more important, with respect to the acquisition of practical knowledge, than how much an individual works.

Examination of the statistical interaction between variables revealed that the relationship between work status and practical knowledge is mediated by school GPA. For students with high GPAs (B+ and above), working was not associated with variations in performance on the practical knowledge test. In contrast, among students with lower GPAs (B and below), workers scored higher than nonworkers on our test of business, money, and consumer information. Perhaps less academically oriented students acquire practical information more readily when it is tied to experience, whereas students with a strong academic orientation learn information just as well without direct experiential support (Steinberg, Greenberger, Garduque, and McAuliffe 1982).

It is appropriate once again, however, to question whether

worker-nonworker differences—in this case, in the realm of practical knowledge—represent preemployment selection factors or effects that are attributable to employment. Perhaps youth who have more savvy about business and money matters have other competencies as well that make them more likely to succeed in finding or holding a job. The data do not support this hypothesis. Among youth who were not working, those who were seeking jobs did not differ from nonseekers in their level of practical knowledge. This finding led us to speculate that practical knowledge does not constitute a basis for selective advantage in getting hired but rather may result from experiences related to working.

Unfortunately, however, our longitudinal study did not confirm this prediction. We uncovered no significant differences in practical knowledge between youngsters who initially were nonworkers but subsequently took jobs and those who remained nonworkers. In this study, it will be recalled, we were able to control for scores on practical knowledge prior to employment. Of course, youngsters who start their first job later than others—as is the case with those in the longitudinal sample—differ in a number of respects from youngsters in the cross-sectional sample. It is difficult, therefore, to interpret the nonconvergence of findings. Nonconvergence may indicate, on the one hand, that working does not lead to improvement in practical knowledge or, on the other hand, that effects of working on practical knowledge depend on a variety of other features of the individual worker.

Some of the most important lessons a young person may learn in the workplace have little resemblance to the kinds of information that are usually assessed by means of paper-and-pencil tests. Experience in some work settings, for example, may lead to subtle and hard-to-measure advances in youngsters' social understanding: their ability to comprehend what people are thinking and feeling, to understand the social institutions and processes in which they are participating, and to get people to respond in ways that meet their own needs or further their own interests (Steinberg, Greenberger, Jacobi, and Garduque 1981). Workplace advocates have hoped that employment would engender not only job skills and practical knowledge but wisdom of this kind.

Interviews with employed youngsters in our sample suggest that some youngsters indeed may deepen their social understanding as a consequence of experience in the workplace. The following excerpts illustrate a number of different themes.

In the following excerpts youngsters talk about what they have learned about the nature and dynamics of relationships between workers and supervisors and among coworkers.

MACHINE SHOP WORKER: You learn how to handle supervisors. . . . If you have a complaint . . . well, you take it to them, in some instances. You gotta see how you're going to talk to them, because if you put it to them really negatively, they may react adversely.

FOOD SERVICE WORKER: A couple of my friends want to work [in this restaurant], but I don't know if I want them to . . . I would be telling them what to do. And they're your good friends, and you think, "I should take it easy." And you can't because you can't play favorites.

CONCESSION STAND WORKER IN AMUSEMENT PARK: Yeah, I get along with my boss. Sometimes the things he tells me to do, I get kinda mad about. I can't do nothing, because he's my boss. . . . I just go ahead and do it. . . . A lot of people kinda dislike him for the things they have to do at work . . . but you're getting paid for it and that's your responsibility . . . that's part of your job, you know; you work your way up eventually. I had to do that. I finally got worked up.

These excerpts suggest that youngsters who are exposed to unfamiliar people at work or to people they might ordinarily not choose to spend time with may develop new social insights.

COUNTER WORKER: I always was able to work with people . . . when everyone was pleasant. When they're not, I used to have trouble with that; I just backed away from the situation if they were mean. Now I can just say "I'm sorry, we'll try to do our best." I've learned to work more with all kinds of people, rather than just the ones I want to work with.

SALESPERSON: People have different views of things, it seems like. You know, at first I couldn't understand that because I thought, well, "my way is the way it should be," you know? But maybe it's not.

FOOD SERVICE WORKER: . . . Things you can say to one person won't affect them, but if you say the same thing to another person, you may really hurt them inside.

In a final excerpt, a youngster speaks to the matter of learning how to handle people in order to achieve a desired outcome: in this case, to keep his job.

SUPERMARKET CHECKER: You know, it pays to kind of ignore them, if they get really ornery. . . . But I try to keep them happy. Like if I don't know where something is, I try to find it. Sometimes, if you don't, they get really mad and they bitch. . . . You can get in trouble if they really want to get you in trouble. . . . You learn how to deal with them.

On the basis of our interview data, we suspect that jobs with certain specific attributes are most likely to promote growth in social understanding: jobs that require young people to shift back and forth among different roles; give them opportunities to control, guide, and influence interactions; and oblige them to deal frequently with strangers. Role shifts—for example, from subordinate vis-à-vis the boss to shift manager in relation to coworkers—can lead the "actor" to appreciate how behavior, feelings, and motives are conditioned by the role he or she is playing. ("I'm not usually irritable, but I get irritable when the people I'm in charge of don't do their job.") Having to deal with strangers or people from different social backgrounds or age groups may make it necessary for the young person to develop greater perceptiveness about the needs and motives of others, more understanding of the social norms that govern behavior in the work setting, and new ways of interacting. Idiosyncratic ways of getting by—ways that may be tolerated by family members and close friends—may prove ineffectual or even offensive in the work setting. And finally, having wide latitude to decide how to conduct an interaction places the burden of responsibility for a successful exchange squarely on the shoulders of the youngster—and thus places his or her social insight and competence at a premium. The situation of a salesperson, whose repertoire of knowledge, understanding of the customer's needs, and tact may make the difference between a sale, commission, and praise from a customer and/or supervisor is very different from that of a food service worker, whose behavioral repertoire is both limited and virtually programmed. Little is at stake when he or she recites some variant of "What can I get you?" "Ketchup or mustard?" "Anything to drink?" "Have a nice day."

The preceding interview segments are compelling and suggest a means by which youngsters in certain kinds of jobs may increase their understanding of social relations. We caution the reader, however, not to conclude that the absence of work experience results in impaired social understanding. We did not interview nonworkers and therefore cannot compare them. It is possible that active participation in the family, in the various activities that take place at school, and in the peer group are equally good contexts for promoting the development of social understanding.

We have discussed so far some of the supplements to education that working may provide—and we have noted those that working seems not to provide. We turn now to the question, "Does working have any costs to adolescents' schooling?" For many people the bottom line is whether students' grades decline. If they do not, then working and schooling are not in conflict. As we shall see, this may be the wrong bottom line. Working may have other effects, on students and teachers alike, that take a toll on learning. Let us begin, however, by examining the relations between working and grade-point average.

Analyses of employment and GPA have focused on both work status—is the youngster employed or not?—and intensity of employment. Studies based on work status, with no statistical control for the number of hours that employed youth are spending on the job, have yielded inconsistent findings on the relationship between working and GPA. Thus in the nationally representative High School and Beyond survey (Lewin-Epstein 1981), sophomores who worked did not differ from their non-working peers in GPA to date; but senior boys who were employed reported lower cumulative GPAs than those who did not have jobs. Or again, students in four Wisconsin high schools who had *never* worked during the school year had higher cumulative GPAs than students who had held jobs (McNeil 1984). However, both of these studies leave some important questions unanswered. Their cross-sectional design, for example, does not allow us to determine whether students with poorer grades are selectively attracted to the workplace or whether working causes students to earn poorer grades. And their methodology does not include controls for the intensity of employment, thus leaving us in doubt about whether observed relations between working and GPA are due to work per se or to amount of work.[7]

Two studies shed some light on the first of these questions: selection versus causation. In one study, tenuous support emerges for the hypothesis that students who perform less well are drawn disproportionately into the labor force. Using the Youth in Transition data set for high-school males, Mortimer and Finch (in press) showed that boys who worked during the tenth, eleventh, or twelfth grades tended to have had lower GPAs as ninth graders—that is, before the typical peak years of youth labor-force participation. This result fell slightly short of statistical significance, however. In our study, based on a more limited, middle-class sample, we found *no* evidence for a selection effect (Steinberg et al. 1982) and no evidence that a change in work status—from never employed to employed during the school year—caused a change in average grades (Steinberg et al. 1982). At best, the notion that academically poorer students are disproportionately likely to hold a job is very weakly supported—and only for males.

Obviously, whether students work is less likely to make a difference in their grades than is how much they work. Being employed for many hours each week may have noticeable implications for academic performance, whereas being employed for just a few hours may leave academic performance unscathed. Once again, however, it is premature to talk of effects before examining the extent to which a selection factor operates, with less stellar students opting for longer hours of work. Unfortunately, no researchers have addressed this issue directly. But we do know, from the High School and Beyond survey, that employed students in the college track work on the average about three hours fewer per week than students in the general or vocational tracks, which suggests that some selection factor may be operative (Lewin-Epstein 1981).

Several studies—but not all—suggest that more intensive

employment actually leads to a drop in school performance. In the cross-sectional component of our study, longer hours of work were associated with lower GPAs. Tenth graders working more than fifteen hours per week and eleventh graders working more than twenty hours had significantly lower grades for that school year than students who worked fewer hours. However, the selection hypothesis cannot be ruled out in this study. Students who do not expect to be rewarded with good grades in school may select into longer hours of work and the accompanying reward of a bigger paycheck. This hypothesis is strengthened by findings from the longitudinal component of our study, which failed to confirm the alternative hypothesis, that working long hours *leads* to lower grades (Steinberg, Greenberger, Garduque, and McAuliffe 1982; Steinberg, Greenberger, Garduque, Vaux, and Ruggiero 1982).

In contrast, a nationwide study of male high-school students, using a different measure of intensity of employment, provides evidence that in certain cases, higher levels of involvement in working do lead to lower GPAs. In the Youth in Transition study, tenth-grade boys were followed up in each of the next two years. Mortimer and Finch (in press) showed that among boys who had begun working in grade 10, those with more extensive work experience had lower GPAs in their last year of high school than those who had accumulated less work experience. GPA in each of the earlier years of high school and family socioeconomic standing were controlled statistically in this analysis. The impact of working on GPA, although statistically significant, was nonetheless small in magnitude.[8]

Other analyses also suggest that employment relatively early in one's high-school career may have a particularly negative impact on GPA. The grades of youngsters who began working in grade 10 showed a decline, whereas the grades of others who began work later did not (Mortimer and Finch, in press). Similarly, a number of hours worked per week in the sophomore year had a negative effect on the GPA earned in the junior year; whereas the number of hours worked in the junior year had no effect on grades earned in the senior year (Finch and Mortimer 1985). In these studies, too, grades in prior years and family social status were controlled statistically. Perhaps intensive employment early in the high-school years signals waning interest in school, which eventually leads to a decline in performance.

To sum up: while there is little evidence to suggest that students who do less well in school are more likely to become workers during the high-school years, there is indirect evidence that they work longer hours than other youngsters. There is also some evidence to suggest that grade-point average is depressed by intensive levels of labor-force participation, especially among youth who begin work early in the high-school years. Although the relationship between working and GPA does not always attain statistical significance, it is consistently negative. In no studies has working been shown to have a positive effect on GPA.[9]

The analyses discussed thus far were based on youngsters' year-to-date or cumulative GPA. Another source of information on the relations between employment and academic achievement is students' perception of whether working has had any impact on the quality of their performance. We asked employed students in our study, "Since you started working, have you noticed any changes in your grades?" Respondents could choose among five response-options: "My grades are much better"; ". . . are a little better"; ". . . are about the same as before"; ". . . have gone down a little"; ". . . have shown a big drop." Twenty-seven percent of our working youngsters claimed that their grades had declined since they began working. This compares with 16 percent who claimed that their grades had risen and with 56 percent who reported that their grades had remained the same. In a study conducted in four southern Wisconsin high schools, a higher proportion of students claimed that working had hurt their academic performance: 44 percent of juniors and seniors currently working claimed that employment was a "moderately" or "very important" source of interference with getting good grades (McNeil 1984).

Students' sense that working hurts their academic performance is somewhat more pronounced than one would expect, based on our review of the effects of working on grade-point average. It is possible that students overestimate the harm that working has caused their GPA, or "misattribute" getting lower grades than they would like to get to the fact that they hold a job. On the other hand, the subjective analysis offered by a substantial proportion of student workers in these studies that working has a negative impact on their school performance is worth heeding. Indeed, their self-analysis may be a more sensitive indicator of the consequences of employment for learning than the "objective" statistical analysis of changes in GPA. The ensuing discussion will show why this is the case.

JOBS AND LOWERED INVESTMENT IN SCHOOL

Adolescents vary over time, and among themselves, in the amount of investment they make in schooling. Their investment can be indexed in a variety of ways—for example, by the time and effort they put into schoolwork and by the number and quality of courses they elect to take. Thus some students opt for meeting the minimum standards for graduation with the minimum amount of effort required to "get by," whereas others exceed the minimum requirements and strive to learn more than what will earn a passing grade. Individual students, of course, may fluctuate in their degree of investment in schooling as the circumstances of their lives change.

It is well known that youngsters' investment in education is determined by a number of factors: their educational goals, academic ability, social class, and the values of their peer group, to name a familiar few. A number of recent studies suggest that work is another factor that influences students' investment in schooling: working seems to reduce their investment. Moreover, years of widespread employment among school-going youngsters may have set in motion a complementary process among teachers. Confronted by a growing number of students who have made working a top priority and who do not meet their academic obligations, some teachers appear to have reduced *their* investment in teaching. These outcomes—lowered expectations on the part of both students and teachers—are potentially far more serious than the minimal effects of working on students' grade-point average.

Educational researcher Linda McNeil (1984), in a report of research involving students and teachers, argues that youngsters' part-time employment during the academic year is one of several factors that causes them to disengage from learning and teachers to disengage from teaching. Her research suggests that many students who work balance the demands of their job schedules by cutting back at school. In turn, some teachers, frustrated by students' failure to meet their expectations, have lowered their standards over the years, gradually accommodating to the emergence of the student worker by simplifying their lectures, assigning less homework, and making the requirements for papers and presentations less demanding.

Surveyed about which of several methods they had used to balance their job and schoolwork, 44 percent of juniors and seniors currently holding a job agreed that taking only the minimum number of courses required for graduation was a strategy of some importance. (Among students who had worked the year before but were not working during the current school year, over one-half said that the wish to take advanced courses in required subjects was of some importance in their decision not to work; and over one-third cited the wish to take elective courses.) Forty-one percent of students currently working responded that choosing easier courses was a strategy of some importance in how they were balancing the demands of work and school. Once enrolled in a course, more-over, the process of accommodation continued. About 60 per-cent of students currently holding a job said that working interfered with doing required reading and written assign-ments; and over 50 percent, that it interfered with "staying alert in class."

Several other researchers, using different data sets, also have examined the link between employment and preparation for class. A study by sociologist Ronald D'Amico (1984), using data from the National Longitudinal Surveys, demonstrated an association between intensive employment and time devoted to homework. As the percentage of weeks out of the school year in which white youth worked in excess of twenty hours rose, time spent on studies declined. The effect of intensive employ-ment on study time prevailed, even after differences in stu-dents' future educational expectations, grade level, and the educational attainment of the head of household had been controlled statistically. That is, these variables did not "explain away" the apparent relationship between intensive jobwork and reduced homework. The findings for minority youth showed a nonsignificant trend in the same direction. The rela-tionship between weeks of less intensive employment (that is, twenty hours or less) and time spent on homework mirrored those for more intensive employment, although it failed to attain statistical significance. As weeks rose in which young-sters worked one to twenty hours per week, time spent on studies declined.

Another national survey, in which a different measure of intensity of employment was used, came to slightly different conclusions. In the High School and Beyond study, students reported simply on the past week's hours of work (Lewin-Epstein 1981). Sophomores reported spending roughly the same amount of time on homework regardless of whether they did not work, worked few hours, or worked many hours per week. Among seniors, however, and especially among male seniors, there was a statistically significant negative relationship between weekly hours of employment and time spent on homework. Boys who worked twenty-two or more hours per week, for example (a category that encompasses 46 percent of all employed male seniors), spent only three hours weekly on homework, compared to the four hours reported by other boys. (Senior boys who were employed, it may be recalled, also had lower GPAs than their nonworking counterparts in this study.)

In both the D'Amico and Lewin-Epstein studies, however, the measurement of intensity of employment and time spent on homework was concurrent. We do not know, therefore, to what extent youngsters who already spend less time on homework select more intensive employment and to what extent intensive employment—however measured—leads to youngsters' spending less time on homework. Our own research suggests that *both* forces are likely to be operative. On the one hand, youngsters who were seeking, but had not yet obtained, their first part-time job already were spending significantly less time on homework than their peers who were not interested in finding employment. On the other hand, taking a job reduced further the amount of time youngsters invested in homework. In the latter analysis, based on longitudinal data, we controlled statistically for the amount of time youngsters spent on homework in the year prior to employment.

In summary, the effects of jobwork on homework parallel those for GPA. When effects are demonstrated—they are not large. However, the effect of jobwork, or any other potentially interfering activity, on homework is *bound* to be limited by the low apparent "demand" for out-of-classroom preparation: the average high-school student nationwide spends less than an hour per day on homework. Also, as in the case of GPA, the relations between jobwork and homework are consistently negative across studies.[10]

Before leaving the issue of working and youngsters' investment in school, it may be worth briefly elaborating the obvious.

Reduced investment in school probably leads to poorer academic performance. Put otherwise, insofar as working leads to a drop in GPA, it may do so by causing youngsters to reduce their investment in school.

In our Orange County study, we constructed a measure of school involvement that is similar in spirit to what we have been calling "investment" in schooling. This measure was a composite, including amount of time spent on homework, amount of time devoted to extracurricular activities, degree of enjoyment of school, and frequency of school absence. We found that investment in school was positively and substantially related to GPA, even after the effects of sex, social class, and grade level were statistically controlled. Moreover, the relationship we had established between intensity of employment and GPA in the cross-sectional component of our study was completely accounted for by youngsters' investment in school: that is, after their scores on this measure were entered into the analyses (with prior controls for sex, age, and social class), the number of hours youngsters worked produced no further improvement in the prediction of GPA.[11]

To conclude: thoughtful commentators on the education of youth have proposed that high-school students could augment what they learn in school by gaining experience in the world of work—presumably without cost to their formal education. *They may be wrong.* Evidence is slim at best to support the notion that the workplace—at least, the naturally occurring workplace in which most youth find jobs—typically promotes the acquisition of new skills or information. The most promising possibility is that certain kinds of jobs may increase youngsters' social understanding. There is little evidence that working provides extensive opportunities to practice the basic cognitive skills that are taught in school. Finally, there *is* evidence, on the other side of the ledger, to suggest that students who work intensively do so at some cost to their education. Declining investment in education is a widespread problem

that has a great many different roots. Youthwork is one cause
—and is, in fact, also a consequence of problems inherent in
the educational system. The "rising tide of mediocrity" that
threatens to engulf the schools (National Commission on Excellence in Education 1983) leads youngsters to invest effort
elsewhere. Nonetheless, it is ironic that the emergence of the
student worker, envisioned as a solution to some of the problems of the high school, in fact may be contributing to its
decline.

Deterring Crime and Delinquency

High rates of crime and delinquency in the youth cohort have
been a source of national concern for many years. Most arrests
occur in the generation of individuals under twenty-five years
of age, and school-going youngsters contribute substantially to
this statistic. Moreover, schools themselves have become an
increasingly common arena for antisocial and illegal behavior,
a fact to which escalating rates of property damage, interpersonal aggression, and drug use are testimony. The public and
the experts both have looked to youthwork as a possible antidote to crime and delinquency.

As we discussed in chapter 1, it is a pervasive theme in
Protestant thought that work has a "moralizing" effect: work
not only is good for people, it makes people good. A related
belief concerns the virtue of keeping busy, or the relationship
between busyness and virtue. If "idle hands are the devil's
workshop," then by implication youngsters who are in the
workplace will stay out of trouble—at least, while they are
there. This could be termed an "opportunity theory" of delinquency according to which working would deter youth from
crime by reducing opportunities for engaging in criminal be-

havior. The following uneasy dialogue, from an interview conducted as part of the Orange County study, illustrates the point:

INTERVIEWER: Do you think it's a good idea for kids Paul's age to have a job?

FATHER: Sure, not so much [because of] what he's doing, it's the time that keeps him from doing other things . . . idle hours permit kids, when they get together . . . Some of them are going to be followers and some are going to be leaders, and if the leaders are heading in the wrong direction, the followers are going to go right with them. . . . Not that that is what [Paul] would do, but it's just removing the temptation.

Sociologists take a different perspective on the relations between working and delinquency. Most delinquency theories imply that working should decrease delinquency either by reducing strains that impel youth into antisocial behavior (Cloward and Ohlin 1960) or by introducing psychosocial forces that act as restraints or controls against delinquent behavior (Hirschi 1969). In the first case, sociologists have argued that delinquency is an expression of conformity to deviant values into which the young person has been socialized successfully. Deviant socialization occurs when access to conventional goals, such as education, occupational mobility, and a position of respect in society, have been blocked. Under such conditions work provides a legitimate means of production and a legitimate means of enabling consumption: the young person with an income derived from employment does not have to turn to crime in order to meet his or her needs. In addition, work is a means of earning status in the larger society.

Control theorists take a slightly different approach. They view delinquency as a consequence of inadequate socialization —in this case, to the conventional or typical norms and values of society, such as living within the law and earning one's way through performance of socially legitimized tasks. From this perspective, work is expected to reduce delinquency by involving youth in conventional economic activity, bringing them into social contact with people who model conventional values and patterns of behavior, and rewarding them for adherence to such values and behaviors.

Research that directly examines the relations between employment and delinquency is surprisingly sparse, given the apparent "rightness" of the connection—or perhaps because of the intuitive certainty that it evokes. However, no empirical evidence can be marshaled to support the view that working reduces delinquency, either among random samples of youth or samples considered to be at risk for delinquent behavior, as a result of economic and social disadvantages and the known demography of delinquency. On the contrary, as we shall see, statistically significant findings occasionally suggest that working promotes some forms of deviant behavior.

We begin with a study of youngsters from inner city, depressed areas, attending schools targeted for special efforts to reduce delinquency by the U.S. Office of Juvenile Justice and Delinquency Prevention. These youngsters were experiencing life circumstances that sociologists typically identify with the sources of delinquent behavior; they were youngsters for whom sociologists have predicted that employment should reduce delinquency.

Sociologist Denise Gottfredson (1985) surveyed a large sample of seventh through twelfth graders—most of them black or Hispanic—from the targeted schools. Respondents were asked about their involvement in three types of delinquent behavior: interpersonal aggression, such as physically assaulting another person; property damage, such as joyriding or breaking and entering; and substance use, including use of cigarettes, alcohol, marijuana, and other drugs and inhalants. They also answered questions intended to reflect their degree of attachment to the conventional social order—questions concerning involvement with peers who get into trouble (a negative indicator); belief in conformity to rules; expectations for continuing their education; and aspirations for conventionally desirable (that is, relatively more prestigious) jobs.

Before describing the findings of this study, some features of its methodology need to be noted. A strength of the study is that delinquency and also attachment to the social order were assessed both prior to and after becoming a worker. This strategy allows the author to control, for example, for previous involvement in delinquent behavior when estimating the effects of employment.[12] There are two problems, however, with the way in which the critical variable, employment, was measured. The first concerns the assignment of youngsters to a single work-status category—that of worker—regardless of whether (1) they were employed in both the current year (1982) and the year before; (2) in the current year only; or (3) in the year before only (that is, not employed in the current year). Subsequent analysis of the impacts of working used 1982 measures of delinquency and social attitudes and did not differentiate between the subgroups of youngsters just cited— a strategy that may mask differences among youth based on the timing and amount of their work experience. Thus youngsters with more years of employment (group 1), or more recent employment (group 2) might show different levels of delinquency in 1982 than those whose employment was more remote in time. This conjecture is based on likely differences in opportunity among the three subgroups of youth to engage in delinquent behavior and on differences among them in experiences that might best promote attachment to the conventional social order.[13]

The second problem concerns the absence of information about the intensity of youngsters' work experience. No data are available on weekly hours of work or the duration of jobs held in one year or the other. For certain outcomes, intensity of employment may be more important than whether, simply, one has held a job. Both strain theorists and control theorists imply that intensity of employment could be a factor in reducing delinquent behavior and deepening ties to the conventional social order. For these effects to occur, how much time a youngster has worked may be far more important than whether the youngster has or has not worked.

In fact, Gottfredson found that working per se did not increase youngsters' ties to the social order nor reduce preexisting levels of delinquency. Neither was there any consistent evidence that working weakened conventional social bonds (although there was a decline in school attendance among a few subgroups) or that working increased delinquency. Working, in short, had no effect on either delinquency or the strength of conventional social bonds. To complete the picture, none of the measures designed to assess strength of ties to the conventional social order predicted delinquency. The best predictor of the extent of delinquency in a given year was the extent of delinquent behavior of the same type a year before. Only race and ethnic background made any additional contribution to the prediction of delinquency.

Two other studies based on national samples of high-school youth also concluded that working does not reduce delinquency. In a national survey of high-school males, youth who worked in grade 11 appeared to have higher, not lower, scores on one of three measures of delinquency a year later (Gottfredson 1982).[14] However, this relationship was reduced to nonsignificance when prior delinquency scores and other predictors of delinquency were controlled statistically. In another study, which traced the criminal career of all individuals born in a midwestern city in 1942 and 1949—and who thus attended high school in the late 1950s and early 1960s—working while in high school was only weakly and inconsistently associated with delinquency. Most relationships disappeared when earlier levels of delinquency were controlled. However, those few relationships that survived tests of statistical significance were *positive*, not negative, as delinquency theorists would expect. Thus the evidence of this study is that employment does not deter delinquency and that, in one or another subgroup of individuals, working actually may *increase* delinquent behavior (Shannon 1982).

The apparent failure of theorists to predict the effects of working on delinquency may not be due to flaws in their theories but to deficiencies in the type of work that is generally available to youth (Ruggiero 1984). For employment to operate as strain theorists suggest, for example, it ideally would provide the means for learning skills and abilities that augured better work opportunities in the future and thus higher social status than youngsters otherwise would enjoy. As we have seen, however, the adolescent workplace is hardly a hotbed of learning or even, for most youth, a firm steppingstone to a satisfactory adult job.

For work to increase young people's ties to the conventional social order, as control theorists propose, several other conditions would have to prevail. Based on data collected as part of our project in Orange County, social ecologist Mary Ruggiero (1984) doubts that they do. She points out that youngsters who are inadequately socialized to the conventional social order would need to come into contact with nondelinquent, "conventional" associates. But as we shall soon see, the workplace also provides contact with associates who do not observe conventional rules of behavior. And the sizable proportion of youngsters who work alone, or virtually alone, end up having little or no contact with either conventional or criminal persons. Ruggiero also argues that if youngsters are to learn conventional values and behaviors that they have not learned before, rewards and punishments must be allocated consistently, unambiguously, and with some degree of repetition. These are the conditions, according to psychologists who study learning, that promote and maintain changes in knowledge and behavior. The relatively sparse interaction of adolescents with persons in a position of authority, documented elsewhere in this chapter, raises doubts, however, about the timely and appropriate allocation of rewards and punishments and thus about the extent of socialization to conventional norms that occurs in the workplace.

The case for the deterrent effects of working on delinquency —a case *not* supported by empirical evidence—generally is directed at lower-class youth. Working, however, has become increasingly and even predominantly a middle-class phenomenon. Ruggiero explored the connections between working and delinquency even though the youngsters in our sample— largely middle class and white—were less likely than lower-class youngsters to encounter delinquent role models or a deviant subculture, to feel frustrated in their present or future aspirations for social status, and to lack the money that allows them to acquire goods legitimately. She hypothesized that working, rather than deterring delinquency in middle-class youth, actually might increase some types of deviant behavior. Because this hypothesis may seem counterintuitive, we shall follow her argument and report her findings in some detail.

According to Ruggiero, characteristics of the jobs adolescents generally hold and of middle-class youth themselves might lead to increases in four types of deviance among youngsters who work. Because most middle-class youngsters do not need their earnings to buy the necessities of life, some of their earnings may be channeled into deviant activities that require money, such as buying and selling drugs and gambling. Moreover, because jobs may be stressful and because adolescence itself is a stressful period of life, employed youngsters with money to spare may engage in illegal and/or unhealthy forms of stress reduction—including smoking cigarettes, drinking alcohol, and using marijuana and other drugs.[15] These stress-reduction techniques, so to speak, are also engaged in by adults, and may appeal to adolescents in part because smoking, drinking, and drug use confer signs of adult status. Third, because the demands of working may interfere with the demands of school, working may elevate certain forms of school-related deviance: being absent from school, cutting classes, and coming to school late; and cheating, copying others' homework assignments, and lying about having turned in assigned work. The former set of behaviors are possible adaptations to working long or late hours, being unprepared for class, or losing interest in school—a topic we discussed earlier. The latter set of behaviors are possible responses to difficulty in keeping up one's school performance. That is, under pressure from work schedules or job stress, youngsters may be more likely to take shortcuts that are considered unacceptable by conventional standards. Let us review the findings in these areas before unveiling the fourth form of adolescent deviance Ruggiero explored.

In Ruggiero's study workers indeed performed more deviant acts involving money, substance use, and school than nonworkers. In all analyses, either work status or "work exposure"— average weekly hours multiplied by number of weeks worked to date—was included, after controlling for the effects on deviance of age and social class. (These effects were negligible, no doubt because of the restricted range of age and social class in the study sample.) Deviant behaviors tended to be more strongly associated with intensity of employment than with working per se, as anticipated. In several instances, moreover, work exposure predicted variation in deviance that was not predicted by a youngster's work status. These findings need to be evaluated, of course, in light of the strengths and weaknesses of the studies on which they are based.

In the cross-sectional study, analyses were conducted for the sample as a whole and for boys and girls separately.[16] These analyses demonstrate that work exposure (but not work status) predicts overall money-related deviance and several individual items on this scale—buying liquor, selling drugs, gambling—

among boys. Work exposure is associated significantly with the frequency of using alcohol, marijuana, and tobacco among both boys and girls. These findings mirror the results of research based on nationally representative samples of high-school seniors (Bachman, Johnston, and O'Malley 1982). Turning to school-related deviance, Ruggiero found that amount of exposure to work also predicted skipping class in analyses of the sample as a whole (that is, both sexes combined). However, work status per se and not amount of exposure to the workplace was associated with several forms of deviant or undesirable behavior. Being employed predicted the frequency of girls' buying marijuana and selling drugs, their use of drugs other than marijuana, and their overall school-related deviance. Being employed also predicted lateness in coming to school and lying about the completion of assigned schoolwork, for the sample as a whole.

Comparisons among workers, nonworkers seeking jobs, and nonworkers not seeking jobs address the question of whether workers' greater deviance precedes their entry into the labor force or emerges after employment. These comparisons "provide considerable support for the conclusion that involvement in drug-, money-, and school-related deviance is a consequence of work experience rather than an antecedent condition affecting selection into the work force" (Ruggiero 1984, p. 362). Of the several aspects of undesirable behavior that we just noted were significantly related to employment status, only cigarette smoking was significantly more frequent among nonworking youth who were seeking jobs than those who were not seeking jobs—a result that suggests that this behavior may predate employment rather than result from working.

The longitudinal study yielded fewer significant work-deviance relationships than its cross-sectional counterpart. We believe, with Ruggiero, that special characteristics of the longitudinal sample may have constrained her search for statistically viable relationships. It will be recalled that the longitudinal sample consists of eleventh and twelfth graders of two kinds: those who have never held a job and those who did not hold their first job until eleventh or twelfth grade. National statistics on the employment of youth suggest that such youngsters— especially those never employed—are atypical; and Ruggiero's data indicate that they are different in important ways from the earlier, cross-sectional sample. Specifically, the longitudinal sample contains proportionately more girls and is measurably less deviant than the cross-sectional sample. Nonetheless, data from this study, in which initial scores on money-, substance-, and school-related deviance were controlled, show that working per se leads to more frequent gambling among boys. Greater work exposure leads to more overall money-related deviance among girls, to more overall school-related deviance among boys, and to two sex-specific increases in particular forms of substance use—alcohol consumption among boys and marijuana use among girls.[17]

It is noteworthy, in contrast, that workers in our sample did not exceed nonworkers in the commission of those kinds of delinquency typically surveyed by other researchers: interpersonal aggression, property damage, and theft. This was exactly what Ruggiero had anticipated. According to her analysis, moreover, it is precisely those adolescents who report the lowest rates of involvement in traditional delinquent activities for whom working is most strongly associated with deviance involving substance use, money, and school. Put otherwise, the least delinquent youngsters in this largely middle-class sample show the greatest "gains" in deviance as a consequence of going to work.

The finding that work increases some forms of deviance leads one to wonder why—what are the mechanisms through which working produces such effects? Ruggiero examined a number of possibilities, including the role of heightened cynicism about work (a possible outcome of employment in low-level jobs), increased income, and the experience of job stress. Analyses indicated that cynicism about the intrinsic value of work was associated with higher levels of deviance. However, increased income and exposure to job stress accounted for most of the variation in workers' deviance scores. Specifically, after amount of income or job stress had been entered into the analyses (with prior controls for age and social class), neither work status nor amount of exposure to working made additional, significant contributions to the prediction of money-, drug-, or school-related deviance. Ruggiero concluded: ". . . it is through the provision of *income* and the production of *job stress* that work may promote [these] particular forms of deviance" among middle-class youth (1984, p. 477, emphasis added).[18]

Job stress may promote deviance through several different means. Stress, for example, may lead to the breakdown of learned, adaptive behaviors, such as rule following. In view of the existence of considerable social support within the peer culture for alcohol and marijuana use, however, this explanation is suspect. Another, more plausible possibility is that money-, drug-, and school-related deviance are outlets for the expression of anger, anxiety, and conflict—emotional experiences that work, under certain conditions, may arouse. Using measures of job stress adapted from Vaux (1981) and reported in a study by Greenberger, Steinberg, and Vaux (1981), Ruggiero found that the stressful features of jobs most consistently related to the forms of deviance just noted were an impersonal work organization, low wage structure, autocratic supervision, meaningless and repetitive tasks, and conflict of work with other roles and responsibilities.

The links between income and two of the three kinds of deviance discussed thus far are obvious: money is required for engaging in "money-related deviance," such as buying drugs for one's own use, or in larger amounts for sale to others; and for frequent substance-related deviance, such as use of alcohol and other controlled or illegal substances. Money that can be spent with considerable freedom—true of the money that youngsters earn themselves—is particularly useful for under-writing such expenses. The link between amount of income and school-related deviance is less direct. Perhaps the experi-ence of controlling a sizable income leads to a heightened sense of power and "adultness" and in turn causes youngsters to rebel in a setting where, traditionally, their power and participation have been limited and their status low.

To sum up: working in the jobs typically available to young-sters does not diminish their prior level of delinquent activity. Among middle-class youth, working may lead to an increase in certain forms of deviant behavior that, although not violent, are nonetheless worrisome. It is an article of faith in many quarters, however, that working *should* deter youth from crime and delinquency. And faith is usually slow to succumb to facts.

Some Unanticipated Consequences of Working

Advocates of work experience for adolescents have focused attention almost exclusively on the good things that working might inspire. They have virtually ignored the possibility that working also might have consequences that no one concerned with improving the adolescent experience would promote de-liberately.

Adolescence is a time of numerous and dramatic changes. Within the span of a few years, youngsters undergo sexual maturation, radical transformations in bodily size and propor-tions, fundamental advances in intellectual ability, and the proliferation of new social roles. These changes have the poten-tial to tax severely youngsters' physical and psychological re-sources, as we know from the amount of sleep they require, from their notorious moodiness, and from increased rates of delinquent behavior and psychiatric problems during adolescence. In this context, it is reasonable to ask whether working —in particular, working long hours—may be stressful and may induce the kinds of health and behavioral problems that are commonly attributed to stress. This possibility was suggested several years ago by Vaux and examined empirically in two studies (Greenberger, Steinberg, and Vaux 1981; Vaux 1981).

There are at least two reasons why working might be stressful for adolescents. First, part-time work consumes time—for some youngsters, quite a lot of time. Concomitantly, many adolescents already have substantial time and energy commitments to other activities: they spend, on the average, thirty hours a week attending school; three to five hours doing homework; and may put time into an extracurricular activity, family responsibilities, and, almost surely, peer relations. It is possible that the addition of extensive working hours to their schedule strains youngsters' adaptational resources and produces undesirable behavioral consequences and health problems.

Second, an abundant literature on adults demonstrates that working may have adverse effects on people's health and well-being under certain conditions. For example, a Special Task Force (1973) that investigated the quality of work in America detailed the dysphoria associated with working in jobs that are perceived as dull, routine, and meaningless. Other researchers have documented the adverse effects of role ambiguity on white-collar workers (Caplan 1971; Kahn and Quinn 1970) and of exposure to physical and chemical hazards on blue-collar workers (Poulton 1978). It is certainly plausible, although arguable, that similar psychosocial and physical stressors might have the same effects on adolescent workers. In fact, conditions that often characterize jobs held by adolescents may clash with special vulnerabilities of this age group. Thus adolescents who typically are confronting issues of autonomy and intimacy may be particularly troubled by work that constrains initiative and affords little opportunity for meaningful contact with others.

With psychologist Alan Vaux, we identified six types of

potential stress in the workplace, based on developmental theory and on behavioral epidemiologist Stanislas Kasl's study (1974) of stress in the adult workplace, and surveyed workers in our study about their job conditions. From their responses Vaux created indices for each of the six domains of job stress: namely, (1) a poor work environment, characterized by time pressure and exposure to heat, noise, and other environmental hazards; (2) meaningless tasks that the adolescent feels are boring, repetitive, and have little effect on others; (3) conflict of work with other roles, such as interference with family, peer, or school activities; (4) autocratic supervision, characterized by low worker input into decisions about what to do and how to do it; (5) an impersonal work organization, in which close attachments are lacking; and (6) a low wage structure, with hourly pay below the minimum wage and little chance of wage improvement.

Because the health and behavioral consequences of job stress had not been studied previously, Vaux selected a range of possible outcomes: minor symptoms of somatic and psychological distress (for example, frequency in recent months of headaches, colds, feelings of tension and irritability, and depressed mood); absence from school and from work; and use of cigarettes, alcohol, marijuana, and other drugs. The rationale for including measures of psychological and physical symptoms is obvious. Absence from school and work were included as indicators of disruptions in the performance of expected activities—a common stress reaction. The frequency of using cigarettes, alcohol, and drugs was examined because such substances may be used to mitigate the physiological and emotional concomitants of stress.

Common sense suggests that the impact of job stressors will depend on the extent of exposure. Consequently, we created "stress exposure" scores consisting of the individual's score on each job stressor index multiplied by the number of hours the individual had spent on that job to date. We will recount first those findings that we anticipated and that we can explain without tortuous argument.

Exposure to all six job stressors was consistently related to alcohol and marijuana use. When the subsample of boys and girls were studied separately, a few sex differences in the job stressors that matter emerged. For boys but not girls, autocratic supervision predicted the frequency of using alcohol and marijuana; for girls but not boys, a poor wage structure and impersonal work organization predicted use of these substances. (The job stressors that fell short of statistical significance were still positively related to alcohol and marijuana use.) These sex differences in sensitivity to particular job stressors are consistent with developmental theories that pinpoint the special concern of boys to achieve autonomy (not something easily realized in an autocratically supervised work environment) and of girls to establish satisfying interpersonal relations (a motive not easily realized in an impersonal job setting).[19]

The relationship between job stress and frequency of use of alcohol and marijuana is impressive for two reasons. First, it persists even after the amount of income available to youngsters is controlled statistically. Second, analyses of longitudinal data imply an actual causal link between exposure to job stress and sex-specific substance use: frequency of alcohol use among boys and marijuana use among girls.

Exposure to job stressors, on the other hand, was not related to the use of drugs other than marijuana (which occurred very infrequently in our sample) and was related inconsistently to cigarette smoking. Two of the six stress exposure indices predicted the latter behavior for the sample of boys and girls together; a third index predicted girls' smoking but not boys', when the sexes were analyzed separately.

Exposure to stressors at work was unrelated, generally, to job absence. The exception was extent of exposure to an impersonal work organization, which predicted girls' job absence but not boys'. (We have noted previously the importance of this aspect of job stress for girls.) As we have observed elsewhere (Greenberger, Steinberg, and Vaux 1981), perhaps the lure of the weekly paycheck is enough to keep youngsters coming to work despite stressful conditions—a possibility that leads us to wonder whether school attendance might be improved by paying youngsters to endure the stressors in that setting! (This idea has been considered seriously by persons who are concerned about keeping poorly motivated and/or economically disadvantaged youth enrolled in school.) Ironically, absence from school is quite consistently related to exposure to job stress, suggesting that youngsters may respond to stress in one setting by failing to meet obligations in another.

Although exposure to job stress appears to have some negative consequences for adolescents' behavior, we found no evidence that it is associated with physical or psychological symptoms—at least, as these are reported by members of our study sample. In the few instances in which we did find a statistically significant relationship between reported health and exposure to a particular type of stressor, the direction of the relationship was actually contrary to prediction. That is, in a few cases, stress exposure of a particular type was associated with *better* mental and physical health. Since these effects were specific to boys, we conjectured that differences in sex-role socialization may be at the heart of this apparent puzzle. On the one hand, it is possible that boys who are experiencing stressful conditions at work simply underreport physical and psychological symptoms, because being able to "handle" hard work supports and validates their gender identity. (Girls would have less motivation to underreport symptoms, according to this argument, because the capacity for taxing work is less central to social expectations for women.) Alternatively, exposure to stress truly may enhance the health and well-being of boys. In support of this proposition an extension of the same socialization argument can be used: namely, exposure to stress enhances the well-being of boys (and not girls) because it supports important social and self-conceptions about their hardiness.[20] Of the two explanations, we favor the first, or underreporting, argument. The fact that boys, like girls, show important behavioral concomitants of job stress—increased frequency of alcohol and marijuana use—tends to undermine the alternative hypothesis, that job stress is actually good for boys' health.

In addition to raising the level of stress in the lives of adolescents, working may nourish the development of certain attitudes that are exactly the opposite of those that work experience is expected to inculcate (Ruggiero 1984). For example, instead of "learning the value of money," in the sense in which this term is generally used, youngsters may learn to value money unduly. Specifically, the novelty and prestige of being able to purchase expensive luxury goods—in an era when the paycheck is not used to help out the family or save—may foster greater materialism. Or again, despite improving youngsters' general work *skills*, experiences in the workplace may nonetheless lead them to develop cynical or contemptuous *attitudes* toward working. Many youngsters, after all, work at jobs that are not intrinsically interesting or challenging and that offer very limited prospects for learning or for significant pay increases and other forms of advancement. In the context of many youngsters' motives for working—not so much for experience or as a steppingstone to future employment as for spending money—they may take away from the workplace a diminished sense that work is a meaningful and satisfying human activity. Finally, rather than socializing youth to conventional values, as some social theorists have speculated, working may promote the adoption of deviant attitudes and behaviors—at least, in certain realms. In particular, working youngsters may become more tolerant of unethical activities in the workplace itself. They are, we know, privy to a variety of deviant, unethical, or irresponsible behaviors perpetrated by both employers and employees. With respect to employers, one of the first deviant behaviors that may come to the attention of a young worker is the hiring of youth to hold jobs during hours and times that violate child labor laws (Ruggiero 1984). We shall have a good deal more to say about employee deviance later. In any case, Ruggiero has conjectured that exposure to illegal practices in the workplace may cause teenage workers to become more tolerant of unethical activities there than they were prior to employment.

Our study provided an opportunity to explore these hypotheses. With Ruggiero, we developed scales to measure materialism, cynicism about work, and acceptance of unethical business practices. Sample items, which were administered as part of the survey questionnaire, are shown in table 3.1.

TABLE 3.1

Sample Items from Scales Measuring Materialism, Cynicism About
Work, and Acceptance of Unethical Business Practices*

MATERIALISM
    My goal in life is to make a lot of money and buy a lot of things. (+)
    It seems that the more money I have, the more things I want to buy. (+)
    Adults who have acquired a lot of wealth really have my respect and
        admiration. (+)

CYNICISM
    People who work harder at their jobs than they have to are a little bit
        crazy. (+)
    There's no such thing as a company that cares about its employees. (+)
    Working gives a person a feeling of self-respect. (−)

ACCEPTANCE OF UNETHICAL PRACTICES
    People who break a few laws to make a profit aren't doing anything I
        wouldn't do in their position. (+)
    In my opinion, it's all right for workers who are paid a low salary to take
        little things from their jobs to make up for it. (|)
    Employers should "look the other way" if people who work for them
        take little things now and then. (+)

*Items are marked (+) or (−) to show whether agreement or disagreement
corresponds to consistency with the attitude being measured.
SOURCE: Adapted from Mary Ruggiero, Ellen Greenberger, and Laurence
Steinberg, "Occupational Deviance Among First-time Workers," *Youth and
Society* 13 (1982): 423–48.

Findings from our cross-sectional and longitudinal studies do not always converge, and effects of working on these attitudinal measures often vary with youngsters' age, sex, and social class. Our initial, cross-sectional analysis showed no differences in materialism between workers and nonworkers; nor did job seekers have a significantly different level of materialism from youth who were not seeking jobs. This pattern of results suggests that in addition to employment having no impact on materialism, the sort of patent materialistic interests that we measured are not a selective factor that draws certain youngsters, and not others, into the labor force. However, the longitudinal analyses indicated that working *does* lead to the development of more materialistic attitudes among boys and among younger workers.[21] In short, the relations between employment and materialism are equivocal and require further study.

A still more complex story surrounds the association between working and acceptance of unethical business practices. Again, no consistent or easily interpretable picture emerges. For the record, it appears that acceptance of unethical practices by youngsters from blue-collar backgrounds (that is, those whose fathers are blue-collar workers) is unaffected by working, whereas tolerance of unethical practices *increases* among youngsters from white-collar or management family backgrounds (again, indexed by father's occupation) and *decreases* among youngsters whose fathers are in the professions. This decrease in tolerance needs to be put in context. Workers from higher social class backgrounds had the *highest* scores on acceptance of unethical business practices prior to employment.

The greatest convergence of findings concerns cynicism. In the cross-sectional study, workers thought of work as less intrinsically rewarding or self-fulfilling than nonworkers. This difference appeared to be due to the experience of working rather than to experiences that predated employment. In the longitudinal study, working—and the amount of exposure to work—led to increases in cynicism for two of three social class groups: youngsters from white-collar or managerial family backgrounds and youngsters from blue-collar backgrounds. In contrast, working led to diminished cynicism among youth whose fathers are in the professions. Interestingly, cynicism about work is related to differences in several aspects of job environments that we previously described as stressful: poor environmental conditions, perceived meaninglessness of work, and the perception that one's social environment at work is impersonal (Ruggiero 1984). Youngsters who work under less benign circumstances, in these respects, are more likely to endorse cynical statements about working.[22]

Deviance in the Adolescent Workplace

Earlier in this chapter we discussed the pervasive but ill founded belief that working deters youth from crime and delinquency. We presented evidence from Ruggiero's study to show that working actually seemed to increase three forms of deviance among middle-class youth: money-, substance-, and school-related deviance. Let us now turn to a fourth type of deviance with which working is associated: deviance in the workplace itself. From the perspective of believers in the delinquency-deterring powers of employment, this is surely an unanticipated consequence of adolescent labor-force experience.

As Ruggiero (1984) anticipated, deviant behavior on the job was not uncommon in our study sample. During the course of their first part-time job, 62 percent of these first-time workers reported committing at least one of nine acts of deviance about which they were surveyed, ranging from minor transgressions (calling in sick when not) to more serious ones (stealing things from the workplace). About 41 percent had committed some form of theft; about 45 percent, some illegal or unethical behavior other than theft (Ruggiero, Greenberger, and Steinberg 1982).[23]

TABLE 3.2

Occupational Deviance Among Adolescents in Their First Job

	Total workers who have done this (%)	Frequency with which workers have done this		
		Once or twice (%)	Several times (%)	Often (%)
Employee Theft				
Given away goods or services	29.9	19.9	7.0	3.0
Taken things from work	18.4	14.9	2.5	1.0
Put extra hours on timecard	9.4	7.4	1.0	1.0
Taken money from work	5.5	5.0	0.5	–
Deliberately short-changed customer	4.5	2.0	2.5	–
Nontheft Deviance				
Called in sick when not	32.2	28.2	3.0	1.0
Worked under influence of drugs or alcohol	16.9	12.4	3.0	1.5
Lied to employer to get or keep job	6.9	5.9	0.5	–
Deliberately damaged property at work	2.0	2.0	–	–

Source: Adapted from Mary Ruggiero, Ellen Greenberger, and Laurence Steinberg, "Occupational Deviance Among First-time Workers," *Youth and Society* 13 (1982): 423–48.

Table 3.2 shows the self-reported frequency of both theft and nontheft occupational deviance among youngsters in our sample. The most common forms of occupational deviance engaged in at least once (column 2 of the table) were, in declining order, calling in sick when not to account for job absence; giving away goods or services for nothing or for less than their market value; taking things from the workplace; working while intoxicated or "high" on drugs; and putting extra hours on one's timecard. Between one and three out of every ten respondents reported having engaged in some form of occupational deviance at least once.

The things youngsters have done at least once are not the same, of course, as the things that they do most frequently. Looking instead at the deviant acts engaged in with the greatest frequency (columns 3 and 4 combined), the rank order changes: giving away goods and services and working under the influence of alcohol or drugs take top honors. By one method of estimation, approximately one-quarter of these young workers could be called relatively frequent offenders (Ruggiero, Greenberger, and Steinberg 1982).[24]

Excerpts from our interview study give some sense of the phenomenon.

> FOOD SERVICE COUNTER WORKER: There was this one guy . . . he was working nights. He'd be on the register, and every night, like there was this order for eleven super tacos, so it was $11.50, and he just took all the money and stuck it in his pocket, he didn't even ring it up. . . . Our manager would come to me the next day, because they'd think I'd been taking the food   because we'd come up short on inventory. . . . He got fired.

> CLOTHING SALESPERSON: Sometimes your friend, like, really wants this ski jacket. And it's not on sale, but I'd mark it down anyway. . . .

> CLOTHING SALESPERSON: . . . my assistant manager, the one that got fired, she wasn't very strict, you know. When I just started working there, she said, "Why do you punch out for lunch? Don't worry about it," so I just took it . . . I'd just take my lunch, you know, because I heard that the office took an hour anyway. . . .

> INTERVIEWER: Sometimes people do things at work that, if your boss knew about it, he'd be pissed. . . . do you do

anything like that, or do you know about people doing anything like that?

GROCERY STORE CLERK: Minors buying beer. The boss may know, but he won't say anything . . . I've taken beer—it's there! Why not? . . . The manager knows but not the boss. . . . The manager even bought it for me. . . . Dan used to come in stoned. He'd be really nice to get along with, but after the stoneness wore off he was . . . not so hot!

Many youngsters, of course, report that they conform to conventional standards of behavior at work, and many no doubt do so. However, some kinds of youngsters are more likely than others to engage in workplace deviance; some jobs are more likely to provide opportunities for or inducements to deviance; and some characteristics of persons and jobs, in combination, generate more workplace deviance than either alone. These predictors tend to differ for theft and nontheft forms of deviance and for boys and girls (Ruggiero 1984).

Among the characteristics of individuals that predict an overall, or summary, measure of occupational deviance are their scores on the three attitudinal measures we discussed earlier. Adolescents who are more materialistic, more cynical about the value of work, and more tolerant of unethical practices in the workplace are more likely to engage in some form of workplace deviance. That is, despite ambiguity about whether these attitudes are themselves affected by working, youngsters' degree of endorsing such attitudes is linked with the commission of more deviant behavior on the job. Among the job characteristics most often associated with one or another form of occupational deviance are conflict between work and other activities and meaningless work tasks—both previously conceptualized as job stressors and shown to predict deviance with money, with substances, and in school; perceived opportunity for theft; and a positive social environment —that is, one in which the young person feels on close terms with others. The meaning of the latter, counterintuitive finding will become clear, we hope, in a moment.

Deviant behavior, like conventional behavior, presumably is functional—it serves a purpose. Two different, but not mutually exclusive, interpretations of the psychological functions of occupational deviance seem plausible. They are based on consideration of which forms of deviance are most commonly engaged in and which features of jobs are most strongly associated with workplace deviance.

First, because several of the job characteristics associated with occupational deviance appear to be stress provoking, deviant behavior at work may be viewed as a means of releasing anger or reducing tension. Certain specific forms of workplace deviance fit this model well—for example, working while intoxicated or stealing from the employer. Alternatively, or additionally, deviance at work may be a means of expressing solidarity with the peer group. Deviance, after all, tends to emerge under positive social conditions at work rather than under conditions where the youngsters feel distant from others; and the closest relations in the workplace are with agemates or near agemates —including "managers" or "assistant managers" who, we have seen, may encourage deviant behavior in the workplace. And the most common forms of deviance involve activities that confirm one's ties to the peer culture: working while "buzzed" on alcohol or drugs—a way of thumbing one's nose at adult expectations for responsible behavior; and giving away things of value to one's friends (Ruggiero 1984; Ruggiero, Greenberger, and Steinberg 1982).

Taken together, increased use of marijuana and alcohol as a function of job stress, increased cynicism about the value of work, and the rapid emergence, among first-time workers, of deviance in the workplace itself constitute a sobering set of outcomes. In view of the level of dissatisfaction many adults express about their work lives and their extent of substance use and occupational deviance, the biggest surprise is that these outcomes of adolescent employment were unanticipated.

Improving Employment Prospects in Adulthood

One of the most important markers of the transition to adulthood is getting a job and earning sufficient income to live independently. A number of youth, however, experience difficulty in "crossing over" to adulthood in these respects. High rates and prolonged periods of unemployment are notorious and constitute a serious and persistent social problem.[25]

There are a variety of structural and individual reasons why a young adult might be unemployed. The strength of the economy and the size of the youth cohort relative to the cohort of older, more experienced workers, are examples of structural factors; the person's race, family background, level of educational attainment, and job skills are examples of individual factors. School critics have concentrated their attention on those individual factors associated with success in the labor force that are amenable to change. As we have noted before, they suggest that overreliance on schooling, compared to other ways of preparing youth for assuming adult roles and responsibilities, has cost youngsters opportunities to develop good work habits, job skills, and contacts for obtaining work. Earlier and more extensive work experience, they believe, would help to remedy these deficits and facilitate the absorption of young adults into the labor force.

The questions that we now turn to are whether employment during the high-school years gives youngsters an advantage in the labor market during the early years of adulthood and whether this advantage (if any) persists over the ensuing years.

Empirical studies demonstrate that youngsters who were employed more intensively during high school indeed fare better than others—at least, over the next four or five years. They experience fewer weeks of unemployment and earn higher hourly wages (Freeman and Wise 1979; Finch and Mortimer 1985; Mortimer and Finch, in press). Economists and other social scientists tend to agree, however, that it is debatable whether high-school employment is the *direct* cause of early labor-force success or whether variation in other, unmeasured factors, such as degree of "drive" or social competence, underlie both high-school employment and labor-force success in the immediately subsequent years. Perhaps both explanations have merit: adolescents with certain characteristics do better in the world of work, and experience in the workplace enhances these characteristics.[26]

Data from the High School and Beyond survey (Lewin-Epstein 1981) provide some hints concerning characteristics of high-school employment that are likely to enhance the prospects for later employment. Seniors were asked whether they had a postgraduation job lined up. As one would expect, based on the studies just noted, students who were employed were more likely than those who were not working—twice as likely, in fact—to answer in the affirmative. Of particular interest, however, is the fact that students' responses varied as a function of the kind of job they were holding at the time. At the low end, about 40 percent of seniors employed in odd jobs, as baby-sitters or as food service workers, said that they had a postgraduation job scheduled; but only a small minority of these youth indicated that it was the same job they were currently holding. At the high end, 75 percent of youth working in the skilled trades, in factories, and in health-related settings said that they had a post–high-school job secured, and nearly half or more indicated that they expected to continue in their current job. Jobs in these three areas appear to provide better prospects for adult careers. They offer better wages, in general, and more paths for advancement than jobs in the "new" adolescent workplace. The frequency with which youngsters' high-school jobs lead directly into jobs after high school is not, however, as great as these figures might suggest. The least attractive "adult jobs"—odd jobs, baby-sitting, food service work—are the ones that nearly half of all high-school students hold. In contrast, fewer than 7 percent of students are employed in the skilled trades and other, relatively more attractive jobs.

The benefits of having worked during high school are more impressive with respect to wages than to rates of employment. Indeed, effects on hourly wages are substantial. One might expect, however, that the positive effect of high-school employment on immediately subsequent wages pertains only to those persons who do not go to college. Persons who go directly into the full-time labor market after high school and are not constrained by the demands of postsecondary education are in the best position to maximize their earnings. (In contrast, adults who are enrolled in school may need to take "jobs of convenience" that allow them the flexibility to pursue their educational goals. In the process, they may have to trade off the opportunity to maximize wages and earnings.) Surprisingly, this is not the case. The positive effects of having been employed in high school show up for *both* groups of young people (Mortimer and Finch, in press). The wage discrepancies between youngsters who worked in high school and those who did not is greatest, moreover, for those with the poorest long-run occupational prospects: high-school dropouts.

The high rate of unemployment over the course of early adulthood makes it important to estimate the impact of different employment histories at the beginning of this period on employment and earnings toward the end of young adulthood. Labor-force economists Richard Freeman and David Wise (1979), summarizing research on this topic, conclude that unemployment at the first stages in the adult life cycle does not have the *major* effects on the entire early adult period that some have feared. The good news is that early unemployment —at eighteen or nineteen, or immediately after leaving school —has almost no effect on subsequent rates of employment. While it is true that employment in one year is statistically related to the likelihood of employment in the next and subsequent years of early adulthood, the correlation is due almost entirely to the persistence of critical individual factors over the years. Once individual differences in motivation, academic ability, educational attainment, and other, similar variables have been taken into account, the effect of variations in prior employment virtually disappears. The bad news is that unemployment in the earliest years of young adulthood *does* take a toll in wages. Persons with periods of unemployment in their early work history are likely to earn lower wages a few years down the road, because wage rates are in part determined by the amount of work experience one has accumulated. Differences in the kinds of "individual factors" just noted also play a part in accounting for variations in young people's wage rates. However, even when these factors are controlled, the effect of amount of prior employment on wages is still substantial.

Earlier in this chapter we described the effects of working during high school on learning and questioned whether what is learned at work may be offset by what is lost in learning at school. We raise an analogous question here: To what extent are short-term gains in labor-force success—amounting chiefly to higher hourly wages—offset by losses in longer-range occupational attainments?

One of the most important determinants of the long-range occupational attainment of adults is education. In general, people with more years of education obtain jobs that not only yield a higher income but are considered higher in prestige or desirability and that lead to greater personal satisfaction (Sewell, Hauser, and Featherman 1976). Even at an early stage in one's occupational history, differences in education matter.

We have mentioned "level of education" repeatedly as one of the individual attributes that make a difference in rates of early adult employment and hourly wages. Consequently, it is important to ascertain whether working during the high-school years has any impact, for better or worse, on adolescents' educational aspirations and accomplishments.

Currently about one-quarter of young people fail to complete high school. In view of the poor long-range employment prospects of high-school dropouts, this is a good place to begin our inquiry. Does having a job and paycheck in hand lure some youngsters into dropping out of school? Alternatively, does the possibility of combining remunerative work with going to school increase the likelihood of persevering until graduation? Or might a good dose of a "bad" job—one characterized by low wages, limited opportunity for learning or advancement, and poor or nonexistent fringe benefits—encourage youngsters to "stick it out" in school?

In the one study we know of that addresses this issue, based on data from the National Longitudinal Surveys, D'Amico (1984) found that intensive employment during tenth and eleventh grades was associated with increased probability of dropping out of school for certain subgroups of students. Specifically, as the percentage of weeks in which they worked more than twenty hours rose, tenth-grade white males and eleventh-grade white females showed greater vulnerability to leaving school. However, less intensive employment was linked with greater educational perseverance for some youngsters. As the percentage of weeks in which they worked one to twenty hours increased, whites of both sexes and black females in grade 11 showed a lower propensity to drop out. A similar but statistically nonsignificant pattern of findings emerged at grade 10. In these analyses, earlier-measured educational expectations were controlled, so that the effects of more and less intensive work experience could be more clearly evaluated.

Based on these findings, D'Amico suggests that employment

in moderate amounts may foster diligence and perseverance—traits that are conducive to completing high school. His argument is not altogether convincing, however. It is unclear, following his logic, why more intensive employment would not foster *still greater* diligence and persistence and thus favor school completion among those youngsters who spend the most time in the workplace. An alternative to D'Amico's explanation is the familiar selection argument. Differences in diligence and perseverance may themselves cause youngsters to make different decisions about how intensively to work. Thus youngsters who have more drive and tenacity—and, we add, who value education more—may protect themselves against a level of employment that might jeopardize their educational goals.

Dropping out of school is the bottom line. But what about the effects of working on the "top line"—the aspirations of adolescents for further education and the level of education they actually attain?

In a nationally representative sample of high-school males in which participants were followed up again five years after graduation, individuals who had a less intensive record of labor-force participation expressed stronger commitment to obtaining further education (Mortimer and Finch in press). As high-school students, their aspirations for postsecondary education were higher; and five years after graduation, they in fact had achieved more years of education.[27] However, their most recent annual earnings were lower than those of their counterparts who had a history of more intensive employment during the high-school years.

The lower annual earnings of young adults who worked less during high school and are investing, or have invested, more time and effort in postsecondary education is predictable from the research we have just reviewed. Five years after high-school graduation, many of these young people were still enrolled in school, full time or part time. (Bear in mind that many teenagers do not go directly from high school into postsecondary institutions.) Also, young adults who obtained postsecondary education are likely to be more recent entrants into the labor force—particularly the full-time labor force; and as we know, wages are determined in part by the individual's amount of prior job experience.

A number of studies indicate that the economic benefits of higher education are not reaped immediately but rather increase as individuals acquire greater job experience (Sewell, Hauser, and Featherman 1976). For example, a recent analysis of data from the National Longitudinal Surveys, focusing on the high-school class of 1972, confirms that the hourly wage rates of young people who ultimately graduated from college or obtained advanced degrees were lower, in the first few years after high school, than the wages of their peers who did not obtain a four-year college degree. However, the crossover point came almost immediately after college graduation for women. By age twenty-one, their wage rates were higher than those of their less-educated peers. For men, in contrast, the crossover point appears to come later. By age twenty-five, the wages of men with a four-year college degree or more still have not caught up with those of men who attained a lower level of education. From age twenty-one onward, however, the wages of college-educated adults of both sexes had a faster growth rate, suggesting that the wages of college-educated men would eventually catch up with, and rise above, those of their less-educated agemates (National Center for Education Statistics 1982).

Labor-force success during the earliest years of the transition to adulthood is a worthy social objective. Other things being equal, it is something we would want to promote for everybody. However, the measurement of labor-force success in terms of weeks of employment and hourly wages may miss the point in some cases. For some young people, "underemployment" and lower-than-maximum hourly wages may be part of a rational strategy for deferred labor-market success. Young people who opt for further education are likely to attain more occupational success and satisfaction in the future.

We have strayed deliberately from the issue of how work experience during high school affects the transition to adulthood, so let us conclude by confronting the issue once again. Whereas a moderate level of work experience during the high-school years appears to be beneficial to youngsters' prospects for earning higher wages in early adulthood, intensive employment also carries risks. Youngsters who become highly absorbed in working appear to invest less in obtaining a good high-school education and appear to obtain weaker educational credentials, in terms of a high-school diploma or the attainment of postsecondary education. Mortimer and Finch (in press) have pointed out that the quality of a young person's high-school education and subsequent educational accomplishments may be far more consequential than early advantages in employment and earnings for adult occupational achievement. Better educational credentials pave the way for entry into more prestigious occupations that have higher earnings and advancement potential. Paraphrasing these researchers' bottom line: Intensive employment during high school may create a short-run advantage in the labor market but set up the conditions for longer-term disadvantage in terms of adult social position and economic attainment.

CHAPTER 4

Beyond Work: The Task of Growing Up

OVER the past thirty years, the social environment of American adolescents has changed dramatically. Once a period of time that was devoted exclusively to school, the middle adolescent years have come to be a time split between the obligations of the classroom and the attractions of the workplace. It is a tug-of-war that has had serious implications for the intellectual, psychological, and social development of young people.

As we discussed previously, the flow of teenagers into the adolescent workplace has not been limited to a minority of deviant or economically disadvantaged youth. Youngsters of the middle class have been transformed into a working class. It is not possible, therefore, to dismiss the phenomenon as affecting only those youngsters who are already disenfranchised from school, or whose families depend on the income from their children's labor, or who are for one reason or another in need of the putative "rehabilitative" impact of holding a job. Indeed, the situation could hardly be more different from this: more youngsters who work are from well-to-do than from poor families, many of them plan to continue their schooling, and most have never shown any apparent need for work's alleged therapeutic benefits.

The findings we have presented—derived from our own studies of adolescents and from those of many of our colleagues working in different parts of the country and with different samples of young people—represent a strong challenge to conventional wisdom and popular belief. They indicate that the negative effects of holding a time-consuming job during adolescence may well outweigh the positive ones. As we have seen, all that goes on in the workplace is not good for young people, many of the lessons learned from part-time jobs are undesirable ones, and the impact of holding a job on youngsters' growth and development can be negative as well as positive. This latter finding is especially true for youngsters who work in large doses —more than twenty hours weekly—among whom the deleterious effect of part-time work appear most consistently.

Many of our findings will undoubtedly surprise those who advocate hefty doses of work experience for young people. Among the most striking of these findings are that extensive part-time employment may have a deleterious impact on youngsters' schooling; that working appears to promote, rather than deter, some forms of delinquent behavior; that working, especially in the high-stress jobs held by many teenagers, leads to higher rates of alcohol and drug use; and that, for many youngsters, working fosters the development of negative attitudes toward work itself.

Although a few studies have uncovered a handful of positive findings that confirm widely held popular beliefs about the benefits of early employment, in general, these findings are not strong. At the very least, the research we have reviewed indicates that the benefits of holding a job during adolescence have been overestimated and the costs, underestimated. Whether this always has been true and was simply not realized, owing to the characteristically uncritical way in which work experience has been viewed, or whether it is peculiar to the age in which we live and the jobs we make available to young people, is a question that we are unable to answer with any certainty. We believe, however, that much of the negative impact that intensive part-time employment may have on young people is attributable to the nature of adolescents' jobs and the larger social context of their employment.

In this chapter we shall try to place the findings we have discussed in perspective. In our view, they say a great deal not only about young people and work but about the changing nature of the transition from adolescence to adulthood, about the problems faced by families and schools in their attempts to socialize and educate young people, and, most of all, about the state of adolescence in contemporary America.

The Transition into Adulthood and
the Inevitability of Discontinuity

In past eras, the transition from adolescence into adulthood was accomplished through a graded series of passages in which the young person assumed, gradually and incrementally, the work, family, and citizenship roles he or she eventually would hold as an adult. Structured apprenticeships led to adult employment; establishing an independent residence from one's family of procreation was preceded by a long period of shared residence with, and semidependence on, another family in the community; power in the community was meted out little by little as individuals proved, typically through economic achievement, worthy of increased status (Katz 1975; Kett 1977). Under these conditions, the most valuable preparation that a young person could receive for adulthood was prior experience in positions that resembled adult roles as closely as possible.

In such societies, in which the transition from adolescence to adulthood was characteristically highly continuous, the prerequisite to adulthood was social maturity: the ability to carry out, on a mature level, the social roles and responsibilities deemed necessary for successful life as an adult member of the community. In essence, the young person's readiness to enter adulthood—and, more important, the success of his or her preparation for adulthood—was defined in terms of demonstrated ability to perform the duties that would be expected in future years.

This is no longer the case. In contemporary society, which is marked by a sharp discontinuity between past and present, present and future, the young person's successful transition into adulthood is not so dependent on having had prior experience in specific adult activities. Rather the passage from adolescence is dependent on his or her having developed the psychological and intellectual wherewithal necessary to face up to the contradictions and confusions, the challenges and choices, that inevitably arise in a rapidly changing world.

Today the successful route to adulthood is as much psychological as it is social; the proper preparation is intrapsychic as well as experiential. In short, the prerequisite to adulthood is psychological, and not only social, maturity. Emerging from adolescence with heightened self-awareness and a healthy orientation toward achievement is today more important than having an extensive record of adolescent employment. The young person who can face adulthood with an internal sense of self-reliance and responsible autonomy is in a far better position to become a successful adult than his or her peer who leaves adolescence with the financial irresponsibility that premature affluence begets. Having had extensive paid employment as an adolescent, moreover, is less important than having developed a clear enough sense of self to know whether one's career choice is a wise and valuable one or having acquired enough sense to know which tack to take should the occupational winds suddenly shift. And the young person who greets adulthood with the resources for social responsibility is better able to contribute to family life and the life of the community than is one whose youth has been spent exclusively in the pursuit of self-advancement.

Much of this was missed, it seems to us, in the various blue-ribbon commission reports issued during the 1970s that proclaimed the value of early work experience. At the heart of these commissions' arguments about the need to involve young people in the workplace was the belief that the transition into adulthood would be made easier by structuring it so that youngsters would have gradual, prior experience in "adult" roles, most notably work roles. Their argument in favor of role continuity derived largely from images of adolescence in prior eras or nonindustrialized societies. Indeed, throughout the commissions' reports and in a variety of similarly argued publications of that period comparisons were drawn between adolescence in primitive and in modern societies, with the former characterized by the continuity in roles they provide their young. In less industrialized societies, the writers noted, children typically are not segregated from their parents and other adults in the community and hence from the society's means of production. But in contemporary America the majority of young people grow up unfamiliar with the day-to-day work their parents perform and with the workplace in which their parents spend most of the day. Consequently, when it comes time for the passage into adulthood, adolescents in modern society are essentially un-schooled in the "real-life" matters of adulthood, having had little meaningful experience in adult roles during childhood or adolescence.

The "continuity" proponents relied heavily on ideas set forth in anthropological studies, like those of Margaret Mead. In *Coming of Age in Samoa*, for example, Mead (1928) wrote:

> Samoan children do not learn to work through learning to play, as the children of many primitive peoples do. Nor are they permitted a period of lack of responsibility such as our children are allowed. From the time they are four or five years old, they perform definite tasks, graded to their strength and intelligence, but still tasks which have a meaning in the structure of society. . . . American children spend hours in schools learning tasks whose visible relation to their mothers' and fathers' activities is quite impossible to recognise. . . . So our children make a false set of categories, work, play, and school; work for adults, play for children's pleasure, and schools as an inexplicable nuisance with some compensations. These false distinctions are likely to produce all sorts of strange attitudes, an apathetic treatment of school which bears no known relation to life, a false dichotomy between work and play, which may result either in a dread of work as implying irksome responsibility or in a later contempt for play as childish. (Pp. 226–28)

The general absence of psychological tumult among the Samoan youngsters she studied, Mead believed, was due to the fact that their society was structured in a way that minimized the stress in passing from childhood into adulthood. By institutionalizing the transition as a continuous one, in which, from an early age, young people were exposed to and prepared for the sexual and work roles they would occupy as adults, nonindustrialized societies were able to transform adolescence into a relatively pacific period. "The stress [of adolescence]," Mead wrote, "is in our civilisation . . ." (1928, p. 235). For the commissions, writing some fifty years later, the "stress of adolescence in our civilization" inhered in the lengthy period of delay between the end of childhood and the entrance into adult roles—a period of delay created by industrialization and extended further by modernization.

The ideas set forth in documents like the President's Science Advisory Committee's *Youth: Transition to Adulthood* (1973) enjoyed widespread popularity. But the commissions made, in our view, three very fundamental errors in their arguments. The first was an error of fact; the second, of judgment; the third, of viewpoint.

As to the first of their mistakes, it is exceedingly clear that American youth had not, as the commissions had suggested, lost touch with workplace. Indeed, as we documented in chapter 1, during the 1960s and 1970s school-going youth entered the workplace in record numbers. At the time the commissions published their reports, in fact, proportionately more school-going youth were in the labor force than at any other period in recent history.

Second, the commissions apparently presupposed a comparability between adolescents' jobs and adults' jobs—and hence, a continuity between them—that simply does not exist in contemporary America. The commissions put their greatest hopes in specially designed work experiences that were tailored to adolescents' developmental needs rather than in "naturally occurring" jobs. Unfortunately, however, the sorts of jobs that genuinely would bridge adolescence and adulthood—the sorts of jobs recommended by these commissions—are for the most part closed to young people, and the available, naturally occurring jobs link youth and maturity very tenuously, at best. As we detailed in chapter 2, the workplace in which today's adolescents are employed bears little resemblance to the one they will encounter as adults. It is by most accounts a genuinely "adolescent" workplace. Those who argue that the jobs most teenagers hold provide opportunities for decision making, foster meaningful contact between young people and their elders, or prepare youngsters for future employment are holding on to an image of a workplace that no longer exists.

We do not take issue with the view that the passage of adolescents into adult work roles is highly discontinuous in this country; indeed, because of the rapidity with which the nature of work continues to change in contemporary society, the transition of young people into adult work roles has become inherently and inevitably discontinuous. But the solution to whatever "transition" problems young people may have is not an expansion of their opportunities for work in the sorts of jobs that have come to characterize the new adolescent workplace. In order to provide a more continuous transition for young people into adult work roles, employers would need to be persuaded to create meaningful work experiences for them that would impart skills and knowledge valuable for adult work roles, and adolescents would need to be persuaded to forsake a certain amount of short-term earning in return for a payoff in long-term learning.

In fairness to the advocates of earlier work experience for young people, it is important to note that never in their writings did they actually recommend that adolescents work in the retail and service jobs that dominate the landscape of the new adolescent workplace. The authors of *Youth: Transition to Adulthood,* for example, came out strongly in favor of the "alternation of school and work" for youngsters fourteen years of age and older, in a pattern of half-time schooling and half-time employment managed under the auspices of existing work experience, career education, and vocational education programs. Perhaps anticipating that employment in such "managed" programs might look different from employment in the naturally occurring labor force, this commission recommended comparing the experiences of youngsters employed in managed programs with those of their peers employed through "ordinary labor force hiring" (p. 160). However, neither did this commission nor others writing in a similar vein caution against the intensive involvement of youngsters in part-time jobs, and their recommendation that schools confront the scheduling problems that hindered many youngsters' labor-force participation led, in many school districts, to the further encouragement of students to work—in whatever jobs were available. Indeed, in many districts, naturally occurring part-time retail and service jobs became placement sites for school-sponsored work experience programs. Clearly, many school officials misinterpreted the commissions' argument, failing to see the distinction between involving youngsters in a deliberately structured transition into adult work roles and simply letting them out into the part-time labor force without guidance, under the pretext of expanding their "educational" opportunities.

Interestingly, although the continuity proponents responsible for the commission reports based many of their arguments on the work of Margaret Mead, the inevitability of discontinuity—and the futility of trying to make our society more continuous—was pointed out by Mead herself. A close reading of *Coming of Age* reveals that she was doubtful about the prospects of integrating Samoan-style transitions into American society, with its heterogenous population, rapid pace of social change, and head-spinning array of choices facing the young person. "[American] society presents too many problems to her adolescents, demands too many momentous decisions on a few months' notice," she wrote. In contrast, "Samoa knows but one way of life and teaches it to her children" (1928, p. 248). The solutions to adolescents' problems in modern society, wrote Mead, involved giving them the intellectual tools necessary to make informed choices about their futures. The means was more and better education, at home and in the school, so that children could "come clear-eyed to the choices which lie before them" (p. 246). Despite the widely publicized (and largely incendiary) criticism Mead's fieldwork has received in recent years, her observations about the differences between socialization in traditional and industrialized societies nevertheless remain valid. In the former (so-called postfigurative cultures), the socialization of young people for adulthood can be accomplished mainly by exposing youngsters to adult roles and activities; in the latter (so-called cofigurative societies), social change is too rapid for such a process to be successful, and didactic instruction rather than observational learning is the preferred mode of education.

The third, and most critical, error made by proponents of the earlier integration of young people into the workplace is that they overemphasized the value of developing social maturity and underestimated the importance of developing psychological maturity. Increasingly, adolescents need more instruction, not more observation, to prepare for their entrance into the world of work. Industrialization did not simply create adolescence, it also necessitated it. By redefining what it meant to be an adult, by stepping up the intellectual and psychological requirements, industrialization not only permitted but also made essential the provision of a longer passage out of youth.

Adolescent Work: Role Experimentation or Pseudomaturity?

The notion that much of the "work" of adolescence is intrapsychic rather than experiential is rooted in Erik Erikson's perspective on the period. Indeed, Erikson suggested that it was society's responsibility to provide a period of time for young people to undertake this intrapsychic work, a period in which "exploration, becoming, growth, and pain"—to use historian Patricia Spacks' phrasing (1981)—could be pursued in relative safety. Erikson called this period of time a psychosocial moratorium and the process of exploration role experimentation. During this respite from excessive responsibility and obligation, young people could introspect, explore, experiment, and figure out who they were and where they were headed—a task that had become increasingly difficult, but increasingly necessary, in contemporary society. As he wrote in *Identity: Youth and Crisis* (1968, pp. 128, 157):

> By moratorium . . . we mean a delay of adult commitments, and yet it is not only a delay, it is a period that is characterized by a selective permissiveness on the part of society and of provocative playfulness on the part of youth. . . . A moratorium is a period of delay granted to somebody who is not ready to meet an obligation or forced on somebody who should give himself time.

How might early work experience fit into an Eriksonian conception of adolescence? The answer is complicated. It is clear that Erikson views the "trying on" of a variety of different personalities, identities, and roles—what has been termed role experimentation—as an integral part of the adolescent's psychological development; only through exploration and experimentation can the young person pursue the tasks of identity clarification and self-definition. As he and others have pointed out, complex societies present individuals with a vast array of identities from which to choose. The task facing the young person is to fashion out of these possibilities a "series of ever-narrowing selections of personal, occupational, sexual, and ideological commitments" (1968, p. 245). Ultimately, the sense of identity that is achieved is both psychological and social; it is the result of a mutual recognition between the young person and society. The adolescent forges an identity, but at the same time, society identifies the adolescent.

Experimentation in different roles and situations is necessary during adolescence in order that the individual ultimately become all that he or she can be. One means of facilitating role experimentation is for adolescents to experience a variety of different settings and relationships while still enjoying the protective cover of the psychosocial moratorium. This experimentation allows individuals to learn about themselves—their strengths and weaknesses, likes and dislikes, hopes and fears—without their mistakes having unalterable consequences. Without role experimentation, adolescents in modern society either remain locked into roles handed to them by their elders or muddle through adulthood with a confused and incoherent sense of who they are.

Many would argue that holding a job during adolescence is an important part of the role experimentation process—a reasonable assumption at first glance. Yet the issue is not so clear-cut. Not all experiences in new roles and settings necessarily lead to psychological growth. Under some circumstances, work experience may indeed facilitate the identity development process, through helping adolescents to discover their unique areas of skill and deficiency, of facility and clumsiness, of grace and ineptitude. Under other conditions, however, working actually may pose a strong impediment to introspection, self-awareness, and psychological growth—by occupying the young person's time and energy in tasks that teach very little, by rewarding shallowness in interpersonal interactions, or by encouraging the development of superficial values and self-indulgence. As we have suggested in earlier chapters, much depends on the nature of the job and, more fundamentally, on the psychological backdrop against which the work is performed. In order to examine the issue further, we shall need to examine some of Erikson's ideas in a more critical light.

Work and Identity Development

The concept of "role experimentation," a term that figures so prominently in Erikson's theory, is something of a misnomer.

The problem, in our view, is in the use of the term role, a concept that has a far more limited definition than Erikson probably intended. A role, strictly speaking, is a socially recognized position with a particular set of behaviors prescribed for it. As such, the term role experimentation has an overly behavioral connotation; it suggests images of adolescents as actors, trying on different costumes, playing with different props, and behaving according to different scripts. But some of the most valuable "experiments" adolescents engage in are not behavioral in nature. Many of the "experiments"—although this word connotes a more systematic phenomenon than probably occurs—are mental; they take the form of daydreaming and problem solving in fantasy. They involve imagining who one might be, without actually trying out future roles; pondering one's place in society, without actually experimenting with being in different places; and devising new strategies for dealing more effectively with others. These internal processes, perhaps unseen by others, play as important a part in the process of self-definition as do more behavioral experiments with roles. Indeed, engaging in this mental work is an important prelude to the development of psychological maturity.

The psychosocial moratorium, then, is not simply a period during which the adolescent can experiment with different props, scripts, costumes—and jobs. Such experimentation may facilitate the development of social maturity but may have little to do with the growth of psychological maturity. In order for this latter type of development to occur, adolescence also must be a time during which the young person can explore, through fantasy and internal problem solving, different modes of thinking about things, different sorts of feelings, different values, and different ways of looking at the world. Adolescents must be provided opportunities to develop, practice, and refine newly emerging cognitive abilities, ego skills, and interpersonal strategies that will prove valuable during adulthood. Indeed, without a period of thoughtful introspection during adolescence to accompany their role experimentation, young people will not be able to bring to these roles either wisdom or a sense of purpose.

The sort of psychosocial moratorium that is beneficial both psychologically and socially requires an environment that challenges the young person to develop more advanced cognitive and emotional equipment, yet at the same time permits and encourages such luxuries as daydreaming, fantasy, and harmless irresponsibility. A premature thrusting of the adolescent into responsibilities and commitments that do not provide opportunities for meaningful learning or intellectual stimulation compromises the youngster's psychosocial development at both ends—it neither encourages fantasy nor facilitates cognitive or emotional growth. As such, it endangers the process of identity exploration in two very important ways.

First, there is the danger of becoming committed to an identity before one has fully thought about the possible alternatives, a danger that Erikson has written about extensively—the youngster who is forced to carry on the family business; the adolescent who marries a high-school sweetheart immediately after graduation; the youngster whose parents select a college and a course of study for their child. Erikson labeled this phenomenon "identity foreclosure." Identity foreclosure is not simply the premature selection of a career or a mate. To think of the phenomenon in these terms is to miss its essence and misunderstand Erikson's viewpoint. Identity foreclosure is, instead, the premature curtailment of the entire process of identity development. It is a foreclosure of the process of self-discovery, not simply the making of premature commitments: "[The] developing individual has settled upon a certain identification or set of identifications as forever characterizing himself in all ways. . . . [Identity foreclosure] is a premature fixing of one's self-images thereby interfering with one's development of other potentials and possibilities for self-definition" (1959, p. 143).

Excessive commitment to a part-time job during adolescence may interfere with a youngster's "development of other potentials and possibilities for self-definition." The process of identity development is sometimes foreclosed by a sheer lack of time or freedom for role experimentation; it is for this reason that Erikson argues for the provision of a psychosocial moratorium to young people. One of the dangers inherent in taking on a job that demands twenty or thirty hours each week, therefore, is that the time commitment compromises the moratorium; the amount of time left over for other activities— activities that could provide for more varied experimentation —is severely foreshortened. It is one thing for a youngster to view a part-time job as one of many potentially valuable after-school activities to be pursued in order to learn more about his or her predilections and skills. But it is quite another for an adolescent to become so wrapped up in being a "worker," and devote so much of his or her leisure time to a job, that few hours, and little energy, are left over for getting involved in other activities that may help along the process of self-discovery. When youngsters curtail their involvement in extracurricular activities, for example, because they have after-school jobs—a pattern that is common, as we noted in chapter 3— they may miss out on the sorts of experiences that often contribute to healthy identity development.

A second danger associated with excessive involvement in the workplace is that of growing up without the cognitive capability or motivation necessary to engage in self-examination; going to work every day in a monotonous job, pursued solely for the paycheck, may deaden the young person's sense of introspection, imagination, and curiosity. Thus for some adolescents the problem with excessive involvement in work is not so much that the time commitment to a job takes away from the time available for other, potentially more valuable forms of role experimentation, but that their involvement in the workplace interferes with their engaging in the sort of

mental exploration that is also important for healthy psychosocial development. Youngsters who have foreclosed the process
of mental exploration may emerge from adolescence possessing
the superficial signs of adulthood—but may lack the necessary
inner equipment to pursue the roles of worker, parent, spouse,
and citizen with zest, competence, and commitment. This
phenomenon, the lamentable companion to identity foreclosure not described by Erikson, is "pseudomaturity."

Pseudomaturity involves the attainment of social maturity—
the assumption of adult roles—without the development of
psychological maturity to go with it. It is not an uncommon
phenomenon in contemporary society; as young as fifteen or
sixteen, many adolescents work, make love, become parents,
use alcohol, own expensive clothes and cars—experiences that
traditionally have been delayed until adulthood. Yet these social "adults" are still psychological adolescents, and the ways
in which they perform these roles suggest—to use sociologist's
Erving Goffman's distinction—that they are "playing at"
rather than "playing" the roles they have hurried to adopt
without any genuine commitment or understanding.

One of the first writers to recognize the dangers of adolescent pseudomaturity was Edgar Friedenberg, in his book *The
Vanishing Adolescent* (1959). Although written some twenty-
five years ago, it is perhaps more compelling today than when
it was first published. Friedenberg noted that instead of doing
the psychological work that genuine maturity required, many
adolescents were merely "undergo[ing] puberty and simulat-
[ing] maturity" (p. 17). Rather than fostering genuine psychological maturity, the social institutions serving young people—
Friedenberg's chief concern was American secondary education—merely layered a thin veneer of adulthood over an imma-
ture psyche. The idealistic, passionate, anguished, ideological
adolescent had disappeared.

Sociologist David Riesman had taken a somewhat similar
stance in *The Lonely Crowd* (1950), in which he described the

psychologically shallow, outer-directed adult. In the introduction to Friedenberg's book, Riesman wrote:

> . . . Traditional adolescence is vanishing, swallowed up at the childhood end by the increasing precocity of the young, their turning of high school into an ersatz . . . suburb, their early if somewhat flat maturity as lovers, consumers, committeemen. . . . The American teenager, able to anticipate adulthood, so to speak, on the installment plan, gives up too readily his search for significance, settling . . . for a pliable and adjusted blandness. (Pp. 10–11)

Society, according to Riesman, asks too little of adolescents: "merely that they 'grow up,' finish school, and get on the payroll." This same view was echoed some ten years later by psychologists Elizabeth Douvan and Joseph Adelson, who had undertaken an extensive study of adolescent psychological development and, instead of self-examination and psychological struggle, turned up the same sort of "adjusted blandness" noted by Riesman. In their pessimistic conclusion to *The Adolescent Experience* (1966), they wrote that young people had "forfeited" their adolescence, becoming teenagers instead: "the passions, the restlessness, the vivacity of adolescence are partly strangled, and partly drained off in the mixed childishness and false adulthood of the adolescent teen culture" (p. 354).

Although the immersion of teenagers in the adolescent workplace came several years after Friedenberg's or Douvan and Adelson's books were published, the cautions raised by these authors several decades ago aptly apply to life in the adolescent workplace. The country-club atmosphere of the suburban high school, already visible by the time *The Vanishing Adolescent* was published, has been exacerbated by the dramatic increase in discretionary income afforded by the availability of part-time jobs for teenagers. The "adjusted blandness" lamented by Riesman has been channeled into the highly routinized patter of counter workers at fast-food restaurants. The "mixed childishness and false adulthood of the adolescent teen culture" has been maintained and strengthened by the mixed childishness and false adulthood of the new adolescent workplace. Indeed, the research we have reviewed suggests that, rather than helping youngsters learn more about themselves and their futures or preparing them for the transition into adulthood, absorption into the new adolescent workplace encourages the development of pseudomaturity.

Work and the "Pseudomature" Adolescent

Consider for a moment the image of a fifteen-year-old worker, employed in her first job, padding the number of hours on her timecard, calling in sick when she isn't ill, or working while "buzzed" on marijuana. Or the sixteen-year-old boy, who, arriving home after a tough afternoon at the fast-food restaurant, downs a few beers and thinks to himself, "People who work harder at their jobs than they have to are a little bit crazy." What does it mean when youngsters so quickly agree with such statements as "My goal in life is to make a lot of money and buy a lot of things," "There's no such thing as a company that cares about its employees," or "People who break a few laws to make a profit aren't doing anything I wouldn't do in their position"?

Why do these sentiments and behaviors, many of which are shared by millions of adults in American society, seem so jarringly out of place among teenagers? Why do we feel uncomfortable seeing youngsters engage in behavior that adults engage in, even when the behavior is something certain to be displayed at some later point in development? It is an uneasiness that journalist Marie Winn writes about in *Children Without Childhood* (1984):

> What's going on with children today? Is everything happening too soon? There is nothing wrong with sex, the modern adult has come to understand well, but what about sex at age twelve? Marijuana and alcohol are common social accessories in today's society, but is sixth grade the right time to be introduced to their gratifications? Should nine-year-olds have to worry about homosexuality? Their parents hardly knew the word until their teens. Lassitude, indifference, cynicism, are understandable defenses against the hardships of modern adult life, but aren't these states antithetical to childhood? (P. 4)

The notion that today's youngsters may be entering into "adult" activities too early and too quickly for their own well-being has been the subject of several popular books written during the past few years, most notably Winn's book and child psychologist David Elkind's *The Hurried Child* (1981). Neither author speaks directly to the issue of the early immersion of youngsters in the world of work. However, it is clear to us that the intensive involvement of teenagers in part-time jobs both furthers and reflects the trend for young people to engage in what appears to be adult behavior at an earlier and earlier age—at the risk of compromising what they really need to develop for successful adulthood. An explanation of why work has had this effect hinges on the distinction between adult and "adultoid" behavior. "Adultoid" behavior simply mimics adult activity without being accompanied by the underlying perceptions, beliefs, or understanding that a person who is psychologically adult would bring to a similar situation.

Thus far we have said a great deal about what psychosocial maturity is not and what it is sometimes mistaken for, but we have only hinted at what we believe psychological maturity actually is. What does it mean to be psychologically adult in contemporary society, and how might we differentiate this attainment from pseudomaturity? In our view, genuine psychological maturity has two components: autonomy and social responsibility. This view of psychosocial development has been elaborated elsewhere (Greenberger 1984; Greenberger and Sorensen 1974) and will be presented here only briefly. In our evaluation of the impact of early work experience on the psychological development of young people, we ask whether, and to what extent, their experiences in the workplace promote healthy autonomy and social responsibility.

The competent functioning of the individual as a separate or independent entity—what we refer to as autonomy—is a focal point of virtually all psychological theories of development (Erikson 1959; Loevinger 1976; White 1959). In our choice-ridden, rapidly changing society, three aspects of autonomy are of critical importance during the adolescent years: the development of self-reliance, because excessive dependence on others interferes with the individual's capacity to make decisions and follow through with them; the development of a positive work orientation, because modern society demands that virtually all adults be capable of performing competently and autonomously in informal and formal work settings; and the development of a clear sense of identity, because a stable sense of self is necessary in order to make sensible and appropriate decisions about future roles in a society in which such choices are often difficult to make.

A society cannot survive, however, if its members will not take responsibility for doing its economically productive, socially integrative, and self-protective work. Accordingly, the other component of psychological maturity concerns the relationship of the individual to his or her society. It is not enough for individuals to be able to function autonomously; they must also possess social responsibility—the ability to take part in ensuring the well-being and survival of society. The capacity for concern with social entities larger than the self or the immediate family has been considered within the framework of several different psychological and sociological perspectives on human behavior (Erikson 1959; Fromm 1947; Inkeles 1968). Although opportunities for adolescents in contemporary society to actually display social responsibility are not so great as are those for them to display autonomy (a case, perhaps, of adolescence imitating adulthood), it is important that young people be given opportunities to develop the prosocial values and attitudes that serve as the foundation upon which adult socially responsible behavior is built. Among other things, this disposition includes cooperation, self-sacrifice, and social commitment—the commitment to helping society flourish, even if doing so means delaying immediate gratification and modifying idiosyncratic, personal goals.

Although many advocates of early work experience claim that working promotes the development of maturity, often it is pseudomaturity, and not real maturity, that is the outcome of experience in the new adolescent workplace. The distinction between the two is seen clearly when we look, for instance, at the way in which working teenagers handle their earnings. Because much of adult life in contemporary society is occupied with earning and spending money, one of the chief arguments made by proponents of teenage employment has always been that youngsters will learn "the meaning of a dollar" through having the experience of earning a salary and making decisions about what to do with it. The argument ostensibly is that engaging in the adult activities of earning and spending money during adolescence help give young people practice in behaviors they will need to perform as adults. But this may not always be the case: whether earning and spending during adolescence help teenagers learn to better manage their money during adulthood depends on the circumstances under which their early encounters with money occur. The issue is whether the form of money management observed among adolescent workers is adult or "adultoid."

The answer, we think, is quite clear. As we have seen, few George Baileys are to be found any longer in the new adolescent workplace: that is, few teenage workers devote their earnings to improving the lot of others. Today the majority of youngsters spend virtually all of their earnings on themselves, on what most would consider luxury consumer items. Youngsters' orientation to money is one of immediate gratification, of self-indulgent consumerism, of "indiscretionary" spending. The lessons learned from this pattern of behavior can hardly prepare teenagers for the sort of money management that will be required of them as adults. Social psychologist Jerald Bachman, in an article entitled "Premature Affluence: Do High School Students Earn Too Much?" (1983a) explains:

> A fairly popular assumption these days is that students should have a great deal of freedom in spending their part-time earnings, so that in making their own choices and occasionally their own mistakes they will get some reality experiences and "learn the value of a dollar." This is an attractive notion, at least in the abstract. In practice, however, it may be problematic. The problem is that the "reality" faced by the typical high school student with substantial part-time earnings is just not very realistic. In the absence of payments for rent, utilities, groceries, and the many other necessities routinely provided by parents, the typical student is likely to find that most or all of his/her earnings are available for discretionary spending. And given that many are earning in excess of $200 a month, it seems likely that some will experience what I've come to call "premature affluence"—affluence because $200 or more per month represents a lot of "spending money" for a high school student, and premature because many of these individuals will not be able to sustain that level of discretionary spending once they have to take on the burden of paying for their own necessities. (P. 65)

What might be some of the short- and long-term effects of this "premature affluence"? In the short term, some of the consequences may be increased cynicism about the value of hard work and a lack of interest in working harder than is absolutely necessary to keep one's job (because the value of work becomes linked solely with making money and "coasting" on a job yields the same size paycheck as does working above and beyond an employer's expectations); increased interest in buying and using drugs and alcohol (the ultimate consumer goods in an affluent adolescent society); and the tendency to develop more materialistic attitudes. Perhaps the best thing that can be said about the short-term effects of young workers' increased spending power is that it enables poor youth who work to participate in an increasingly pricey peer culture. In a period of life when peer approval is critical to youngsters' development, the importance of being able to wear the same kinds of clothes as others, and participate in some of the same leisure activities, should not be dismissed lightly. In any case, the affluence enjoyed by many working adolescents permits them to engage in a variety of "adultoid" behaviors that otherwise might be unavailable—or at least constrained.

In *Children Without Childhood,* Winn contrasts the activities and possessions of youngsters a generation ago with those of their counterparts today, with examples drawn from a satirical piece in the *National Lampoon:*

> The child of a generation ago . . . spent his typical Saturday afternoon "climbing around a construction site, jumping off a garage roof and onto an old sofa, having a crabapple war, mowing the lawn." The agenda for today's child, however, reads: "Sleep late, watch TV, tennis lesson, go to shopping mall and buy albums and new screen for bong, play electronic WW II, watch TV, get high." The bulging pockets of the child of the past are itemized: "knife, compass, 36 cents, marble, rabbit's foot." The contemporary tot's pocket, on the other hand, contains hash pipe, Pop rocks, condom, $20.00, 'ludes, Merits. (Pp. 3–4)

Similarly, Elkind describes youngsters' fascination with expensive designer fashions, their use of clothing and cosmetics to appear more adultlike, and their responsiveness to the millions of advertising dollars spent promoting music and movies. What neither Elkind nor Winn does say, however, is that the trips to the shopping mall, the record albums, drugs and drug paraphernalia, the cigarettes, the designer jeans and expensive cosmetics—not to mention the pocketful of quarters needed to feed the video game or the $20.00—have become a part of the contemporary teenager's life partly through the affluence generated by part-time work.

The long-term effects of premature affluence are likely to be the more serious ones, however. Bachman and his colleagues speculate that such early affluence leads to later disappointment with one's financial state. As a part of their Monitoring the Future investigation, the annual study of American high-school seniors, these researchers have conducted follow-up surveys a few years after high-school graduation. These surveys indicate that young adults' satisfaction with their standard of living declines steadily during the years following graduation—presumably because individuals, once forced to face a few of life's financial obligations, find that only a fraction of their earnings can be put toward luxury consumption. What troubles Bachman, however, is more than simply the dissatisfaction expressed by individuals in the early years of adulthood:

> [The adolescent] pattern of spending a large proportion of income on relatively immediate sources of personal pleasure may reduce the ability to "delay gratification" . . . The sometimes expensive tastes developed in the teen years may be very hard to give up a few years later. If so, then saving for the "big ticket" items, particularly housing, is likely to be stunted. That, in turn, is likely to have substantial impacts on society as a whole, not to mention parents who find young adults moving back home or never leaving home. (1983a, p. 67).

In our view, extensive involvement in the adolescent workplace may interfere with the development of healthy autonomy and social responsibility. Although some youngsters may better their self-management skills as a result of working, and many have opportunities to exercise autonomy over the money that they earn, the sort of autonomy that early work experience appears to foster is only a pale version of what autonomy could mean. It is autonomy only in the most cynical, most individualistic, sense of the word; it is not the sort of autonomy that supports the goal of moving toward adult self-sufficiency. Thus youngsters get themselves to work punctually, but once there, rarely do more than the minimum that is expected of them; they enjoy substantial control over the money they earn but show little interest in saving for long-term expenditures and spend it mainly on their immediate gratification; they score higher on measures of self-reliance and work orientation but direct little of this gain in self-management capability toward meeting a higher level of responsibility at school. As for the impact of adolescent employment in today's workplace on social responsibility, the picture is even more negative. Indeed, the findings concerning workers' increased drug and alcohol use, cynicism about the intrinsic value of working, tolerance of unethical business practices, self-indulgent patterns of spending and consumption, and initiation into occupational deviance speak for themselves.

SOME COUNTERARGUMENTS AND RESPONSES

In the course of presenting our findings concerning the relation between early work and pseudomaturity to audiences of adults —often, adults who were trained as child psychologists—we ran into two classes of counterarguments that are worth considering in some detail here. One set of arguments, frequently voiced, concerns the absence of evidence that the negative concomitants of working persist. Basically, some audiences dismissed the seriousness of the findings by suggesting that since the jobs we were studying were merely "adolescent" jobs, the consequences of working in them would not last very long and surely would disappear by the time youngsters entered "real" jobs. Why worry about the effects in the absence of evidence that individuals are permanently affected?

This question seems misdirected, for several reasons. Proponents of early work experience for youngsters have based their argument on the assumption that the lessons acquired through adolescent jobs will carry over into adulthood and improve the quality of adult workers. (This was certainly the assumption behind the recommendation for early work made by the President's Science Advisory Committee [1973].) But surely one cannot argue that the good work habits, such as self-reliance or punctuality, that youngsters may develop through working persist into adulthood, while the cynicism, personal extravagance, and workplace deviance do not. If early work experience does have a long-term effect on youngsters' development and behavior, it is clear that this effect is, at best, likely to be mixed and, at worst, more negative than positive.

Moreover, although no studies are available that indicate there are direct links between adolescent work experience and adult behavior, we do know that some of the immediate effects of adolescent work may themselves have a carry-over impact in adulthood. There is ample evidence, for instance, that patterns of adult drug and alcohol use are influenced by patterns of use during adolescence (Kandel 1978); to the extent, then, that excessive employment during adolescence may lead to increased substance abuse during adolescence, excessive employment may have an indirect long-term impact on adult alcohol and drug consumption. Similarly, it is well documented that academic achievement during adolescence is predictive of subsequent educational attainment, which, in turn, is related to occupational attainment during adulthood (Featherman 1980). Because working may have an adverse impact on youngsters' school involvement, it therefore may have a long-term indirect effect on their occupational attainment. Put in more general terms, although we do not know about the long-term consequences of excessive employment during adolescence, we do know that some of the immediate effects of adolescent employment have important sequelae.

Suppose, however, that most of the effects of early work experience, both negative and positive, are indeed temporary —that once young people leave their jobs in the adolescent workplace, they leave behind the attitudes they have developed and the lessons they have learned there. If this is the case, why worry at all about teenagers' involvement in the workplace? Youngsters will outgrow whatever habits—"good" or "bad"— they pick up. They may use a little more alcohol and drugs than they would otherwise but they will escape without permanent scars; they may feel under a certain degree of stress from having to manage the pressures of work and balance the demands of a job with the obligations of school, but, as the expression goes, "they'll live."

This line of reasoning strikes us as worrisome for underneath it lies a latent hostility that adults feel toward children in our allegedly "child-centered" culture. After all, why is "bad" all right just because it is temporary? Some years ago sociologist Christopher Jencks (1972) argued in favor of improving the quality of youngsters' school experiences, even in the absence of evidence that such improvements had long-term effects on later achievement. It is an argument worth repeating. One does not need evidence linking stressful or unpleasant life circumstances in childhood with long-term harm or stunted development in adulthood in order to justify correcting noxious childhood circumstances. One only need be concerned about the immediate quality of life for young people. Apparently, gone are the days in which adults saw themselves as charged with protecting youngsters from having to see and experience unnecessarily things that are painful or ugly or stressful. Now our attitude toward young people seems to have shifted—as Winn puts it, from an age of "protection" to an age of "preparation"—and we are willing to permit youngsters to do whatever they are interested in doing, so long as we do not have any proof that they suffer long-term ill effects.

The second set of counterarguments came from individuals who insisted that teenagers' negative experiences at work, and worrisome responses to these experiences, amounted to education for reality. Noting that cynical attitudes about work, occupational deviance, and use of alcohol and drugs to alleviate job stress are seen frequently in surveys of working adults, it was suggested that the inevitability of these attitudes and behaviors excused their early development. Indeed, some adherents of this viewpoint went so far as to suggest that the sooner youngsters learned the "hard facts" about working life (these "facts" apparently include skepticism about the value of hard work, winking at occupational deviance, and unwinding with alcohol after a hard day at work), the better off they would be. If one has any doubts that the age of protection with respect to the young has come to a close, these arguments appear to lay such doubts to rest.

It is certainly true that, like the teenagers in our studies, many adults feign sickness to avoid work, steal from their employer, ignore rules and regulations in the workplace, and view their jobs cynically. Millions of adults unwind from the stresses of work each day with alcohol or other drugs. In some respects, advocates of earlier work experience for young people, in arguing that experience in the workplace would help "prepare" youngsters for their adult work careers, could not have been more correct.

We do not find persuasive, however, the argument that it is good for working youngsters to be exposed at an early age to the cynicism, questionable ethics, and stress-reduction techniques of the workplace on the grounds that they eventually are going to learn these attitudes and behaviors. Stress in the workplace, worker absenteeism, and job dissatisfaction may have become commonplace among American adult workers, but they are not goals for which we should provide early socialization.

The view that the inevitability of worker alienation and job dissatisfaction excuses—or makes desirable—their early appearance ignores very important cognitive and emotional differences between adolescents and mature adults. No one would suggest that a child and an adult are affected in the same way by going through a divorce, or by moving to a new neighborhood, or by failing at something that is important to them. The adult has the ability to place events into perspective, to take the broader view, to make sense out of the puzzling or troubling things he or she sees by drawing on past experience or inner wisdom. It matters a great deal *when*, developmentally speaking, individuals have the experiences that they have, because it is their developing intellectual and psychological capabilities that give the experiences their particular meaning. Adults are better able than children to call upon compensatory defense mechanisms to protect their own self-esteem, balance short-term effects against long-term consequences in making decisions, and understand the complexity of motives that drive human behavior in interpreting the actions of others. Social scientists have demonstrated repeatedly, for example, that our abilities to understand ourselves, our relationships with others, and the workings of social organizations improve measurably throughout the adolescent years (Barenboim 1981; Hill and Palmquist 1978; Selman 1980; Turiel 1978). It is one thing for a blue-collar worker to become hardened after twenty years on an assembly line; it is quite another to hear the same cynicism from a youngster after only a few months on her first job.

We do not have a great deal of empirical evidence on the costs of early immersion in quasi-adult activities, but several writers, writing about very different activities, have speculated that such behavior may have deleterious long-term consequences for youngsters' psychological and social development.

As we mentioned, Erikson argued that hurrying youngsters into intense involvement in adult roles leads to identity foreclosure—a premature closing off of the role experimentation process in favor of insufficiently considered commitments. (Empirical studies do indicate that individuals exhibiting identity foreclosure show other signs of psychological immaturity, including low scores on measures of autonomy and high scores on measures of need for social approval [Bourne 1978].) In their 1966 study, *The Adolescent Experience,* Douvan and Adelson noted that early and intensive involvement in dating among some of the girls in their sample appeared to foster superficiality in interpersonal relations rather than hasten the development of higher levels, or increased capacity for, intimacy—as some might have predicted. Bachman, in his article on premature affluence, speculates that early experience in earning a great deal of money fosters the development of juvenile, rather than mature, patterns of spending and saving. Winn, in *Children Without Childhood,* quotes psychoanalyst Peter Neubauer: "Children who are pushed into adult experience do not become precociously mature. To the contrary, they cling to childhood longer, perhaps all their lives" (p. 199). As Winn writes:

> Because of the precocious knowledge, the wordly savoir-faire, the independence, the assertiveness, the confident sense of equality in communicating with adults that characterize so many children today . . . it is easy to get the impression that children are also more mature these days. Indeed, the child growing up under more protective, old-fashioned circumstances may seem more "bratty," more "spoiled," more demanding than the hardy, self-sufficient child. . . . But whether the greatest level of maturity is reached when one has a shorter rather than longer period of dependence and protection is the great unanswered question. Based on the evidence of contemporary children, it appears than while a certain level of sophistication and suavity is achieved when a child is forced to take [on adult responsibilities] it is not at all the same thing as maturity. As the child grows older, true maturity, defined by an

ability to share, to empathize, to sacrifice, to be generous, to love unselfishly, and to nurture and care for children of his own, may prove elusive, and in its place attention seeking and narcissism become the characteristics that define his adult life. (1984, p. 198).

Why do early adultlike experiences not facilitate the speedier acquisition of autonomy and social responsibility, of genuine maturity? One answer to these questions is psychoanalytic in origin; the other is Piagetian. The psychoanalytic version emphasizes the development of so-called ego skills—coping mechanisms, in today's jargon. The Piagetian version emphasizes the development of reasoning skills and, in particular, the ability to put experiences into perspective, to take the long view. Both viewpoints lead to the same conclusion: a prolonged period of moratorium is needed, prior to adulthood, during which individuals' energies are turned inward and focused on developing intellectual and intrapsychic skills. Such skills, so critically important for coping with problems, stresses, and decisions at later points in life, need time to grow and mature, and they develop more fully when the child is somewhat protected from undue stress and conflict and presented instead with age-appropriate challenges.

This maxim applies to settling into an identity without ample role experimentation, jumping into a serious dating relationship at a young age, coming into affluence prematurely, or becoming overcommitted to a job. Young people often lack the ego strength and foresight necessary to reject identities selected for them by someone else and hence are susceptible to the dangers of identity foreclosure. Adolescents may lack the self-confidence and interpersonal understanding needed in order to refuse to "play the game" while out on a date, and therefore are in danger of adopting the shallow quality of adolescent courtship patterns as part of their interpersonal repertoire if their involvement in dating is not kept in check. Teenage money-earners typically do not have the impulse control and long-term planning abilities necessary for wise consumer behavior and are vulnerable to advertising pitches and peer pressures, so long as guidance or advice is not forthcoming from parents or other authorities. And, we think, adolescent employees may lack the wisdom and vision necessary to resist overinvolving themselves in part-time jobs—and forsaking developmentally more beneficial activities—simply because they have become enamored with the idea of receiving a paycheck. Parents and other adults, influenced by conventional wisdom about the virtues of working, may not offer the protection youngsters need in this arena.

This vision of the value of prolonged adolescence is antithetical to the "school of hard knocks" viewpoint so often advanced by work-experience advocates. Introducing children to the "hard facts" of the "real" world, however, may harden them, force them into adult behavior for which they are not ready, and deprive them of opportunities for psychological growth.

In *The Hurried Child*, Elkind argues that our society's fascination with moving youngsters quickly out of childhood and into a state of quasi-adulthood is stressful to the young and evokes a wide range of social and psychological problems: drug and alcohol abuse, delinquency, declining academic performance, psychological disturbance, psychosomatic problems, even suicide. Consistent with this line of reasoning, we have seen that working a great deal during the school year often is associated with higher rates of drug and alcohol use, higher rates of delinquent activity, diminished academic performance, and increased absence from school. Even more in line with Elkind's argument are findings that alcohol and drug use, occupational deviance, and school absence are especially prevalent among teenagers who work in high-stress jobs.

Work and the Other Contexts of Adolescence: Some Recurrent Themes

The movement of young people in great numbers into the part-time labor force has not been without repercussions for the other contexts in which teenagers spend time, namely the school, the family, and the peer group. Some of these repercussions are related to, and reflective of, shifting values and priorities in American society and are worthy of detailed and careful consideration in this light. When we turn to an examination of these issues, we find, interestingly, that the discussion turns not to "new" problems brought about by the immersion of youngsters in the workplace but to all-too-familiar concerns about the socialization of young people in this country—the declining academic competence of American youngsters; the increased orientation of youth to their agemates; and the continued erosion of parental contact with, and authority over, their adolescent children. In each of these three cases, the intensive involvement of teenagers in part-time jobs has further aggravated a disturbing trend.

WORK AND SCHOOL: RAISING THE RISING TIDE

The publication a few years ago of *A Nation at Risk* (1983), the National Commission on Excellence in Education's indictment of American secondary education, drew widespread attention to deficiencies in this country's high schools and, consequently, in the intellectual abilities of its high-school students. "The educational foundations of our society are presently being eroded by a rising tide of mediocrity," the commission warned. It noted: "If an unfriendly power had attempted to impose on America the mediocre educational performance that exists today, we might well have viewed it as an act of war. As it stands, we have allowed this to happen to ourselves. . . . We have, in effect, been committing an act of unilateral educational disarmament" (p. 5).

According to the commission, scores on the Scholastic Aptitude Test have shown a "virtually unbroken decline" from 1963 on, including a decrease in both the proportion and number of students with superior scores. Marked deficits in higher-order intellectual skills were estimated to afflict nearly 40 percent of all seventeen-year-olds. Only 33 percent of seventeen-year-olds could solve mathematical problems that require several steps, and only 20 percent could write a persuasive essay. In a recent comparison with adolescents from other industrialized countries, American youngsters scored last on more than one-third of the nineteen tests given, and never came in first or second (National Commission on Excellence in Education 1983).

The strikingly poor performance of American youngsters, the report noted, was due in part to the steadily declining demands made on them by their schools. While students' scores on standardized tests of achievement had been declining, their grades had been increasing, and the amount of homework being assigned had fallen continuously over the past twenty years. (Although adolescents' standardized test scores have shown small upturns recently, their rate of improvement is so slight that, if continued at this pace, it would take until 2010 for scores to return to 1962 levels.) "In many schools," the commission wrote, "time spent learning how to cook and drive counts as much toward a high school diploma as time spent studying math, English, chemistry, U.S. history, or biology" (p. 22). Textbooks had been written down to "ever-lower reading levels." More than 40 percent of all students were enrolled by 1979 in a "general" rather than college preparatory or vocational curriculum—up from about 10 percent in 1964; one-quarter of the "academic" credits earned by students in the "general" track are in physical and health education, personal service and personal development courses, and work experience outside school. The report noted that because graduation requirements were so slim in many high schools, students were taking a relatively large number of elective courses and were selecting courses that were typically undemanding of their time and energy.

Although the report did not mention the extent of youngsters' involvement in part-time jobs as a factor in their declining levels of intellectual and academic achievement, the findings that we have reviewed indicate that the two trends are likely related. Indeed, when viewed alongside the plummeting levels of student achievement and lowering of high schools' expectations, the increasing involvement of middle-class teenagers in jobs that are not intellectually stimulating, career-related, or financially necessary paints a rather grim picture of the state of adolescent education in the United States.

Several years ago we met with a number of European education and labor officials to learn more about the part-time employment of young people in other industrialized countries. As we noted in chapter 1, far more American high-school students work than do their European peers. As mentioned, one very important reason is that European youth have much more demanded of them by their schools—in and out of the classroom—than do Americans. Indeed, a Belgian sixteen-year-old we spoke with was amazed to learn that American teenagers had so much time to work. She was kept busy with school until four or five in the afternoon some days and was assigned—and expected to complete—about four hours of homework each evening.

We have noted that the association between working and schooling is generally negative, although more modest than one might expect. One would think that holding down a job for twenty or twenty-five hours each week—often during after-school hours and on weekday evenings—would interfere significantly with a student's ability to study and complete school assignments. Why, given the large number of hours that most students now invest in their jobs, does working not take a greater toll on youngsters' academic performance? Because working is so widespread, one cannot claim that there is something unique about youngsters who work that "buffers" them from its school-related consequences—either, for example, that workers are already performing so poorly in school that their grades have nearly bottomed out or that workers are so much more able than their classmates that they are able to maintain good grades even while holding a job.

The answer, we believe, is provided in *A Nation at Risk* and in McNeil's study of "lowered expectations." Students have been able to fashion academic programs for themselves that are so unchallenging, and schools have become so undemanding, that adolescents are able to invest considerable hours in their jobs without jeopardizing their school performance. The youngster whose academic program includes reading assignments at a far lower level than he or she is capable of, whose teachers assign only a few hours of homework weekly, and whose curriculum includes a hefty dose of simplified "personal growth" courses is understandably able to put down his or her books at the end of the school day, don a fast-food uniform, and not think about school again until the next morning.

The fact that working has only modest effects on youngsters' school performance—at least in terms of their grades—is hardly a sign that holding a job is an innocuous activity. Rather it suggests that parents, school administrators, teachers, and students have collaborated tacitly in allowing students to work long hours without ill effects on their school performance. Support for students' employment comes from parents, many of whom believe that the "lessons" learned on a job are more valuable than those learned in the classroom (an overwhelming majority of the parents we surveyed in our Orange County study were pleased with their children's employment), and from school administrators, who have "an interest in the orderly functioning of the school and its public image" (McNeil 1984, p. 37). As McNeil explains:

> Many administrators were grateful for the positive, constructive contacts which working students made with the local business community. These are much more desirable than news about students' auto accidents, drinking, shoplifting, or general hanging around shopping centers or parks. . . . One assistant principal felt that jobs for seniors were good for school discipline in that they help clear seniors out of the halls and away from school grounds during afternoon classes and after school. (P. 37)

Although not always supportive of student employment, teachers have little recourse in response to the diminished involvement in school that working appears to generate. One teacher complained to McNeil that "he missed having students who 'overachieve.' Now that effort goes into pleasing the manager at McDonald's" (p. 36). According to this study, most teachers eventually accommodate to what are perceived as the changing priorities of students by "gradually reducing out-of-class assignments, shortening reading assignments, or simplifying lectures" (p. 5).

> One of the factors helping shape teachers' instructional decisions, at least as many of them explained, was their own perceptions of what might reasonably be expected of students. *Students' part-time jobs were a key factor in lowering teachers' expectations that students would take lessons seriously, would exert effort in preparing assignments, would merit teachers' efforts in structuring meaningful activities* (p. 7, emphasis added).

Adolescents themselves, of course, have played a role in the process of lowering expectations in the classroom. Ultimately, a vicious cycle has been created. "The more students worked, and for longer hours," writes McNeil, "the less some teachers required of them at school. The more school became boring and less demanding, the more students increased their work hours" (p. 5).

One might well ask why teachers have acquiesced to the values and priorities of their students. Although not mentioned by McNeil, it seems clear to us that one reason is the sheer number of students who work. In the past, when faced with the relatively few youngsters who were investing more time on a job than in schoolwork, a teacher might consider the decision rational, in view of their family's economic needs or their limited academic talents; in other circumstances, a teacher might give a youngster his or her just desserts for letting school responsibilities slide. But when confronted with a classroom full of working students, who together present a united front of apathy and restlessness, whose minds are on earning and spending money—and who are the sons and daughters of the community's professional and middle-class families—there may be little that an individual teacher can do, especially without the support of parents or administrators.

It is not clear to what extent the "rising tide of mediocrity" engulfing our schools is due to the undermining of students' involvement in school by their commitment to part-time employment and to what extent, in contrast, students' commitment to their education has waned, and interest in the workplace has grown, because of the mediocrity of the schools. Rather than debate the merits of these arguments, it seems more prudent to assume that both processes are at work (a view for which there is some empirical support), that they fuel each other, and that neither says anything especially encouraging about the present state of American secondary education.

This is not the place to offer recommendations for improving the quality of American high schools; at least a dozen reports on this topic have been issued by "blue-ribbon" commissions over the past five years, and these are replete with specific proposals for school reform. What we wish to add to these proposals is the observation that youngsters' enormous investment of time in part-time jobs during the school year in order to earn discretionary income, juxtaposed with their mediocre record of academic achievement, indicates that schools are not sufficiently challenging, stimulating, or demanding of their students. In the early 1970s, the answer to problems in schools was to encourage students to find their learning experiences in the world of work (Illich 1970). We disagree vehemently with this solution. The learning experiences at work typically are *not* rich enough to warrant the school's blessing. Indeed, we strongly concur with those recent commissions that have recommended that schools require students to take more difficult classes, demand more from youngsters in the classroom, and insist that schoolwork occupy a substantial amount of their time out of school. We wonder how the achievement scores of American students might look today if youngsters were to spend twenty hours each week behind a stack of books rather than behind the counter of a fast-food restaurant.

One final point on the issue of work and school. We have argued in earlier chapters that adolescents have strong developmental needs to experiment—to try out different, albeit sometimes fleeting, aspects of the self. If youngsters are to profit from these activities, we have suggested, they also need time and encouragement to reflect on what they are doing and to draw lessons from their experience. We have asked whether the workplace provides opportunities for experimentation and introspection, and we have found it wanting. It seems only fair to comment on how the schools might measure up on these same dimensions.

The heyday of the open-space school, the school with a radically innovative curriculum or authority structure, and the school without walls between it and the community is long since gone. These educational ventures represented efforts to provide students with more room—often literally as well as figuratively—to decide what they wanted to learn more about and to go about finding it out with less structuring of the problem (and the answer) by the teacher. Under the pressure of an increasingly diverse student population in many areas of the country, including large numbers of children for whom English is a second and recent language; under the constraints imposed by shrinking school budgets; and under the influence of public opinion that increasingly favors a back-to-basics approach to education, schools today would seem to have reduced incentives to encourage, much less champion, experimentation and introspection. We ourselves have jumped on the bandwagon with those who favor more demanding schools and higher levels of achievement by students. It is by no means clear, however, that schools have to discourage youngsters from more energetic and responsible "playing with" ideas or possible fields of interest, or from trying to make sense of these experiences, in order to meet more stringent educational objectives. In fact, one could argue that these are exactly the kinds of activities that contribute to learning and accomplishment.

Practices that call for experimentation and reflection generally hinge upon allowing students some room for failure and making them more active participants in the teaching-and-learning process. In the first category fall strategies such as allowing students a limited number of pass/fail options, so that they may experiment with a subject that they might otherwise shun. The potential gain for students is the discovery of more interest or talent or perseverance than they had anticipated— or confirmation of previously held views of lack of interest or ability. Both outcomes can yield educational benefits and useful additions to self-knowledge. Even within the structure of a regularly graded course, moreover, some allowance can be made for an occasional, ambitious "flop." For example, students can be given the option of treating one assignment as an ungraded experiment, if they want to try something new and risky: a scientific invention, a musical composition, or a poem dealing with themes broadly relevant to the course. Students who are willing to reach high should be allowed to fall short and to escape a punishing grade.

Encouraging more active participation by students in their

own education is a goal as laudable as it is vague and hard to implement. Some years ago, education critic Charles Silberman (1970) described a typical classroom scene in these terms:

> Exhaustive studies of classroom language in almost every part of the country, and in almost every kind of school, reveal a pattern that is striking in its uniformity: teachers do almost all the talking, accounting, on average, for two-thirds to three-quarters of all classroom communication. . . . Equally significant, analyses of student and teacher conversation indicate that the student's role is passive, being confined, for the most part, to questions or statements. (P. 149)

The goal of making students more "active" is generally framed in terms of better classroom morale and better learning. Empirical studies have shown that active involvement in a task brings better prospects of learning and retention of the material at hand. Here we wish to point out the importance of students' active engagement for the progress of their "identity work" as well as their schoolwork.

It seems to us, by definition, that youngsters who speak, argue, reveal themselves, challenge, and defend—and who are argued with, challenged, and, hopefully, at times supported—are likely to learn important lessons about how much they really know and what they really care about. A recent empirical study also suggests they may develop a firmer sense of connection between themselves and others. In a study of high-school students, those youth who described their classroom environments as providing greater opportunities for challenge, decision making, and discussion of values scored significantly higher on measures of perceived competence to influence others, social responsibility, and anticipated level of future political participation (Newmann and Rutter 1983). Although the study was not designed to test causal relations between these "developmental opportunities" in the classroom and youngsters' psychosocial attributes, such a relation is at least plausible. The association between developmentally challenging classrooms and students' sense of social responsibility was independent of family socioeconomic status, prior level of school achievement, and the degree to which the same, favorable developmental opportunities were present in the home and on the youngster's job.

Recent reports show that high-school students are surprisingly poor at evaluating the soundness of an argument, at weighing conflicting evidence, and at drawing sound conclusions from the information that has been presented (National Commission on Excellence in Education 1983). Greater activity in the classroom might help to sharpen these important cognitive skills, at the same time that it sharpens youngsters' understanding of themselves and their sense of social solidarity. Methods of teaching that put a greater responsibility on students, however, are easier to applaud than to implement. Students who are accustomed to taking a passive role in the classroom and who have been overrewarded for docility and obedience usually find it difficult to rise to the occasion. In many respects, it is easier, although not more productive for students, for teachers to run the whole show themselves.

Work and the Peer Group: Strengthening the Youth Culture

Many reports on the status of youth written during the past fifteen years have warned that young people had become isolated from meaningful contact with adults. The fragmentation of the nuclear family, the demise of the extended family, mobility patterns that create instability in neighborhoods and communities, the decline of the apprentice system, and the increasing number of households in which both parents work all were cited as contributing factors. The President's Science Advisory Committee (1973), as well as other commissions, claimed that integration of youth into the workplace would help to reverse the trend toward increased age segregation, bringing young people into contact with the older generation and creating opportunities for youth to encounter adults who could, and would, serve as teachers, models of adult roles, and helpers in times of stress.

It was also felt that the dispersion of young people across a wide array of work settings, rather than their concentration in a limited number of age-segregated schools, would help break down—or at least weaken—what was perceived by the committee to be a strong and troublesome youth culture (Timpane et al. 1976). This youth culture, at least as it was described by sociologist James Coleman writing for the committee, was characterized by its "inward-lookingness" (not to be confused with introspection). Coleman's notion was that young people had become more likely to look to each other as sources of friendship and support, entertainment, information, and influence on matters of dress, recreation, and personal consumption. The committee attributed the growth of "inward-lookingness" to three factors: the increased size of the youth population, the prolonged attendance of youth in age-segregated educational institutions, and the increasing affluence of young people.

As we noted in chapter 2, the work environments inhabited by young people today have not served the age-integrating function envisioned by most proponents of early work experience. The reasons seem clear enough once one looks beyond the generalized "workplace" referred to in the various commission reports and focuses instead on the actual settings in which youngsters work. It matters very little that adults are present in the "workplace" if work environments themselves are highly age segregated. On most jobs, adults are simply not available to young people. For example, adults may be employed in the business office of a restaurant but have little meaningful contact with the young people working at the food counter. Moreover, there must be opportunities during the work day for informal socialization and interaction to occur, which, as we have seen, is not usually the case on most adolescents' jobs. In a job environment in which tasks are highly structured and time pressure is intense, even individuals who are working side by side have few chances to interact in a meaningful way (that is, for one to instruct or confide in another).

Finally, and perhaps most important, in order for work to provide a basis for meaningful intergenerational socialization, the adults in the work setting must have some stake or interest in devoting time to socializing the young people with whom they work. Adults' stake in socializing nonfamilial adolescents depends on the degree to which they perceive themselves to be mentors to young people and on the degree to which they are likely to maintain contact with their charges in the future. Consider, for instance, the difference between a high-school teacher, who occupies a formal role as an educator or socializer, and a work supervisor, who does not; or between a work supervisor who lives in the youngster's community and knows his or her family and a supervisor with no links to the youngster's life outside the work setting. The former is more likely to have future dealings with that young person and, consequently, some reason for taking an interest in the youngster's socialization. In the new adolescent workplace, however, adolescents' work supervisors often are only a few years older than their employees and seldom see their workers outside of work, partly because the mobility of the young has made possible their employment in neighborhoods away from home. The new adolescent workplace is clearly not providing opportunities to break down age barriers in any meaningful sense, nor is it helping to integrate youngsters into adult society.

The sort of informal intergenerational contact envisioned by the President's Science Advisory Committee's Panel on Youth is likely to be extremely limited and difficult to achieve in highly industrialized work environments where the ratio of workers to supervisors is very high and where there is such a highly stratified division of labor that novices rarely work with more experienced employees. In the old adolescent workplace, in which children worked alongside their parents or other adults, the conditions necessary for meaningful intergenerational contact to develop were likely to be found. In the new adolescent workplace they are not.

But not only has the involvement of young people in the new adolescent workplace failed to foster intergenerational contact —it actually has strengthened the very youth culture that social commentators like Coleman had looked to the workplace to weaken. This is true with respect to the social contacts that adolescents have at work, the values and attitudes they express as a result of their experience in the labor force, and the behaviors—in and out of work—that employment appears to foster. Several lines of evidence point in this direction.

First, it is clear that for many young people—especially those holding the prototypical "adolescent" jobs in the retail and service industries—the work environment serves as a setting in which socializing with agemates can continue after the school day has drawn to a close. At fast-food restaurants, movie theaters, and convenience stores, young people typically work with, and wait on, their peers. The topics of conversation among workers are precisely those over which "youth culture" opponents have expressed concern: clothing, dating, popularity, purchases. Far from breaking down the age barriers erected by schools, we have managed in the new adolescent workplace to create a setting that is equally age-segregated.

Second, data on youngsters' patterns of spending show that earnings typically are not being put toward "adult" purchases —like further education—but are spent on the accoutrements of adolescence. As noted in earlier chapters, more than half of all working teenagers spend nearly all of their earnings on immediate personal needs and activities—clothing, stereo equipment, records, movies, recreation (including drugs and alcohol), hobbies, and car expenses—all important aspects of the youth culture. Most of them spend none of their income at all on family living expenses and report that they do not save any income at all for future education or other long-term anticipated expenses. The Panel on Youth was doubtless correct in suggesting that the youth culture has been strengthened by young people's affluence and thus their ability to indulge their tastes for records, clothes, movies, and other commodities made for and often by the young.

The argument that the workplace has strengthened, rather than weakened, the youth culture is also buttressed by studies of work and delinquency. If work were indeed a help in socializing youngsters into adult values, one would expect to find that rates of delinquency would be lower among youngsters with jobs. But as we saw in the last chapter, this is not the case. Indeed, the specific forms of delinquent and deviant behavior working does appear to promote among middle-class youth— buying and using drugs and alcohol, cutting school, skipping classes, lying about the completion of assigned homework—are behaviors that do not suggest the internalization of adult standards and values, but the further solidification of antiestablishment norms within the peer group.

Finally, the findings concerning occupational deviance among middle-class workers suggest that illicit behavior in the workplace serves to validate membership in the youth culture (Ruggiero, Greenberger, and Steinberg 1982). Although deviance in the workplace was found to be related to stressful aspects of working, there was one noteworthy exception: occupational deviance was more common in work settings described as having a *positive* social environment—an environment in which youngsters reported having ample opportunities to meet people, to confide in others, and to socialize with coworkers outside of the work setting. Working while intoxicated or "stoned" and giving away goods and services, the reader may recall, were two of the most prevalent forms of occupational deviance reported. Drinking and drug use are important social activities in the peer group, and the recipients of "giveaways" are often teenagers (Ruggiero 1984). Both of these acts, we suspect, serve to bond adolescents with each other. The cynicism toward work expressed by many teenage employees, along with their illicit behavior on the job, suggests a collective "nose-thumbing" at adult conventions.

Work and Family: The Continued Erosion of Parental Authority

There is widespread recognition among observers of contemporary American family life that the authority parents have over their children—especially their adolescent children—has eroded considerably (Lasch 1979). The explanations are legion (although some are without empirical foundation): permissive child-rearing has increased the susceptibility of youngsters to the influence of peer pressure; the "breakdown" of the American family has left children with fewer adults to whom to turn for advice and guidance; maternal employment has left children with less vigilant supervision; the overall democratization of society has blurred status boundaries between youngsters and adults, including their own parents.

Whatever the reasons, many parents simply feel out of control. Consider, for example, this mother's response in an interview about her thirteen-year-old's behavior:

I don't really think any parent today can really stop a sixth- or seventh-grader from smoking pot or getting into sex. The pot is so available, the kids have the money, and they have so much freedom, so little supervision, what with all of us having to work just to survive. . . . I just don't think there's any way to control these kids once they reach puberty. (Winn 1984, p. 27)

The ability of a parent to influence his or her child's behavior rests on three things: the degree of emotional intimacy between parent and child; the degree of contact between parent and child; and the degree to which the parent is able to exercise control over the child. Emotional intimacy is important because through it children internalize their parents' values and standards; contact, because through it parents stay informed of their children's behavior and remain in a position to monitor it; and control, because parents occasionally need to fall back on their power when closeness and contact fail.

It is beyond the scope of this book to address whether parents and children are less close today than they have been in past eras and whether diminished intimacy is a factor in the erosion of parental authority. Certainly, it appears as if a different kind of closeness between parents and children, one based on egalitarian relationships, has become more prevalent in American families (Winn 1984); and there is some evidence that adults today place relatively less importance on their role as parents than did their counterparts previously (Yankelovich 1981). But it seems incontrovertible that today parents have less day-to-day contact with their youngsters and relatively less control over their behavior.

The extensive involvement of youngsters in part-time jobs is related in several ways, we believe, to the erosion of parental authority over adolescent children. Youngsters themselves tell us this, in so many words. More than half the youngsters we studied in our Orange County sample report having gained either "a lot" or "a little" more freedom since taking on a job —as opposed to only 4 percent who report having "less" freedom. (About 40 percent report no differences on this dimension.) One reason for the subjective sense of greater freedom may be that working teenagers simply see their parents less often. Many working youngsters report that they eat dinner with their family less frequently (thus losing one of the few times of the day during which parents and children can "catch up" on each other's activities). About half the youngsters reported that they help out around the house less often since they became employed, and a fair number indicate that the frequency with which they and their families spend leisure time together has dropped off as a result of working.

A second reason for working youngsters' subjective sense of greater freedom from parental control is that money buys a certain degree of independence from parental influence. For one thing, much of the money that youngsters earn goes toward car and car-related expenses—over two-thirds of working youngsters we studied drive themselves to their jobs—a form of expenditure that both diminishes contact between adolescents and their parents and reduces parents' ability to monitor their youngsters' behavior. (It also removes a salient reward—turning over the keys to the family car—and a salient punishment—"grounding"—from the repertoire of actions that many parents use to influence the behavior of their adolescent children.)

Moreover, as we noted earlier, adolescents feel freer to spend as they please money they have earned than money their parents have given to them as an allowance. This may come as little surprise to most readers. What is more interesting, however, and particularly relevant to the issue of the erosion of parental authority, is the frequency with which parents of working youngsters report that they do not have the "right" to control what their youngsters do with their earnings. In this respect, one of the most important sources of power that parents have over dependent children—economic power—has been substantially diminished by the ample discretionary income of working teenagers. The belief, by the way, that parents do not have the right to control their youngsters' earnings represents an important departure from English common law, under which a father was entitled both to the services and earnings of his minor children, in return for the duty of support (Greenberger 1983a). Many parents also may be surprised to learn that under current law in most states, they in fact do have a right to their youngsters' earnings from a job, if arrangements are made before the youngster begins that job.

It became clear to us in the course of interviewing the mothers and fathers of working youngsters that many parents no longer feel sufficiently interested, able, or empowered to deny their children's acquisitive desires. As the mother of one worker told us: "I would like to have my son give me the money and let me dole it out. But I'm afraid to say that, because that tells him that somebody is governing [his] spending. . . . You can't do that." Often, when asked why their child was working, parents told us that their child wanted something (a stereo, a car, a vacation) that they felt was an unnecessary expenditure. In some families—certainly in many families some years ago—the standard parental response to such a request has been "We do not think you need it." Today more often than not the response is likely to be "If you want it so badly, go out and get a job." Rather than exercise their authority, many parents prefer to shift the responsibility for the spending decision onto the shoulders of the teenager. Parents also may find it difficult to steer their children away from working or restrict their youngster's work hours in order to direct them toward what they believe might be more valuable activities.

Many parents feel that decisions about purchases, about working versus not working, or about how many hours one ought to invest in a job should be made by the adolescent, ostensibly in order to teach the young person certain lessons about making decisions and about making mistakes. For these parents, the line is drawn on the issue of safety. As long as the adolescent is not in any danger, there is no apparent need for parental intervention. Yet simply watching out for youngsters' safety—rather than, say, watching out for their psychological development as well—transforms the parental role in a very important way. It reduces parenting solely to its most basic, custodial function. This transformation has been a tremendous loss to adolescents, who, surrounded by custodians all day long, are hardly in need of additional ones at home.

Finally, it is worth noting once again, as we did in chapter 1, that the flow of teenagers into part-time jobs has occurred at the time when maternal employment also has increased substantially. The increased involvement of mothers in the labor force has had important implications for who is left at home and thus for where parents believe that teenagers might best spend their time. Concerned about adolescents' potential for doing things that they do not approve of and feeling powerless to monitor their youngsters' activities while away from home, parents may feel that the workplace is a better place for a teenager than an empty house—or at least, a house not supervised by an adult. (Little did twenty-year-old fast-food shift managers know that they would be called upon to function *in loco parentis.*) Teenagers, too, may find their home a less attractive, lonelier place to be than the workplace.

CHAPTER 5

Improving the Adolescent Experience

W E began our examination of the part-time employment of American adolescents by noting that the involvement of youngsters in the labor force reflects an important transformation that has taken place in the nature of adolescence in contemporary society. It is a transformation that has followed, and in its own way has abetted, many changes that have occurred over the past twenty-five years in schools, in family life, and in the social world of young people.

In the preceding chapters we have taken a critical stance toward intensive school-year employment in the naturally occurring workplace. Our arguments inevitably lead to a number of questions, such as:

1.   How does school-based work experience compare with the jobs youngsters find and negotiate on their own? This question is based on the possibility that school-run employment programs should be expanded and that the lessons learned from them might point to ways that jobs in the naturally occurring workplace could be improved.

2.   How does volunteer work stack up against paid work? This question is motivated by two quite different considerations. First, traditional volunteer work centers on giving service to others and therefore might have certain unique consequences for participants. Second, it is possible that youngsters who are willing to forego pay for other opportunities may be able to gain entry into more stimulating and mind-expanding work environments than youth who require pay for their services.

3.   Are there activities that youngsters might engage in that would yield greater developmental benefits than work, whether paid or unpaid? This question often is raised in the context of time- and energy-consuming involvement in extracurricular activities, such as sports and interest-oriented clubs, but has another source as well: people who may grant that intensive employment leaves much to be desired as a prescription for the adolescent years sometimes fall back on the premise that it is better for youngsters to work than to have "nothing to do."

4.   Are there ways that we can make the jobs available to adolescents better? This question is prompted by the conviction that adolescents are not going to stop working—a conviction we share.

Criteria for Evaluating Teenage Activities

We will try to respond to these questions in terms of a common set of criteria. In our view, both work and nonwork activities can be evaluated usefully (but not exhaustively) along six dimensions according to the extent to which they: (1) promote growth in autonomy; (2) increase cooperation and social responsibility (social "connectedness"); (3) lead to learning and mastery of useful skills and information; (4) advance youngsters' occupational development; (5) provide opportunities for experimentation and integration of experience (identity clarification); and (6) bring youngsters into contact with adults who can contribute to these ends. These six criteria are related in complex ways. Our discussion of why they constitute a reasonable framework for evaluating youngsters' work and nonwork involvements will necessarily reflect this conceptual overlap.

Autonomy and social connectedness have been described as the two major goals of human development: good outcomes, because they optimize both the individual's interests and well-being and because they bode well for the smooth functioning of society (see chapter 4). At the core of autonomy are the capacities to be self-governing rather than controlled by others or their wishes and the capacity to exist independently. To be self-governing, it is essential, by definition, to have a clear sense of the self one is: what one values, enjoys, wants. The nonautonomous self, in contrast, is the repository of "received identities" that are experienced as alien or coming from others. Experimentation, exploration, and reflection upon one's experience play an important role in the development of autonomy, since they are avenues through which the adolescent may learn not only about the contents of the self but about ways of expressing it—and what they may cost in terms of other valued goals. To be self-governing, it is also necessary to develop initiative and confidence in one's powers of decision making.

To grow in the capacity to exist independently, on the other hand—the second meaning of autonomy—requires additional experiences and the development of other competencies. Youngsters need to acquire a broad array of information about how society and its institutions operate and about how to interact with others in ways that lead to the satisfaction of one's needs and aspirations. And they need to acquire knowledge and experiences of the occupations available to persons with their particular interests, abilities, and resources. Autonomy, of course, can be realized only to a degree. As members of society we necessarily experience constraints on self-definition, self-government, and self-expression.

As we have noted previously, our social connectedness is not just an impediment to autonomy but a source as well of feelings of well-being. Societies, in turn, have a stake in producing adult members who can perform the productive, cooperative, and altruistic activities that ensure its survival. The experiences that we have described as likely to promote autonomy also are likely to promote social connectedness. For example, the experimentation that leads, in favorable cases, to identity development is not a matter of defining who one is in isolation from a social context; on the contrary, identity attainment includes the development of a social self, the establishment of a meaningful place for oneself in the larger world. The acquisition of job skills and of an occupational identity, to mention two other examples, enable one to participate in the work that society values and play a substantial role in organizing one's social relations. Or again, aspects of autonomy such as the ability to decide on a course of action and to initiate it may be put to the service of social rather than personal goals, including goals that benefit others more than oneself. Considering the individualistic orientation in American life and the results of our research into the effects of working on adolescents' psychological and social development, it seems that activities which foster feelings of social connection and responsibility may be scarce.

If so, they are an especially important criterion for evaluating the developmental benefits that youngsters might reap from one activity as opposed to another.

We have proposed, additionally, that adolescents' activities should be evaluated in terms of the opportunities they offer for contact with adults. It should be noted that we qualified this criterion by specifying contact with adults who are themselves psychologically and socially mature. There is no reason to think that adults who are neither autonomous nor socially responsible will be good models or teachers of these ways of being. There is also no reason to think that these functions can be performed only by adults. Adolescents may learn a great deal from each other about how to be independent and how to be a responsible member of the group.

Before turning to a discussion of how work and nonwork activities measure up on these six criteria of evaluation, we wish to clarify our expectations. No single activity should be asked to provide some "minimum daily requirement" of each of these developmental nutrients. Instead, we might look across the range of activities that absorb youngsters' time and energies and ask which specific ones are good in which respects and in which specific areas youngsters' developmental opportunities need to be supplemented or enhanced.

Work Through Structured Programs

Over the past century, American educators have developed and set in place a myriad of work experience programs for young people. These programs include school-sponsored efforts, such as vocational education, work-study, and career education; and government-sponsored efforts, such as the Comprehensive Employment and Training Act (CETA) and various other youth employment and training programs. In our examination of students' experiences in the part-time labor force, however, we have focused exclusively on "naturally occurring" jobs—that is, jobs that are created by economic and market forces and not by educators or policy makers who have the socialization and education of young people in mind. Work programs coordinated by schools or government agencies, in contrast to naturally occurring jobs, are designed specifically to facilitate the transition from school to work, by imparting information about careers, teaching job skills, providing the credential of an employment history, or placing youngsters in contact with potential full-time employers. Some readers may wonder whether these sorts of work experiences affect adolescents in different ways from experiences in naturally occurring jobs. Are the findings we have reported in this volume, drawn from studies of youngsters in the naturally occurring labor force, generalizable to students who are employed in structured work experience?

Although direct comparisons of naturally occurring jobs and structured work experience programs have not been conducted, the indirect and descriptive evidence amassed to date suggests that the actual job experiences of young people in school- and government-sponsored programs are not very different from those of their peers working in naturally occurring jobs. In work experience programs, as in naturally occurring jobs, adolescents typically perform highly routinized, repetitive work with few opportunities for decision making or learning. One team of researchers (Farrar, DeSanctis, and Cowden 1980), for example, observed youngsters working in jobs obtained through career education programs. Most youngsters spend their time in unskilled manual labor (cleaning, digging holes, and so forth) or low-level clerical tasks (for example, photocopying). Similar reports come from evaluations of youth employment and training programs (such as Manpower Demonstration Research Corporation 1980).

Because work activities do not differ substantially between naturally occurring and program-sponsored jobs, one might expect to find that the impact of employment on youngsters' development does not differ very much either. This is essentially the case. The findings derived from several recent evaluations of career education programs, discussed by education researcher Thomas Owens (1982), are fairly representative of the results reported across the entire literature on work through school-sponsored programs. The only positive finding reported consistently is that students enjoy participating in work experience programs and look back more positively on their high-school experience than do students who did not participate in career education—a finding that, in light of the activities occupying youngsters' time on these jobs, may say more about the dreariness of school than the attractiveness of work. There is no evidence that participating in school-based work programs has any enduring impact on helping youngsters to develop responsibility, acquire important job skills, make better career decisions, or enter more successfully into the full-time labor force following the completion of their schooling.

The results of research on the impact during adolescence of work in government-sponsored programs also are consistent across a variety of types of programs (Steinberg 1982). Research points to three conclusions. First, it appears that programs which do not maintain strong links between the school and the workplace (by mandating proper school attendance as a condition for employment, for example) have an adverse impact on adolescents' school attendance, involvement, and performance. This finding is reminiscent of what studies of youngsters in naturally occurring jobs reveal, namely that extensive involvement in the workplace (natural or structured) can undermine involvement in school. When regular school attendance and the maintenance of a satisfactory GPA are required as conditions for getting and staying on in a job, however, students may be less likely to allow job commitments to draw their energies away from school responsibilities. One way to achieve this goal is to require that all enrolled high-school students produce annual work permits signed by an official of their school, and perhaps by their parents as well, as a precondition to their being hired. Schools and parents could refuse to sign a permit if the student had not been complying with the mandated educational requirements.

Second, as with school-sponsored programs, work experience through government-sponsored efforts does not help adolescents develop personal or social responsibility, foster self-esteem, impart positive work attitudes, deter youngsters from delinquent activity, or teach lasting job skills (Steinberg 1982). Finally—and perhaps most important—work experience through government-sponsored programs has no significant impact on adolescents' subsequent employment or earnings (Mangum and Walsh 1978; Taggart 1980). This is true across the board, for school-year and summer programs, part-time and full-time programs, and programs targeted at in-school and out-of-school youth. Indeed, it is safe to say that very few government-sponsored work programs for adolescents ever have been successful. As one recent evaluation team disappointingly concluded, "[The structured] work programs had no significant long-term impact on the earnings, employment, criminal activity, or drug abuse of the youth group. The program's benefits for youth fell short of its costs" (Manpower Development Research Corporation, cited in Auletta 1982, p. 230).

It appears, therefore, that the impact of working through structured experiences is not appreciably different from the impact of working in the naturally occurring labor force. There is little evidence that working through structured programs has any more "character-building" benefit than does working in naturally occurring jobs. Adolescents may learn about the world of work through sponsored work programs, but this knowledge does not appear to be translated into enhanced employability or a more successful transition into full-time employment later on. And, as with overcommitment to a part-time job, extensive involvement in a work experience program may have a deleterious impact on school performance and school involvement.

The reasons for the disappointing evaluation of structured work experience programs seem clear enough when one examines them in light of the themes we outlined earlier. It matters little if the work experience is orchestrated by schools or government agencies if the experience itself offers little of educational or psychological value. Jobs that provide only limited opportunity for decision making or cooperation are not likely to foster healthy independence or social responsibility. Jobs that are clearly recognizable as "adolescent" jobs, and that have little connection with the occupations youngsters will enter as adults, are unlikely to serve as effective bridges into enduring employment. And jobs that involve youngsters in repetitive, unstimulating tasks are not likely to facilitate the growth of higher-order intellectual skills; prepare youngsters for adult employment; inspire feelings of self-esteem, mastery, and competence; or foster a clearer sense of identity.

Alternatives to Adolescent Employment

There are those who undoubtedly will question what we believe youngsters could, or should, be doing with their free time if they were not working. Some readers may contrast a picture of youngsters employed in restaurants or shopping malls with one of youngsters who are not employed and who are "hanging out"—at home, in front of the television set, or in the very same restaurants and shopping malls in which they could be working. "Why *shouldn't* teenagers be working," the question goes, "if the alternative is simply wasting time doing nothing?"

We have several responses to this argument. The first is a reminder that studies which have contrasted the development of working youngsters with that of representative samples of their peers—many of whom, presumably, are doing "nothing," —favor youngsters who are not working. Thus despite the common assumption that idleness breeds laziness, or that "hanging out" is at the root of youngsters' problems with drugs and alcohol or involvement in crime and delinquency, the available evidence simply does not support the proposition that holding a part-time job is substantially better for adolescents' development than doing "nothing." Indeed, the reader should recall that working adolescents are more, not less, likely to use drugs and alcohol; more, not less, cynical about the meaning of work; and more, not less, involved in certain deviant activities than their peers who are not employed.

Our second response takes a somewhat different slant. What may seem on the surface to the uninformed adult observer as "nothing" may be quite important psychologically to the adolescent. Thus we are not convinced that doing "nothing" for part of the day is necessarily a bad thing for young people to do, nor do we believe that it is accurately characterized as "nothing." Being unburdened from the responsibilities and time demands of a job leaves time for fantasy, for "working through" the day's experiences, for leisure, and for building and strengthening relationships with friends, all of which can contribute in very healthy ways to adolescents' psychosocial development. Recent research by a team of investigators from the University of Chicago (Csikszentmihalyi and Larson 1984), in which adolescents' moods and psychological states were monitored across a variety of settings and activities, indicates that for high-school students a moderate amount of solitude (during which daydreaming is a central activity) is related to psychological adjustment. And, as we noted earlier, fantasy and daydreaming are important components of the process of identity exploration; adolescents who are denied these luxuries inadvertently may be foreclosing the process of identity development.

Involvement in leisure activities—whether they be playing basketball in the schoolyard, practicing the electric guitar in the basement, or sharpening the latest dance steps in the solitude of one's bedroom—can help build youngsters' sense of mastery and competence in ways in which working at a repetitive, routinized job cannot. The learning that takes place on the typical adolescent job is accomplished very quickly, as we have seen, and there is often little room for further growth once the acquisition of the rudimentary requisite skills has been accomplished. As a consequence, on many adolescents' jobs there may be little opportunity for the development of mastery or competence. In contrast, there is always room for improving a jump shot, learning a new chord fingering technique, or mastering increasingly difficult dance routines. Pushing oneself to improve—in virtually any kind of activity—can teach the adolescent important lessons about the value of self-control, the necessity of perseverance, and the pride of accomplishment. These are lessons that are more likely to be learned through leisure and recreation activities than on the average part-time job.

To the extent that working takes time away from peer relations, it may interfere with some of the important interpersonal work of adolescence. Many adult readers will balk at the idea that adolescents need more time for peer relations than they currently have. This is understandable; after all, we hear a great deal about the overexposure of adolescents to their agemates and about the lack of contact between adolescents and their elders. But there is a difference between simply being exposed to the peer group (which most adolescents certainly experience in hefty doses) and being involved in close and enduring friendships with agemates (an experience enjoyed by fewer adolescents). Thus, despite the concern that is frequently voiced over the excessive peer orientation of contemporary youth, most theorists still agree that adolescence is an enormously important time for the development of such interpersonal skills as intimacy, empathy, trust, and cooperation, and that these skills develop in the crucible of close relationships with peers. The adolescent whose afternoons and evenings are largely devoted to earning money may be missing out on critical interpersonal experiences, so often underestimated in value by adults (who perhaps have forgotten the importance of these relationships during their own adolescence) but so important to the young person's long-term growth and development.

Our most critical argument about alternatives to paid employment, however, is this: the choice open to young people is not simply a choice between holding a part-time job and doing "nothing." There are activities available, or potentially available, that may be more beneficial than working, and we believe that parents and educators should take a more active role in steering young people toward these activities. These activities include reading and studying outside of school, becoming involved in extracurricular activities, and taking on the responsibilities of unpaid volunteer work or community service.

Data derived from our surveys of young workers indicate that commitment to a part-time job interferes with participation in extracurricular activities, because such activities usually are scheduled during adolescents' prime work hours. This interference may be unfortunate, because participation in extracurricular activities involving athletics, the arts, school government organizations, or special interest clubs may facilitate youngsters' psychosocial development in ways that a part-time job does not. For example, research indicates that participation in extracurricular activities during adolescence enhances youngsters' occupational ambitions (Kleiber and Rickards 1985)—an outcome that does not appear to result from part-time employment. Persistence and success in an extracurricular activity during high school is a strong predictor of academic success, leadership, and social accomplishments in college (Otto and Alwin 1977).

What might an adolescent be missing by opting for a job rather than for extracurricular participation, and why may such participation be important for future success? First, extracurricular activities seem to provide opportunities for role experimentation and, consequently, for growth in the realm of identity. Special interest clubs, for instance, permit young people to discover unique talents and learn more about their interests and abilities—both of which can contribute to their self-esteem and self-confidence.

Second, many extracurricular activities require adolescents to exercise independence and self-control and to learn about cooperation—activities and lessons that, as we have seen, are unlikely to take place very often on most jobs in the new adolescent workplace. But in contrast to most job experiences, through activities such as working on a school newspaper or yearbook youngsters presumably learn to make decisions and work together and have opportunities to see a product develop from start to finish. Lessons about personal and social responsibility may also be derived from participation in organized sports: athletes need to establish training routines and stick to them despite a variety of competing interests and cross-pressures. And through athletic participation youngsters may experience the rewards of making a commitment to a larger organization, of placing importance on group goals in addition to personal achievement. As two experts on leisure recently wrote, "The context [of high school athletics] is a deliberately structured test of strength, courage, endurance, and self-control. One learns to be aggressive without being hostile, to persist and be resourceful. Even losing has its virtue in teaching one to manage failure and disappointment" (Kleiber and Rickards 1985, p. 302).

Finally, because many extracurricular activities are "open-ended" or relatively flexible with respect to content (Which stories will the school paper report? Which activities will a service club take on?), new opportunities for learning continue to emerge, providing intellectual stimulation and a basis for the further development of mastery and feelings of competence. Interestingly, the University of Chicago study found that adolescents' moods were most positive and their activity levels higher when participating in arts, hobbies, or sports than in any other activity, including working at a part-time job (Csikszentmihalyi and Larson 1984). Indeed, the desire of adolescents to be doing something *other* than what they were doing at the time their mood was assessed was lowest in extracurricular activities and greatest when working at a job. These findings suggest that even adolescents recognize that the benefits of having a part-time job are likely to be extrinsic (the job is a source of income) rather than intrinsic (the work itself is enjoyable or interesting).

Benefits similar to those associated with extracurricular activity also may accrue from participation in service activities. In many parts of the country there exist programs that place young people in volunteer settings in the community, usually without pay. In communities in which formal programs do not exist, there nevertheless are almost always opportunities for young people to become involved as volunteers. Some work as volunteers in human service organizations such as schools, nursing homes, day-care centers, peer counseling centers, hospitals, and institutions for the mentally or physically handicapped. Some volunteer their services in public works efforts designed to clean up their community's environment or refurbish its infrastructure. Others work as political activists, involved in special interest causes or election campaigns (Conrad and Hedin 1981; Hamilton 1981).

Students who tutor others, who are responsible for dependent individuals in child-care and health settings, or who engage in efforts to improve the physical appearance of the community might be expected to become more altruistic, more favorable to community participation, and more humanitarian in outlook. Although we do not have a great deal of information about the impact of community service work on adolescent development, the few existing studies indicate that such involvement can be more developmentally beneficial than paid, part-time employment—*but only when it is coupled with simultaneous or follow-up opportunities for discussion and reflection* (Danzig and Szanton 1986). For example, in one study sixth-grade youngsters who tutored mentally retarded children and had a supervisory seminar showed increased empathy, whereas similar youngsters who did not have a seminar developed more negative attitudes and teaching behaviors in relation to the children they were supposed to be helping (Conrad and Hedin 1981).

In general, though, when service programs are accompanied by seminars and other opportunities for reflection and discussion, participants tend to show gains in the domain of social responsibility—a domain that appears unaffected by work in the part-time labor force. In one series of studies (Conrad and Hedin 1981), participants in service activities gained in their ability to empathize with another person, understand the nature of someone else's problem, and suggest a sophisticated and reasoned solution to it. In addition to these interpersonal benefits, youngsters who participated in programs that combined structured classroom experiences with service activities also showed gains in their sense of duty, concern for social welfare, self-esteem, and feelings of competence. Participants in these programs also showed significant changes in their attitudes toward adults, with program participation associated with more positive attitudes. Finally, it should be noted that many youngsters are able to use volunteer experiences to learn more about future occupations, a lesson that is possible because adolescents may be placed more often in positions of greater challenge and responsibility when employers need not be concerned about getting their money's worth out of the adolescent's work.

It is important to reiterate that in the absence of opportunities to reflect on volunteer experiences, the psychosocial gains associated with service work are likely to be insignificant (Newmann and Rutter 1983). Nevertheless, the findings indicate it is indeed possible to provide adolescents with out-of-school experiences that benefit them psychologically and that benefit society as well.

The prospect of a large number of adolescent volunteers—in hospitals, schools, child-care programs, community maintenance activities, and the like—may cause concern in some quarters because of the potential displacement of adult workers. There are two forms of response to this concern. First, it is important to note that *paid* adolescent workers, too, are not exempt from the charge that they take jobs away from their elders. The fact that youth can be hired legally at a minimum or subminimum wage reduces the likelihood that the jobs they typically fill will be upgraded to full-time positions at a living wage—positions more attractive to adults. School-going adolescents who work may contribute especially to unemployment and underemployment in the just-older, young-adult cohort whose level of job skills and job experience exclude many from all but jobs of modest quality. Second, serious effects of adolescent volunteerism on adult employment are likely only in the event that adolescent volunteer work should become epidemic. In that unlikely case, safeguards could be devised to protect adults' jobs. Settings where teenage volunteers work could be enjoined from substituting volunteer labor for work that is normally paid and required to observe limits with respect to the number of volunteer hours they accept.

Although engaging youngsters in extracurricular and service activities may offer psychosocial benefits that working in a paid job does not, steering adolescents toward these activities does not, of course, address the main reason that youngsters seek employment—to acquire spending money. We are not suggesting that parents take on the task of subsidizing their youngsters' acquisitive urges. How, then, should parents respond to pleas for designer clothes, stereos, ten-speed bicycles, and sports cars, if not with the standard response "If you want it so badly, why don't you go out and get a job?"

We recognize that parents are in a difficult position. Yet we believe they can play a more active role than they currently do in shaping their children's values and attitudes toward money and its uses—and, consequently, in shaping their children's attitudes toward the work of growing up—by discussing the youngsters' requests with them and helping them determine what is, and what is not, necessary to buy. It is undoubtedly easier for parents to direct their youngsters into the labor force than it is to teach them that they can survive without the latest in headphones, or the newest style of cashmere sweater, or front-row seats to every concert in town. Yet adolescents, who are easily impressed with the status afforded by material possessions, need to be taught by their parents about the shallowness of conspicuous consumption and the importance of being able to delay gratification. One way to accomplish this is for parents to insist that a portion of their youngsters' earnings be saved for longer-term needs. Parents also might consider encouraging their working youngsters to contribute a portion of their earnings toward family expenses, particularly in cases in which such a contribution would actually make a difference. The difficulty parents experience in saying "no" to their adolescents' requests has become increasingly common as more and more teenagers have entered the labor force and as standards have risen for what the "necessities" of a "comfortable" adolescence are. As virtually every parent knows, it is always easier to behave permissively than to set limits and guidelines on children's behavior, particularly when what is being permitted—in this case, taking on a job for the purpose of earning spending money—seems so innocuous. But perhaps parents should reconsider this strategy in light of what we now know regarding some of the potential costs of excessive employment and of the values that may be communicated to youngsters by encouraging them toward higher and higher levels of consumption.

Several comments are in order at this point about the varied needs of young people from different socioeconomic backgrounds. We have focused our attention largely on school-going youngsters whose families are sufficiently affluent for their children not to have to work long hours. These are the young people who, as we noted earlier, are disproportionately overrepresented in the part-time labor force. The majority of these youngsters, particularly those who are college-bound, would profit, we believe, from curtailing their involvement in part-time jobs and turning their time and energies toward other activities, including volunteer and service activities, extracurricular programs provided by schools, and the pursuit of intellectual, artistic, and athletic interests during nonschool hours. Youngsters who must work in order to help support their families and those adolescents who do not have to work because of financial circumstances but who wish to work in order to gain experience in the labor force should be encouraged by parents and school personnel to select jobs that are likely to have an educational as well as an economic pay-off. These youth should be assisted in their attempts to find employment but should be steered mainly toward jobs that are likely to improve their chances of succeeding in the adult labor force, by providing direct bridges into full-time employment, teaching valuable work skills, or helping in the process of occupational identity exploration. Schools can provide such direction through existing work-study and student employment programs. Instead of simply posting available employment opportunities, however, individuals in charge of such programs might also provide direction and guidance to job seekers. Many students would benefit from counseling before taking on a part-time job. Such counseling should be aimed toward helping them find good matches between available part-time work experiences (or, perhaps, nonwork experiences) and their long-term educational and occupational aspirations. Later we suggest ways in which school personnel might help youngsters develop formal employment histories that could be useful when the time comes to enter the full-time labor force.

Improving Experiences in the Adolescent Workplace

The fascination of youngsters with work, and with the spending money it generates, is not going to disappear, and neither is the adolescent workplace. It would be foolish, therefore, for us to suggest that the problems of adolescent employment will recede simply by our encouraging youngsters to become involved in nonwork activities that are likely to benefit them more psychologically than financially. The economic forces that have drawn youngsters into the workplace and encouraged them to invest considerable time there will not vanish, nor is it likely that they will weaken. Ours is, and will continue to be, a consumer society, and it is unreasonable to suppose that youngsters will not follow the behavior of the adult models to whom they are exposed. The advertising and marketing industries will continue to promote young people's consumption of luxury goods, and as long as there are avenues through which teenagers can acquire discretionary income, they will certainly rise to the bait. Nevertheless, there are measures that policy makers, employers, educators, and parents can take that may minimize some of the costs of adolescent employment and perhaps even maximize some of the benefits. In this final section, we discuss some of these measures.

POLICY MAKERS: CONTINUE TO LIMIT YOUNGSTERS' HOURS ON THE JOB

Our findings, and those of other investigators, suggest quite clearly that it is the amount of time youngsters spend in the labor force, and not simply whether they work, that is the critical factor affecting their behavior and development. Specifically, the psychological costs of working while in high school are primarily dependent on how much time youngsters spend in the labor force. Several implications follow from this conclusion.

First, it is clear that, at the very least, we ought not to adopt any policies that encourage youngsters to work more than they are already working. Lowering the minimum wage for young people, as one example, is likely to do just this (Greenberger and Steinberg 1982). We know that youngsters work mainly for the discretionary income it provides, and reducing their hourly wages would only require them to work more hours in order to realize the same amount of spending money. In view of the findings we have reviewed, then, any policy that would increase the number of hours youngsters work would exacerbate already existing problems in the schooling, family life, and social activities of American adolescents—more mediocrity in the schools, less contact between young people and their parents, and, perhaps, higher rates of drug and alcohol abuse. The argument that the subminimum wage would help solve the "youth unemployment" problem is erroneous; it fails to distinguish between middle-class youth, who do not have an unemployment problem, and impoverished youth, who constitute the majority of the unemployed. In other words, the argument fails to recognize who is working, and why. Second, it appears to be the case that formal and informal measures are still needed in order to keep a cap on the number of hours that youngsters work. Without such restrictions, many will continue to work more hours than is likely to be good for them.

Proponents of the deregulation of child labor, or of liberalizing current restraints, argue that concerns voiced decades ago by child protectionists—that working would imperil children's health, interfere with their education, and lead to juvenile delinquency—are no longer valid. They claim that today the situation is, if anything, exactly the reverse (Mnookin 1978; Minnesota Law Review 1975). The evidence we have reviewed, however, does not justify these optimistic conclusions. Indeed, continued efforts to prevent the overworking of adolescents during "prime time" for their socialization and development are still warranted and are in the best interests of both young people and society. We should not be misled by those who continue to call for doing away with or relaxing child labor restrictions, under the guise of removing unnecessary "protection" and behind the "children's rights" banner.

EMPLOYERS: OPTIMIZE ADOLESCENTS' WORK ENVIRONMENTS

In the naturally occurring workplace, the profit motive will continue to prevail over concern for whether young workers (or older workers, for that matter) are deriving psychosocial benefits from employment. Nonetheless, some employers will find the prospect of improving youngsters' jobs personally rewarding—and perhaps even profitable. Especially in those industries that rely heavily on part-time adolescent workers and where rapid turnover is a problem, employers may want to make jobs better. Such efforts may pay off in reducing on-the-job mischief and deviance by young workers.

Perhaps the most important contribution employers can make is to limit their adolescent employees' hours of employment. The preference of employers for young workers who are willing to work long hours is understandable. The fewer employees they have on the payroll, the lower their training costs and the fewer their scheduling problems. But research suggests that fifteen hours a week may be an appropriate ceiling for work by high-school sophomores; twenty hours for seniors. By implication, freshmen and juniors should work less than, or at least no more than, their just-older peers. Employers also might consider increasing opportunities for even less intensive weekly employment—such as eight to ten hours. Through these shorter hours, employers may attract youngsters into the labor market who are now precluded from participation. Youngsters who spend appreciable amount of time on studies and in extracurricular activities might be particularly well-motivated and competent employees.

Another way in which some employers could improve the job experience of youth is by introducing greater variety into the job environment. Job rotation would provide more opportunities for experimentation, identity exploration, and mastery of new information and skills. Of course, the different wages and entry-level skills associated with different jobs put a lid on the feasibility of job rotation on a large scale. Nevertheless, possibilities do exist: most jobs adolescents fill in fact require very little training. Some employers even have found ways to give novices a taste of more demanding jobs. In some settings, for example, employees rotate the job of shift manager—the same youngster who is an "ordinary" waitress four days out of five serves as shift manager on day five. A policy of this kind enables more adolescents to learn supervisory skills. Employers also might encourage youngsters to take an occasional shift at other jobs of an equal or lower skill level, for the sake of familiarizing themselves with the range of work in the organization. Obviously, this suggestion offers opportunities for abuse by employers. Continued employment should not be contingent on the young person's agreement to perform other work, nor should the person's hourly wages suffer. Finally, youngsters who have proven themselves dependable and competent employees might be invited to attend occasional planning or policy meetings that "the boss" attends—a privilege that could be offered at no wages—with a view toward increasing young people's knowledge of how a business is run.

Increased variety in their lives on the job may be good for youngsters in a number of ways. First, greater variety would mitigate our criticism that extensive commitment to one's job —or better, to *one* job—interferes with young people's developmental needs for self-testing and self-clarification. Youngsters who have the kinds of enriched work environment we just described are more likely than others to have experiences from which they learn what they like and find interesting and what they do not; what they are good at and what they are not. Second, youngsters who have had personal experience with the tasks performed by different members of the organization might well develop a deeper appreciation of the perspective of others. Our research, it may be recalled, suggests that when youngsters' jobs require them to shift roles and types of social interaction, they grow in social understanding. Similarly, exposure to the roles of other people in the work setting may promote growth in cooperation and a greater sense of solidarity. In addition to the gains for youth, employers stand to benefit from greater interpersonal understanding and cooperation among their employees. And by increasing opportunities for learning and role experimentation, employers may achieve a payoff in increased employee motivation and loyalty. Youngsters may perform beyond the call of duty more often if their employers, by trying to optimize their work environment, have done the same.

In view of widely shared hopes that working should, or at least could, be a maturity-enhancing experience, one other issue deserves consideration. As we have noted, many youngsters work mainly in the company of their peers; older people who might serve as mentors, or at least role models, are in short supply. Employers whose staff is highly age segregated could look for ways to alter the age distribution in the workplace. For example, it might be possible, within the limit of the existing pool of employees, to impose rules about the minimum ratio of youth under, versus over, age eighteen on any one shift— to juggle work schedules, in other words, for the purpose of decreasing the concentration of minors. More ambitiously (and admittedly, less likely), a number of part-time slots could be collapsed into full-time positions at better pay, for which older employees, perhaps in the post–high-school, next-older cohort, might be hired. Our earlier suggestion that managers and supervisors reward dependable and competent employees by inviting them to attend occasional management-related meetings is also relevant to modifying the peer-saturated work environment.

SCHOOLS: INTEGRATE ADOLESCENTS' WORK EXPERIENCES INTO SCHOOL ACTIVITIES

Schools can, and should, play a role in helping to make part-time employment a more valuable experience. Efforts to improve the integration of the work experience into a broad range of classroom activities and innovations in counseling seem most to the point. Teachers can help increase the educational value of students' experiences in the part-time labor force by integrating discussions of these experiences into existing classes in almost any subject: for example, social studies, economics, business, and psychology. In so doing, educators can help guide and stimulate adolescents' thinking about the world of work and add an intellectual component to their employment experiences. As we noted earlier, the most successful volunteer programs for young people are those that integrate service activities with structured classroom discussion. The same is also likely to be true for work experience.

Counselors have a potential role at three junctures. First, they can direct information about the pros and cons of school-year employment to students who are contemplating working or are likely to do so: entering freshmen are the obvious target. Based on issues we have raised, counselors can discuss the features of work that make one job better than another. They can educate students about the possible costs of overinvolvement in work. And for the many students who do not need to work for financial reasons, they can suggest alternatives to paid employment. Some counselors may be interested in developing high-quality placements for students who are willing to volunteer their time.

All of these counseling functions pertain as well to students who already have school-year jobs. For these youngsters, it is pertinent to inquire whether they are really interested in their work, whether they are still learning anything, and whether they are growing in self-knowledge as a result of their experiences on the job. If not, and if they cannot improve their work conditions, it may be time to look for another job. Again, alternatives to work might be explored. Has the youngster thought of spending some time previously devoted to working to participation in school athletics, or replacing a few hours of paid work with volunteer work in an area that holds some promise for a future career? Counselors also should inquire about the methods by which students manage to balance their commitments to work and to school. They should be especially sensitive to clues that students who work may be selecting easier courses, or doing less well, than they would if their commitment to the job were less substantial.

Finally, and perhaps most different from the activities they now engage in, school counselors could help youngsters to establish an employment history and a record of their credentials as an employee. This history could be useful to students as they try to move into higher-quality jobs over the course of their high-school years and as they move into full-time or part-time jobs after graduation. Let us consider this suggestion in more detail.

One of the short-run benefits of early work experience is that it makes youngsters more marketable in the early adult years, when they are at their greatest risk for unemployment. Yet, we venture, few youth who work during their high-school years keep a careful record of their employment, buttressed by employers' verification and evaluation of their job performance. It seems plausible that youngsters who bring the best credentials to the early adult job market will have an advantage over others in obtaining employment, and perhaps, better wages (Bachman 1983b). Such credentials may be especially valuable to those youth with the poorest post–high-school employment prospects—those who dropped out of school before graduation or had relatively little employment experience during the high-school years.

Counselors could provide an important service by encouraging timely and uniform record keeping—especially, but not only, by youth who expect to go into the full-time labor force after high school. Job evaluations that have a useful level of detail are best gotten at the time of employment, not a year or more later, for reasons intrinsic to the adolescent workplace. Most teenagers' tenure in a given job is relatively brief, by adult standards, and a supervisor contacted for evaluation well after a youngster has left the job may not recall his or her particular competencies. Additionally, turnover and job mobility are likely to be high among the young adults who typically supervise teenage employees.

Perhaps the most concrete step counselors could take to encourage better record keeping by students would be to provide job-evaluation forms—ones that are appropriate and that students and employers are likely to use.[1] Standard forms, requiring only checked ratings of various proficiencies, are probably least troublesome for employers. For example, employers might rate whether the youngster's punctuality, level of initiative, and other work-related skills are below average, average, better than average, or far superior to those of other students employed in the same or similar jobs. Use of such forms would not preclude the addition of more individualized comments about the youngster. The encouragement of frequent—perhaps quarterly—job chronicling and evaluation, with standard items of evaluation, would yield a number of benefits. Each "entry" would form the basis for potentially useful discussions between youngsters and their employers and, if desired, between youngsters and their school counselors. The record would constitute a report card detailing progress as a worker and as such would be useful to young people and to prospective employers as well. Finally, in communities where standard evaluation forms are in use, prospective employers would have additional information on which to compare potential new employees. Taking this proposal one step further, we suggest that counselors might encourage students to keep their job records on file at school, to be used by students whenever they wish and by counselors (for example, for recommendations) only with the student's permission. The file would leave with the student when he or she leaves school or graduates.

PARENTS: MONITOR YOUNGSTERS' EMPLOYMENT
MORE CAREFULLY

In chapter 4 we noted that some of the deleterious consequences of youngsters' excessive involvement in the part-time labor force may result from the ensuing diminished contact with their parents. It stands to reason, therefore, that increasing the involvement of parents in the labor-force activities of their children may minimize some of the costs of working and increase some of the benefits. We can suggest several ways of achieving these ends. First, parents should play an active role in helping their children decide whether to work and should initiate discussion of alternatives to working that might be pleasurable, interesting, and growth-promoting. Together they should discuss the activities the adolescent will be forced to give up in order to take on a job.

Second, parents of a youngster who wishes to work should help their child decide what sort of job to take on and how many hours each week to commit to a job. Parental involvement at this stage should take the form of a discussion about the youngster's perceived financial needs, a plan for the income derived from working, and a discussion of the pros and cons of different sorts of jobs. Because so many of the adverse effects of employment are related to the number of hours a youngster is employed, parents should pay special attention to this issue in discussing their child's potential work involvement.

Third, parents should remain involved in their child's work experience after he or she has entered the labor force. Discussions about working conditions, conflicts on the job, business operations, and the like can help to turn what may be a fairly uninteresting job into more of an educational activity than it otherwise would be.

Finally, parents periodically should reassess their child's employment situation in terms of its apparent impact on the youngster's behavior and attitudes. Does the job seem to occupy more of the adolescent's time and energy than it should? Has the experience of working made the child overly concerned with money and with material possessions? Is the youngster showing signs of disengagement from school, from important extracurricular interests, or from close friends as a result of involvement in the labor force? These may all be signs that the adolescent's commitment to the job has become excessive.

Concluding Comments

We indicated earlier that the factors that make a difference in youngsters' work experience are its educational, economic, and social contexts. It is clear that in these three areas, the jobs available to young people in the new adolescent workplace do not generally provide environments conducive to psychological growth and development. Indeed, we would argue that the counterintuitive findings presented in this volume—for example, that working is more likely to interfere with than enhance schooling; promotes pseudomaturity rather than maturity; is associated in certain circumstances with higher, not lower, rates of delinquency and drug and alcohol use; and fosters cynical rather than respectful attitudes toward work—can be explained by deficiencies in the work experiences typically available to youngsters. It is precisely because the typical adolescent's experience in the new workplace is educationally irrelevant, economically unnecessary, and largely age segregated that adolescent employment has the impact that it does. It promotes autonomy only in its most individualistic sense and social responsibility, little or not at all.

We think it unlikely that bad jobs in the new adolescent workplace can be turned into very good ones. They are inherently discontinuous with youngsters' future careers and hence largely irrelevant to education for adult work. They tend to be located in middle-class neighborhoods and thus more accessible to youngsters whose employment is least economically necessary—a situation that compromises the young worker's sense of productivity and altruism. And because these jobs are usually unattractive to adult workers, they are unlikely to foster a great deal of intergenerational contact. As long as work environments remain deficient in these respects, they will continue to produce the unanticipated, and undesirable, consequences we have described.

Although we have recommended ways in which employers might upgrade young people's jobs, it is unreasonable to expect dramatic changes in the nature of the new adolescent workplace. We can do a great deal more, however, to educate young people about the costs and benefits of various types of work experience. Leaving it to young people to handle it themselves —to select their own jobs, set their work hours as they see fit, dispose of their earnings according to their own desires, and try to make sense out of their experiences—with little guidance or protection from parents or teachers—almost certainly ensures that intensive work experience during the school year will do youngsters more harm than good.

Writing about child labor some fifty years ago, two social critics observed that youngsters from poor families go to work "with no plan . . . their jobs usually anything they can get, having nothing to do with their interests and their capacities, only with business demand . . ." (Lumpkin and Douglas 1937). Intending to arouse sympathy for these children, they asked, "What would the average middle-class parent say to such an 'educational' program for his adolescent boys and girls?" (p. 44). Ironically, middle-class parents today appear to have sanctioned just such an educational program for their youngsters, imputing to the typical teenage job a host of benefits for which there is little evidence.

The belief that work—under virtually all circumstances—is "good" for young people, and a good deal of work even better, is deeply entrenched. For this reason it is not easy to win a hearing for our argument that the benefits of extensive school-year employment have been overestimated and the costs, underestimated. We have tried to demonstrate that the nature of the jobs available to young people today, the characteristics of the workplace in which these jobs are located, and the motives that impel many young people to seek jobs limit the benefits that are likely to result from intensive work experience. On the positive side of the ledger, we show that youngsters report better work habits after holding a time-consuming job, and girls who work intensively report greater feelings of self-reliance. Intensive work experience pays off, too, in lower rates of unemployment and higher wages during the first several years of high school, but there are compelling reasons to believe that these advantages do not persist and, moreover, are obtained at a price. Indeed, as we have shown, the gains that may accrue to young workers are accompanied by a number of costs. Experience in the adolescent workplace often breeds contempt for the idea that work can be enjoyable and satisfying. Extensive involvement in a job takes a toll on young people's education, and lower educational attainment has implications for young people's long-run occupational success and life satisfaction. Intensive work leads to increased use of alcohol and marijuana, especially when jobs are stressful. And because the paychecks that reward long hours at work are unencumbered by adult responsibilities, youngsters experience premature affluence: they engage in a level of consumption that is inconsistent with the obligations that many of them will face in the ensuing years. Finally, long hours spent in the workplace curtail opportunities for other, developmentally productive activities.

Adults have a strong interest in seeing that adolescents ready themselves for the transition to adulthood. A youngster who is able to get and hold a job is taking a step in that direction— but in light of the changed conditions of work, perhaps not the giant step it is generally thought to be. It is tempting to see the ability to play adult roles, such as worker, as a sign of maturity. However, those who are, by social definition, adult may nonetheless remain psychologically adolescent, playing roles they have been eager to win with little perception or understanding and little sense of meaning. Paraphrasing David Riesman's comments on American teenagers of the previous generation (in Friedenberg 1959), we are concerned that adolescents today, hurried to "grow up" and get on the payroll, are settling into "adjusted blandness" at a time of life when they ought to be more spirited. Their jobs may make them economically rich, but may also make them psychologically poor.

Details of Studies
Cited in Chapter 3

THE *Greenberger and Steinberg study* referred to throughout the book was conducted at four high schools in Orange County, California, selected to provide a range of students with respect to ethnicity and family social class. The initial pool of individuals contacted for this study were 3,100 youngsters —all tenth and eleventh graders present in school on the day of testing. From this group we selected all youngsters currently holding their first part-time, school-year job (most, their very first steady job). With a 67 percent consent rate, 211 youngsters formed the target sample for our cross-sectional study and were compared with 319 youth who had never held a steady job. Data collection was carried out in 1978. Of the study sample, 82 percent was white; 10 percent, Hispanic; 8 percent, black or Asian (chiefly the latter), conforming well to the ethnic distribution in the standard metropolitan statistical area from which the high schools were drawn. Approximately 25 percent of the youngsters came from family backgrounds in which the father holds a job in the professions; 33 percent, from white-collar backgrounds; 42 percent, from blue-collar backgrounds. A year later we contacted the nonworkers from the cross-sectional study and readministered the survey questionnaire to 71 percent of these youth. The sample of continuing nonworkers in this longitudinal phase of the Orange County study numbered 101; workers, 75.

Participants in the project were studied by a variety of methods: survey questionnaires, on-site observations, and interviews. They supplied information on a wide range of topics, including work history and reasons for working; involvement in school; family and peer relations; involvement in deviant and criminal behavior; and a variety of attitudes and traits.

In addition to the study directors, Mary Ruggiero and Alan Vaux have drawn on this data set.

The *Youth in Transition* study, under the direction of Jerald Bachman at the University of Michigan's Institute for Social Research, began in 1966 and continued through 1974. The study was based on a national sample of 2,213 tenth-grade boys attending public high schools, who were resurveyed periodically until 1974.

The study focused both on the causes and consequences of young men's educational aspirations and attainments. In addition to data on education, information on a wide variety of attitudes and behaviors was obtained.

Researchers who drew on this data set are Mortimer and Finch (in press) and Finch and Mortimer (1985). They studied the initial (1966) sample of over 2,000 tenth-grade boys, who were resurveyed as juniors and seniors and then again, five years after graduation, in 1974.

The *High School and Beyond* survey is a longitudinal survey of U.S. high-school sophomores and seniors that began in 1980 with a sample of more than 58,000 students. The study is directed by Samuel S. Peng at the National Center for Education Statistics. Schools in the nation were stratified by size and were selected for participation proportional to their size. Thirty-six sophomores and thirty-six seniors were drawn randomly from each selected school. The study concentrates on young people's educational and labor-force activities and accomplishments.

Noah Lewin-Epstein (1981) analyzed findings from the first wave of data collection, before the survey had generated longitudinal data.

Monitoring the Future is a yearly survey of high-school seniors at the University of Michigan's Institute for Social Research (Johnston, Bachman, and O'Malley 1982). Its full title is *Monitoring the Future: A Continuing Study of the Lifestyles and Values of Youth.* The survey was begun in 1975 and is ongoing. Participants are drawn from 125 to 140 schools nationwide and selected to be representative of all seniors in the continental United States. Between 15,000 and 18,000 students have been surveyed each year.

The project is designed to track changes in values, behaviors, and life-style orientations in successive cohorts of high-school seniors. A subsample of seniors each year is followed up at a later time. Survey content includes religious, political, and social values; family plans; concern with various social problems; education and work behaviors; a number of personality measures; and drug use and attitudes toward drug use. The latter two topics are those that receive the most coverage in this survey.

McNeil's study (1984) was conducted in four "middle-class" high schools in southern Wisconsin. A survey was administered to 1,577 junior and senior students to supplement ethnographic data collected earlier at these sites. Most students were surveyed in social studies classes. Although the sample is not, strictly speaking, representative of all students in the school, it provides a good mix of students in terms of gender and academic ability. Ninety-five percent of the sample was white. Median family income, as estimated by respondents, was $25,-000 to $34,999. Youngsters who were currently working, had worked the year before but were not currently working, and those who had never worked received somewhat different questions about their present work situation and reasons for it, and the impacts or anticipated impacts of working on a variety of school-related outcomes.

The *Gottfredson project* (1985) is part of the School Action Effectiveness Study, funded by the U.S. Office of Juvenile Justice and Delinquency Prevention to operate education projects designed to reduce delinquency. The study draws on youngsters in sixty-nine schools in seventeen cities. Selected schools were located, for the most part, in depressed, inner-city areas with a predominantly minority population. Although the study began with random sampling of students from each school, later constraints imposed on the researchers interfered with this sampling plan. In addition, considerable sample attrition occurred, because many students were not enrolled in the same school over the two years of the project. The final sample consisted of 1,400 youngsters in grades 6 to 12 and is therefore considerably younger, on the average, than students in the other studies reported in this chapter.

In this study respondents were surveyed about their involvement in different types of criminal behavior; attributes of their close peers; a variety of attitudes and behaviors assessing commitment to school; belief in conventional roles; and employment status. Youngsters were surveyed initially in 1981 and again in 1982.

The *National Longitudinal Surveys* (also called the National Longitudinal Survey of the Labor Market Experience of Youth) have been conducted yearly since 1979 by the Ohio State University's Center for Human Resource research. A national representative sample of fourteen- to twenty-one-year-olds constitutes the survey group.

Ronald D'Amico (1984) used data from the 1979 to 1982 waves of the survey. From the more than 1,200 respondents, he drew 5,000 who met the condition of being enrolled in high school in 1979.

NOTES

Chapter 1 / *Teenage Work in America*

1. These estimates are based on population projections from a national survey of students conducted by the National Center for Education Statistics as part of its High School and Beyond project (Lewin-Epstein 1981).

2. See the English Factory Act of 1833, described in Vulcan (1968).

3. Among the relevant factors in the post–Civil War nineteenth century: large waves of immigration from Europe to the cities of the United States and large numbers of rural dwellers moving to the cities as a consequence of farm mechanization; and, as a consequence of the two, an ever-increasing supply of cheap labor in urban areas, which kept wages down.

4. Federal legislation regulating child labor that had been proposed in 1916 and 1919 was declared unconstitutional by the U.S. Supreme Court, on the grounds that it represented an intrusion upon state power (Lumpkin and Douglas 1937; *Minnesota Law Review*, 1975). Both state and federal legislation address the minimum age at which youngsters can work, specify hours of work during the school year and other times of the year, and prohibit certain types of work. Where state and federal laws vary, the stricter regulations prevail.

5. The terms employed and in the labor force have specific and distinctive meanings in the reporting of labor statistics. "Employment" means that the individual worked at least one hour in the week prior to the survey. Labor-force participation, or being "in the labor force," means that the individual was employed or looked for work in the week prior to the survey. We generally discuss adolescent work

in terms of labor-force participation; however, for enrolled and nonenrolled youngsters, only employment data were collected during the 1940 decennial census of the population.

6. See previous note on distinction between "employment" and "labor-force participation."

7. Although Census data on enrolled fourteen- to fifteen-year-olds are available for 1950, methods of data collection differ substantially from those used by BLS, as do estimates of labor-force participation.

8. Figures for 1947 are taken from Reubens, Harrison, and Rupp (1981), based on unpublished BLS data. Figures for other years are from the *Employment and Training Report of the President* (Office of the President 1982), Table B-9.

9. It is arguable whether national data sources on children and youth employment are accurate. They are almost surely inadequate. The Bureau of Labor Statistics provides monthly data on employment by sex and by age, but gives no student/nonstudent breakdown on either variable. Data on hours of employment (and on earnings), moreover, do not differentiate between youngsters who are and are not enrolled in school, between youngsters of different ages, or between boys and girls. U.S. Census data are better elaborated but still far from complete. They describe employment status and hours of employment for students and nonstudents, separately for boys and girls, year by year between ages fourteen and twenty-one. Distinctions between in-school and out-of-school youngsters are not made, however, with respect to earnings and type of employment; and data on earnings are grouped by age fourteen to fifteen and collapsed for all individuals sixteen and over. The biggest limitations of U.S. Census data, obviously, are the infrequency with which information is collected and the subsequent lag between collection and dissemination.

10. Information on weekly hours of employment of school-going youngsters, broken down by age and sex, was first collected by the U.S. Census in 1960; by the BLS, in 1967. Using BLS data for October 1967, 1970, 1980, and 1982, we note that changes in intensity of employment differ to some extent by sex, age, and the nature of the youngster's work: agricultural or nonagricultural.

Overall, there was relatively little change in the average number of hours per week worked by school-enrolled boys between 1967 and 1980. For girls, however, the picture during that period was quite different. Among fourteen- and fifteen-year-olds employed in non-agricultural jobs, mean hours of work increased 21 percent between 1967 and 1980, with little change (though the small observed change was *upward*) in average hours of work in agricultural jobs. Among sixteen- and seventeen-year-old girls, there was a 19 percent increase in weekly hours of work in nonagricultural jobs and an 11 percent decline in hours of work in agricultural occupations (from data supplied by Anne M. Young, Bureau of Labor Statistics, personal communication). Thus the single biggest increase in hours of work was found among younger girls in nonfarm jobs. Since 1980 students' average hours of work per week have declined for all subgroups except older boys in agricultural occupations.

Although tangential to our purposes, it is worth noting that youngsters who hold agricultural jobs (many, presumably, on farms owned by their family) work considerably longer hours than their peers who have nonagricultural jobs. This was so in 1967 and continues to be so. The difference is especially marked among younger students, among whom farm workers in 1980 put in approximately twice the number of hours as their friends working in nonfarm jobs. In addition, girls in the fourteen- to fifteen-year age group work considerably more hours per week in agricultural jobs than their male counterparts, a pattern that is also visible—though less striking—among older boys and girls before 1980. This fact makes interesting food for thought, in view of the consistent, and contrasting, finding that adult men work longer hours than women (Greenberger and Steinberg 1983) and of recent research that uncovers the "invisible" work of women on farms (Sachs 1983).

11.   In contrast to discrepancies in their estimates of how many youngsters are in the labor force, the BLS and surveys based on adolescents themselves yield rather similar estimates of youngsters' weekly hours of employment. For example, 1980 BLS data, in which fourteen- to fifteen-year-olds and sixteen- to seventeen-year-olds are considered, indicate that the average boy in the former age group works 11.5 hours per week (from data provided by Anne M. Young for October 1980). Data from the High School and Beyond study, based on the report of high-school sophomores and seniors in 1980, yield a figure of 14.8 hours for the former group. In view of the facts that sophomores tend to be somewhat older than fourteen to fifteen, on the average, and that older students work longer hours, the two sets of figures do not seem much out of alignment.

12. In the United States, as well, more students work during the summer than during the school year. Reubens, Harrison, and Rupp (1981, p. 288) note that summer and school-year workers are sufficiently nonoverlapping that they should be treated separately.

13. The triple-barreled item to which people responded leaves some doubt about what they actually were agreeing to. The item was "We never know what tomorrow will bring, so I think it is important to enjoy life today, even if you have to incur some debts to do it."

14. Our sense that young people have become more materialistic could be contested. In some studies, for example, a substantial proportion of respondents express the view that they would "welcome less emphasis on money" (American Life Insurance Survey 1978; Yankelovich 1973). In light of far more substantial evidence of increased emphasis on making money and enjoying what it can buy, we do not interpret such responses as signs of diminishing materialism. Rather we view them as a possible indication that the pursuit of material goals has psychological costs of which many people are aware.

15. The two peak periods of increase in employment of women with children under eighteen are matched by peaks in fourteen- to seventeen-year-olds' employment; and within this age group, growth in youth employment is greater among girls. The first large increase in the employment of women with children occurred between 1940 and 1950 and reflected wartime and postwar economic factors. The increase in boys' employment over this decade was substantial, as indicated earlier, but the increase in girls' employment was considerably greater—especially among older youth. The second peak period of increase for women with minor children was 1970 to 1980. In this period there was also substantial increase in fourteen- to seventeen-year-olds' employment—greater than that from 1950 to 1960 or 1960 to 1970. The gain in girls' employment, among both fourteen- to fifteen-year-olds and sixteen- to seventeen-year-olds, was dramatic compared to the gain in boys' employment.

16. These panels and commissions included, among others, the Panel on Youth of the President's Science Advisory Committee (1973); the National Panel on High School and Adolescent Education (1974), whose efforts were sponsored by the U.S. Office of Education; the Carnegie Council on Policy Studies in Higher Education (1980); and the National Commission on Youth (1980), sponsored by the Kettering Foundation. Among the members of some of

these groups were James S. Coleman, sociologist; Zvi Grilliches, economist; Joseph Kett, historian; Urie Bronfenbrenner, psychologist; B. Frank Brown, educator; George Gallup, public opinion researcher; and Dennis Gallagher, manpower expert.

17. Any decrease in contact with the world of work may be specific to poor and minority adolescents, who are less likely to live where the jobs are today. Government labor statistics, however, do not provide information on possible changes in the social origins of student workers over the past four decades.

18. For a thorough critique of the reports of the President's Science Advisory Committee, the National Panel on High School Education, and the National Commission on Youth, see Timpane, Abramowitz, Bobrow, and Pascal (1976).

Chapter 3. / *Working and Adolescent Development: The Research Evidence*

1. In our cross-sectional studies, however, we devised a method that takes a step toward distinguishing likely causal effects of working from factors that differentiate workers and nonworkers from the start —and that may predispose youngsters to self-select into the labor force. When we found a significant worker-nonworker difference on any outcome variable—scores on a measure of personal responsibility, for example—we looked more closely at our sample of nonworkers. We knew which of the nonworkers were seeking jobs and which were not. Job seekers, we reasoned, are probably more like actual workers than are youngsters who do not want to work—at least on dimensions that predispose them to be interested in employment. Consequently, if job seekers differed significantly from unemployed youngsters who were *not* seeking jobs on the variable of interest, in the same manner as workers and nonworkers had differed, we inferred that the worker-nonworker difference probably predated employment. Put otherwise, we inferred that differences between workers and nonworkers which were foreshadowed by comparable differences between job seekers and youth not seeking jobs probably were not a consequence of working. On the other hand, if a worker-nonworker difference was *not* foreshadowed by a similar difference between job seekers and nonseekers in the sample of unemployed youth, we inferred that the worker-nonworker difference might well be an actual result of work

experience rather than an antecedent or predisposing factor that draws youth, selectively, into the workplace.

2. We observed youngsters who were employed as food service workers, manual laborers, retail sales clerks, machine operatives and skilled laborers, clerical workers, and cleaners. These kinds of jobs, along with babysitting, were the most common kinds of work in which our sample was employed. Babysitters were excluded from the observational study, however, on the grounds that it would be too intrusive to observe youngsters at work in private homes and too likely to alter the natural flow of events.

3. In comparisons of workers and nonworkers, youngsters' age and social class were typically controlled. In the longitudinal study, initial or time 1 scores on variables that working was predicted to affect (e.g., self-reliance) also were controlled.

4. The work orientation and self-reliance scales are subscales of the Psychosocial Maturity Inventory. The reliability and validity of these scales are described in Greenberger and associates (1975) and Greenberger and Bond (1976).

5. Observers were university students who had been trained to apply a one hundred-item behavioral code to the events they saw. Using a portable electronic event recorder, they produced a detailed chronicle of what took place, with whom, and for how long (Greenberger, Steinberg, and Ruggiero 1982; Ruggiero and Steinberg 1981).

6. About two-thirds of the test content concerned money and banking, and consumer matters. The internal consistency of this measure, as indicated by Cronbach's Alpha statistic, is 0.78.

7. The finding that senior boys, but not girls, who work have lower GPAs than their nonworking counterparts (Lewin-Epstein 1981) provides a case in point. We know from another source that boys take their first steady, part-time job at a significantly earlier age, and work longer hours in their first several jobs, than girls (Greenberger and Steinberg 1983). Taken together, these two facts imply that senior boys, on the average, will have spent more time in the workplace than their female peers. Thus the effects of works status are probably confounded with the effects of intensity of employment in Lewin-Epstein's study.

8. Results of this study must be viewed, however, with some caution. As the authors themselves note, the measure of work experience is rather crude. Youngsters were asked in grades 10, 11, and 12 whether they were working at the time of the survey. Respondents

who answered no were considered not to have worked during that entire school year. In view of the fact that high-school students make fairly frequent moves in and out of the labor force, such classification is no doubt imperfect. Overall, the researchers are likely to have underestimated employment.

9. Standardized achievement test scores would provide a much better basis for assessing the effects of employment on learning. Unfortunately, however, few studies to date have utilized, or had available, such measures. Students' grades are a notoriously imperfect indicator of learning. Even as a measure of performance rather than learning, grades are subject to a host of nonintellective factors, among them, students' effort and conduct and local norms about what constitutes an "A" or a "C." Research on employment and GPA would be strengthened, despite these limitations, if investigators entered into their analyses some measure of the demands of individual students' curriculum. Students' grades may be differently affected by employment as a consequence of the school track they are in (college-bound, general curriculum, et cetera) or the number of courses they take in excess of minimum graduation requirements.

10. One exception is Gottfredson's study (1985) of junior high and high-school youth from schools targeted for special efforts to reduce delinquency. In these largely inner-city schools, employed males reported spending more time on homework than they did prior to employment. Gottfredson described this finding as "counter-intuitive" and eschewed further interpretation.

11. Several lines of evidence suggest that lower "school involvement" or investment in schooling is not merely a factor that predisposes youngsters to join the labor force or to participate intensively. We have reviewed at length studies on working and time spent on homework. These suggest that intensive employment actually leads to a decline in homework. Although we found no effects of working on participation in extracurricular activities in the Orange County study, D'Amico, using a much larger and nationally representative data set, found otherwise (Steinberg, Greenberger, Garduque, and McAuliffe 1982; D'Amico 1984). Greater intensity of employment, measured as the percentage of weeks in which a student worked more than twenty hours per week, was associated with spending less time at school, before and after hours, among white males and minority females. A significant negative association between weeks of less intensive employment and the amount of free time spent at school

was also noted for white males. In all of these analyses, the potentially confounding effects of a number of student and family background characteristics and time spent at school *prior* to employment were controlled.

In Gottfredson's study of youngsters attending, for the most part, inner-city schools (1985), she found little or no evidence that working affected school attendance or "attachment" to school. In our study of middle-class youth, we found that workers were absent more often and liked school less than nonworkers. Analyses of job seekers and youngsters who were not seeking employment suggested that school absence and lack of enjoyment of school were not initial selection-to-work factors but rather might be consequences of involvement in work. Although subsequent analysis of the longitudinal sample did *not* confirm the notion that working, or working long hours, led to increased school absence, it *did* support the concept that longer hours of work led to a drop in school enjoyment.

12. Delinquency has been shown to be highly stable from one year to the next. Hence studies that fail to include prior level of delinquency in the prediction of current delinquency run the risk of overestimating the importance of variables that are correlated with youngsters' earlier level of delinquency but that have no predictive utility once earlier delinquency is taken into account.

13. One could argue that youths with more cumulative experience in the workplace have had the least opportunity to engage in delinquent behavior (an argument of time and place) and the most exposure to the conventional order; and that among youths who worked in only one of the two years surveyed, those who worked during the same year as the final assessment of delinquency had less opportunity to engage in delinquent behavior and more recent exposure to experiences that might raise their stake in the conventional social order. The author's treatment of the data makes it impossible to discern the proportion of youngsters in each of the three subgroups of workers.

14. Again, we question the rationale for predicting delinquency from nonconcurrent or noncumulative work experience, the procedure that was used in this study.

15. These effects of exposure to job stress had been proposed earlier by Vaux and reported in Greenberger, Steinberg, and Vaux (1981) and Vaux (1981).

16. Performing separate analyses for boys and girls allows one to note possible sex differences in the relations between working and various forms of deviant behavior. These differences may be masked in analyses where boys and girls are combined. Analyses of the combined group, on the other hand, may highlight relationships that are not strong enough to attain statistical significance when the smaller subsamples of boys and girls are considered separately.

17. At the level of specific acts of deviance, workers in the cross-sectional study were more likely than nonworkers to buy marijuana and other drugs, sell marijuana, buy liquor, gamble, drink alcohol, smoke cigarettes, use other drugs, miss school, come late to school, skip classes, lie about having turned in assignments, and "cut up" in class. In the longitudinal study, similar particulars are more frequent gambling and consumption of alcohol among boys who work and more marijuana use among girls.

18. Bachman, Johnston, and O'Malley (1981), studying older youth from a broader social spectrum, found that the association between intensity of employment and frequency of using illicit drugs did *not* disappear when income was controlled. They suggest that youngsters who work more have greater exposure to other young workers, "including some slightly older and thus more experienced in the use of drugs" (p. 67).

19. Certain work stressors are harmful to both boys and girls. As noted elsewhere, "Males and females alike are adversely affected by exposure to work settings characterized by high levels of noise, dirt, heat, time pressure and other similar environmental stressors: and to a lesser extent, by work that involves meaningless tasks and conflict with other roles" (Greenberger, Steinberg, and Vaux 1981, p. 700).

20. We have not mentioned a third possible explanation—that girls are less able than boys, physically and psychologically, to withstand the effects of stressful experiences—because there is no evidence to support this still-popular view of differences between the sexes.

21. That is, after controlling for sex, grade level, social class, and work status, significant interactions between working and students' gender and between working and grade level were detected. Analysis of subgroups revealed that boys and younger students showed increases in materialism if they had been employed.

22. Using a different measure of social class, Ruggiero (1984) found that neither work status nor amount of exposure to work was associated with materialism or acceptance of unethical business practices, but that work status was significantly related to cynicism about work, in the direction we have indicated.

23. The only other scholarly research on occupational crime by youngsters was done twenty years ago. In this study (Myerhoff and Myerhoff 1964; reported in Ruggiero 1984), a participant observer of eighty fifteen- to eighteen-year-old in-school youths reported that adolescents talked of stealing often and regularly from their employers.

24. Responses of "often" were scored 3; "several times," 2; and "once or twice," 1. Summing over the nine deviant acts, we categorized as relatively frequent offenders youngsters who had total scores of at least 3: that is, one deviant act committed often, or three deviant acts committed once or twice, or one deviant act committed several times, and another, once or twice.

These self-report figures probably underestimate the true extent of deviance in the workplace. Individuals tend to underreport information that puts them in an unfavorable light. In addition, the most deviant workers may be more likely to have been detected and to have lost their jobs. If so, the most deviant youths would be underrepresented in our sample of workers. The limitations of self-report data that we have just noted also apply, of course, to reports of other kinds of deviance described in this and other studies.

25. The problem of unemployment among eighteen- to twenty-five-year-olds is more complex than the phrase "the problem" suggests. On the one hand, it is indeed a serious concern. Young adults have far higher rates of unemployment than older adults—about three to five times higher for different race/sex subgroups. On the other hand, unemployment is much more pervasive in some groups than others. It is especially high among blacks, whose employment situation also has deteriorated markedly over the past thirty years (unlike that of whites), among individuals who reside in areas with high poverty rates, and among persons with lower-than-average educational attainment for their age. Although a serious problem, unemployment in the young-adult cohort nonetheless has a somewhat different character than it does for older adults. To begin with, the greatest source of unemployment in young adulthood is the frequency of job changes (Freeman and Wise 1979). This activity ap-

pears to be a normal part of job-search activities during the early phases of the individual's occupational life cycle, and there is a limit to how successful social interventions would be at reducing this particular source of disturbance in labor-force participation. Additionally, almost half of all eighteen- to twenty-five-year-olds are going to school and thus making an investment that presumably will pay off in better future employment and earnings. A good many young adults, furthermore, do not have dependents and at the youngest ages may be living with their parents—some of them by necessity, not choice, to be sure. These factors tend to reduce the personal and social costs of unemployment in the young-adult cohort compared to its costs among older adults.

26. In general, few *selection* effects have been documented. We noted earlier in this chapter that youngsters with lower educational expectations appear to select into more intensive employment. We did not find selection-to-work effects based on self-reliance or work orientation in our Orange County study. In several studies summarized by Freeman and Wise (1979), however, selection effects of "motivation," an unmeasured construct, are noted. Also, few positive *causal* effects of early work experience have been demonstrated on variables that differentiate young adults with better and worse employment histories; in our study we found that high-school year employment increased self-reliance among girls and work orientation for youngsters of both sexes, but led to an offsetting greater cynicism about the rewards of working.

27. It is not known whether family socioeconomic status or youngsters' academic ability may affect this and other outcome measures in the Mortimer and Finch study. As they found no effects of family social class and academic ability on selection into the labor force during high school, they did not control for these variables in subsequent analyses. However, it is still possible that family background and ability may have an impact on youngsters' educational ambitions and attainments.

Chapter 5. / *Improving the Adolescent Experience*

1. The evaluation form might begin with a section to be filled out by the employee. The youngster would enter his or her name; job title; the period covered by the ensuing evaluation; average weekly

hours of employment; hourly wages; and average total weekly earnings (for example, from wages and tips). The employee also would
enumerate the various tasks he or she performs as part of the job. This
information would be validated by the employer's or supervisor's
signature. The employer also would rate the young worker on specific
aspects of job performance. In light of the adolescent developmental
issues we have discussed and in light of employers' needs, we suggest
the following criteria for evaluation: absenteeism; punctuality; dependability with respect to performing assigned tasks; willingness to
accept additional responsibilities when asked; initiative; ability to
accept supervision, including criticism; cooperativeness with other
employees; social skills in dealing with customers or clients; mastery
of information or knowledge necessary for carrying out the job; appro-
priateness of employee behavior; interest shown in learning more
about the job or business; motivation to perform well on the job. As
noted in the text, ratings of below average, average, above average,
and far superior to most high-school students employed in the same
or similar jobs would be an appropriate standard of evaluation. Additionally, evaluators might be asked to rate how strongly, if at all, they
would recommend the employee for a similar job elsewhere, for a job
requiring a somewhat higher level of skill, and for a job requiring
somewhat more responsibility than the current job.

REFERENCES

American Council on Life Insurance. 1978. *Youth '78.* Washington, D.C.

Astin, Alexander. 1982. *The American freshman, 1966–1981: Some implications for educational policy and practice.* Paper prepared for the National Commission on Excellence in Education. Los Angeles: University of California (mimeo).

Auletta, Ken. 1982. *The Underclass.* New York: Random House.

Bachman, Jerald. 1983a. Premature affluence: Do high school students earn too much? *Economic Outlook USA:* Summer: 64–67.

―――. 1983b. Schooling as credential: Some suggestions for change. *International Review of Applied Psychology* 32: 347–60.

Bachman, Jerald; Lloyd Johnston; and Patrick M. O'Malley. 1981. Smoking, drinking and drug use among American high school students. *American Journal of Public Health* 71: 59–69.

Bakan, D. 1972. Adolescence in America: From idea to social fact. In J. Kagan and R. Coles, (Eds.), *Twelve to Sixteen: Early Adolescence,* pp. 73–89. New York: Norton.

Bandura, Albert. 1964. The stormy decade: Fact or fiction? *Psychology in the Schools* 1: 224–31.

Barenboim, Carl. 1981. The development of person perception in childhood and adolescence: From behavioral comparisons to psychological constructs to psychological comparisons. *Child Development* 52: 129–44.

Behn, William H.; Martin Carney; Michael A. Carter; Joyce C. Crain; and Henry M. Levin. 1974. School is bad; work is worse. *School Review* 82: 49–68.

Bourne, Edmund. 1978. The state of research on ego identity: A review and appraisal. Part I. *Journal of Youth and Adolescence* 7: 223–51.

Brenner, Marshall H. 1968. Use of high-school data to predict work performance. *Journal of Applied Psychology* 52: 29–30.

Cain, Glenn. 1982. Married women in the labor force. In L. G. Reynolds; S. H. Masters; and C. H. Moser (Eds.). *Readings in Labor Economics and Labor Relations*. Englewood Cliffs, N.J.: Prentice-Hall.

Caplan, Robert. 1971. Organizational stress and individual strain: A social-psychological study of risk factors in coronary heart disease among administrators, engineers, and scientists. Ann Arbor, Michigan: Unpublished doctoral dissertation, University of Michigan.

Carnegie Commission on Policy Studies in Higher Education. 1980. *Giving Youth a Better Chance*. San Francisco: Jossey-Bass.

Cloward, R. A., and Lloyd Ohlin. 1960. *Delinquency and Opportunity: A Theory of Delinquent Gangs*. New York: Free Press.

Coleman, James. 1961. *The Adolescent Society*. New York: Free Press.

———. 1972, February 5. The children have outgrown the schools. *Psychology Today:* 72.

Conrad, David, and Diane Hedin. 1981. *National Assessment of Experiential Education: A Final Report.* St. Paul, Minn.: Center for Youth Development and Research, University of Minnesota.

Crane, R. T. 1911. *The Futility of Higher Schooling: An Address to College Students.* Chicago: A. C. McClurg & Company.

Csikszentmihalyi, Mihaly, and Reed Larson. 1984. *Being Adolescent.* New York: Basic Books.

D'Amico, Ronald. 1984. Does working in high school impair academic progress? *Sociology of Education* 57: 157–64.

Danzig, Richard, and Peter Szanton. 1986. *National Service: What Would It Mean?* Lexington, Mass.: D. C. Heath.

Dorfman, John. April 26, 1982. "Did inflation whip you?" *Forbes* 129: 96.

Douvan, Elizabeth, and Joseph Adelson. 1966. *The Adolescent Experience.* New York: Wiley.

Elkind, David. 1981. *The Hurried Child.* New York: Addison-Wesley.

Erikson, Erik H. 1959. Identity and the life cycle. *Psychological Issues* 1: 1–171.

———. 1968. *Identity: Youth and Crisis.* New York: Norton.

Farrar, Eleanor, John DeSanctis, and Peter Cowden. *The Walls Within: Work, Experience, and School Reform.* Cambridge, Mass.: Huron Institute.

Finch, Michael D., and Jeylan T. Mortimer. 1985. Adolescent work hours and the process of achievement. In Alan C. Kerchoff (Ed.), *Research in Sociology of Education* 5: 171–96.

Freeman, Richard B., and David A. Wise. 1979. *Summary Report: Youth Unemployment.* Washington, D.C.: National Bureau of Economic Research.

Friedenberg, Edgar. 1959. *The Vanishing Adolescent.* Boston: Beacon Press.

Fromm, Eric. 1947. *Man for Himself: An Inquiry into the Psychology of Ethics.* New York: Rinehart, 1947.

Fullerton, Kemper. 1959. "Calvinism and capitalism: An explanation of the Weber thesis. In Robert W. Green (Ed.), *Protestantism and Capitalism: The Weber Thesis and Its Critics,* pp. 6–20. Boston: D. C. Heath.

Gilbert, James. 1984. Mass Culture against the Family. Paper presented at the meeting of the Organization of American Historians, Los Angeles, California. Mimeo, Department of History, University of Maryland, College Park, Md.

Gillis, John R. 1981. *Youth and History.* New York: Academic Press.

Gintis, Herbert. 1971. Education, technology and the characteristics of worker productivity. *American Economic Review* 61: 266–79.

Ginzberg, Eli. 1977. The job problem. *Scientific American, 237:* 43–51.

Gottfredson, Denise C. 1982. *A test of a student-environment interaction hypothesis in a model of delinquency.* Unpublished manuscript, John Hopkins University, Center for Social Organization of Schools, Baltimore.

———. 1985. Youth employment, crime, and schooling: A longitudinal study of a national sample. *Developmental Psychology* 21: 419–32.

Greenberger, Ellen. 1983a. Children, families, and work. In N. Dickon Reppucci; Lois A. Weithorn; Edward P. Mulvey; and John Monahan (Eds.), *Mental Health, Law, and Children,* pp. 103–22. Beverly Hills, Calif.: Sage.

———. 1983b. A researcher in the policy arena. *American Psychologist* 38: 104–11.

————. 1984. Defining psychosocial maturity in adolescence. In P. Karoly and J. J. Steffen (Eds.), *Adolescent Behavior Disorders: Foundations and Contemporary Concerns*, pp. 3–39. Lexington, Mass.: D. C. Heath.

Greenberger, Ellen, and Lloyd Bond. 1976. User's Manual for the Psychosocial Maturity Inventory. Mimeo. Irvine, California: University of California.

Greenberger, Ellen; Ruthellen Josselson; Claramae Knerr; and Bruce Knerr. 1975. The measurement and structure of psychosocial maturity. *Journal of Youth and Adolescence* 4: 127–43.

Greenberger, Ellen, and Laurence Steinberg. 1981. The workplace as a context for the socialization of youth. *Journal of Youth and Adolescence* 10: 185–210.

————. 1982. Statement on proposed changes in child labor regulations. Hearings of the House Subcommittee on Labor Standards, Washington, July 28.

————. 1983. Sex differences in early labor force participation: Harbinger of things to come. *Social Forces* 62: 467–86.

Greenberger, Ellen; Laurence Steinberg; & Mary Ruggiero. 1982. A job is a job is a job . . . Or is it? Behavioral observations in the adolescent workplace. *Work and Occupations*, 9: 79–96.

Greenberger, Ellen, Laurence Steinberg; and Alan Vaux. 1981. Adolescents who work: Health and behavioral consequences of job stress. *Developmental Psychology*, 17: 691–703.

Greenberger, Ellen; Laurence Steinberg; Alan Vaux; and Sharon McAuliffe. 1980. Effects of part-time employment on family and peer relations. *Journal of Youth and Adolescence* 9: 189–202.

Grossman, Allyson S. 1981. Working mothers and their children. *Monthly Labor Review* 104, 49–54.

Hamilton, Stephen. 1981. Adolescents in community settings: What is to be learned? *Theory and Research in Social Education* 9: 23–38.

Hill, John P., and Wendy Palmquist. 1978. Social cognition and social relations in early adolescence. *International Journal of Behavioral Development, 1,* 1–36.

Hirschi, Travis. 1969. *Causes of Delinquency.* Berkeley: University of California Press.

Illich, Ivan. 1970. *Deschooling Society.* New York: Harper & Row.

Inkeles, Alex. 1968. Society, social structure, and child socialization. In J. A. Clausen (Ed.), *Socialization and Society*, pp. 72–127. Boston: Little, Brown.

Jencks, Christopher. 1972. *Inequality.* New York: Basic Books.

Johnson, Barbara L., and Elizabeth Waldman. 1981. Marital and family patterns of the labor force. *Monthly Labor Review* 194 (10): 36–38.

Johnston, Lloyd; Jerald Bachman; and Patrick O'Malley. 1982. *Monitoring the Future: Questionnaire Responses from the Nation's High School Seniors, 1981.* Ann Arbor, Michigan: Institute for Social Research.

Kahn, R., and R. Quinn. 1970. Role stress: A framework for analysis. In A. McLean (Ed.), *Mental Health and Work Organizations.* Chicago: Rand McNally.

Kandel, Denise, and Gerald Lesser. 1972. *Youth in Two Worlds.* San Francisco: Jossey-Bass.

Kandel, Denise (Ed.). 1978. *Longitudinal Research on Drug Use: Empirical Findings and Methodological Issues.* New York: Wiley.

Kasl, Stanislas. 1974. Work and mental health. In J. O'Toole (Ed.), *Work and the Quality of Life.* Cambridge, Mass.: The MIT Press.

Katz, Michael. 1975. *The People of Hamilton, Canada West: Family and Class in a Mid-nineteenth-Century City.* Cambridge, Mass.: Harvard University Press.

Kett, Joseph. 1977. *Rites of Passage: Adolescence in America, 1790 to the Present.* New York: Basic Books.

Kleiber, Douglas, and William Rickards. 1985. Leisure and recreation in adolescence: Limitation and potential. In Michael G. Wade (Ed.), *Constraints on Leisure*, pp. 289–317. Springfield, Ill.: Charles C Thomas.

Lasch, Christopher. 1979. *The Culture of Narcissism: American Life in an Age of Diminishing Expectations.* New York: Norton.

Lerner, Richard M., Michael Karson, Murray Meisels, and John R. Knapp. 1975. Actual and perceived attitudes of late adolescents and their parents: The phenomenon of the generation gaps. *Journal of Genetic Psychology* 126: 195–207.

Levitan, Sar A., and Richard S. Belous. September 1981. Working wives and mothers: What happens to family life? *Monthly Labor Review* 104: 26–30.

Lewin-Epstein, Noah. 1981. *Youth Employment During High School.* Washington: National Center for Education Statistics.

Loevinger, Jane. 1976. *Ego Development.* San Francisco: Jossey-Bass.

Lumpkin, Katharine DuPre, and Dorothy Wolff Douglas. 1937. *Child Workers in America.* New York: International Publishers.

Macdonald, Dwight. 22 November 1958. Profiles: A caste, a culture. *The New Yorker* 34.

McNeil, Linda. 1984. *Lowering Expectations: The Impact of Student Employment on Classroom Knowledge*. Madison, Wis.: Wisconsin Center for Education Research.

Mangum, G., and J. Walsh. 1978. *Employment and Training Programs for Youth: What Works Best for Whom?* Washington: U.S. Department of Labor.

Manning, David L. 11 March 1980. Inflation, education, and the after-school job. *The Wall Street Journal*, 24.

Manpower Demonstration Research Corporation. 1980. *The Quality of Work in the Youth Incentive Entitlement Pilot Project*. New York: Manpower Demonstration Research Corporation.

Markham, Edwin, Benjamin B. Lindsey, and George Creel. 1914. *Children in Bondage*. New York: Hearst's International Library.

Mead, Margaret. 1928. *The Coming of Age in Samoa*. New York: Morrow.

Minnesota Law Review. Child labor laws—time to grow up. 1975. *Minnesota Law Review* 59: 575–608.

Mnookin, R. 1978. *Child, Family and State: Cases and Materials on Children and the Law*. Boston: Little, Brown.

Modell, John; Frank Furstenberg, Jr.; and Theodore Hershberg. 1976. Social change and transitions to adulthood in historical perspective. *Journal of Family History* 1: 7–32.

Mortimer, Jeylan T., and Michael D. Finch. In press. The effects of part-time work on adolescent self-concept and achievement. In K. Borman and J. Reisman (Eds.), *Becoming a Worker*. Norwood, New Jersey: Ablex.

Myerhoff, H. L., and B. G. Myerhoff, 1964. Field observations of middle class "gangs." *Social Forces* 42: 328–36.

National Association of Secondary School Principals. 1974. *The mood of American youth*. Reston, Va.: National Association of Secondary School Principals.

National Center for Education Statistics. November 1982. *Bulletin*. Washington, D.C.: U.S. Department of Education.

National Commission on Excellence in Education. 1983. *A nation at risk: The imperative for educational reform*. Washington, D.C.: U.S. Department of Education.

National Commission on Youth. 1980. *The Transition of Youth to Adulthood: A Bridge Too Long*. Boulder, Colo.: Westview Press.

National Panel on High School and Adolescent Education. 1976. *The Education of Adolescents.* Washington, D.C.: U.S. Government Printing Office.

Newmann, Fred, and Robert Rutter. 1983. *The Effects of High-School Community Service Programs on Students' Social Development.* Final Report to the National Institute of Education. Madison, Wis.: Center for Education Research, University of Wisconsin.

Office of the President. 1981. *Economic Report of the President.* Transmitted to the Congress, February 1981. Washington, D.C.: U.S. Government Printing Office.

Office of the President. 1979. *Employment and Training Report of the President.* Washington, D.C.: U.S. Government Printing Office.

Office of the President. 1981. *Employment and Training Report of the President.* Washington, D.C.: U.S. Government Printing Office.

Office of the President. 1982. *Employment and Training Report of the President.* Washington, D.C.: U.S. Government Printing Office.

Otto, Luther, and David Alwin. 1977. Athletics, aspiration, and attainments. *Sociology of Education* 42: 102–13.

Owens, Thomas. 1982. Experience-based carreer education: Summary and implications of research and evaluation findings. *Children and Youth Services Review,* 4: 77–91.

President's Science Advisory Committee, Panel on Youth. 1973. *Youth: Transition to Adulthood.* Chicago: University of Chicago Press.

Poulton, E. 1978. Blue-collar stressors. In C. Cooper and R. Payne (Eds.) *Stress at Work.* New York: Wiley.

Reubens, Beatrice G.; John A. C. Harrison; and Kalman Rupp. 1981. *The Youth Labor Force 1945–1995: A Cross-National Analysis.* Totowa, NJ: Allanheld, Osmun, and Co.

Riesman, David. 1950. *The Lonely Crowd: A Study of the Changing American Character.* New Haven: Yale University Press.

Rothbart, Dean. March 2, 1981. Allowances stay flat, candy rises— and kids lose their innocence. *The Wall Street Journal,* 1.

Ruggiero, Mary. 1984. Work as an impetus to delinquency: An examination of theoretical and empirical connections. Unpublished doctoral dissertation, University of California, Irvine.

Ruggiero, Mary, & Laurence D. Steinberg. 1981. The empirical study of teenage work: A behavioral code for the assessment of adolescent job environments. *Journal of Vocational Behavior* 19: 163–74.

Ruggiero, Mary; Ellen Greenberger; and Laurence Steinberg. 1982. Occupational deviance among first-time workers. *Youth and Society* 13: 423–48.

Sachs, Carolyn E. 1983. *The Invisible Farmers: Women in Agricultural Production.* Totowa, N.J.: Rowman & Allanheld.

Savage, David G. November 27, 1983. Japanese Math Lead Growing Study Finds. *Los Angeles Times,* 1.

Selman, Robert. 1980. *The Growth of Interpersonal Understanding: Developmental and Clinical Analyses.* New York: Academic Press.

Sewell, William; Robert A. Hauser, and David L. Featherman. 1976. *Schooling and Achievement in American Society.* New York: Academic Press.

Shannon, Lee W. 1982. *Assessing the Relationship of Adult Criminal Careers to Juvenile Careers.* Washington, D.C.: U.S. Department of Justice. (Microfiche No. NCJ 77744, available from the National Juvenile Justice Clearinghouse of the National Criminal Justice Reference Service, Washington, D.C.).

Silberman, Charles. 1970. *Crisis in the Classroom.* New York: Random House.

Smelser, Neil. 1959. *Social Change in the Industrial Revolution; An Application of Theory to the British Cotton Industry.* Chicago: University of Chicago Press.

Spacks, Patricia. 1981. *The Adolescent Idea.* New York: Basic Books.

Special Task Force to the Secretary of Health, Education, and Welfare. 1973. *Work in America.* Cambridge, Mass.: The MIT Press.

Statistical Abstract of the United States. 1981. Washington, D.C.: U.S. Government Printing Office.

Steinberg, Laurence. 1982. Jumping off the work experience bandwagon. *Journal of Youth and Adolescence* 11: 183–205.

Steinberg, Laurence; Ellen Greenberger; Maryann Jacobi; and Laurie Garduque. 1981. Early work experience: A partial antidote for adolescent egocentrism. *Journal of Youth and Adolescence* 10: 141–57.

Steinberg, Laurence; Ellen Greenberger; Alan Vaux; and Mary Ruggiero. 1981. Effects of early work experience on adolescent occupational socialization. *Youth and Society* 12: 403–22.

Steinberg, Laurence; Ellen Greenberger; Laurie Garduque; and Sharon McAuliffe. 1982. High-school students in the labor force: Some costs and benefits to schooling and learning. *Educational Evaluation and Policy Analysis* 4: 363–72.

Steinberg, Laurence; Ellen Greenberger; Laurie Garduque; Mary Ruggiero; and Alan Vaux. 1982. Effects of working on adolescent development. *Developmental Psychology*, 18: 385–95.

Stephens, William. 1979. *Our Children Should Be Working*. Springfield, Ill.: Charles C Thomas.

Taggart, Robert. 1980. Lessons from program experience. In B. Linder and R. Taggart (Eds.), *A Review of Youth Employment Problems, Programs, and Policies, Volume 1: The Youth Employment Problem: Causes and Dimensions*. Washington: The Vice-President's Task Force on Youth Employment.

Tanner, D. 1972. *Secondary Education*. New York: Macmillan.

Timpane, M.; S. Abramowitz; S. Bobrow; and A. Pascal. 1976. *Youth Policy in Transition*. Santa Monica, Calif.: Rand Corporation.

Turiel, Eliot. 1978. The development of concepts of social structure: Social convention. In J. Glick and K. A. Clarke-Stewart (Eds.), *The Development of Social Understanding*, pp. 25–107. New York: Gardner.

U.S. Bureau of the Census. 1940. *Sixteenth Census of the United States*. Characteristics of the Population. Washington: U.S. Department of Commerce.

U.S. Bureau of the Census. 1950. *Seventeenth Census of the United States*. Characteristics of the Population. Washington: U.S. Department of Commerce.

U.S. Bureau of the Census. 1960. *Eighteenth Census of the United States*. Characteristics of the Population. Washington: U.S. Department of Commerce.

U.S. Bureau of the Census. 1970. *Nineteenth Census of the United States*. Characteristics of the Population. Washington: U.S. Department of Commerce.

U.S. Bureau of the Census. 1980. *Twentieth Census of the United States*. Characteristics of the Population. Washington: U.S. Department of Commerce.

Vaux, Alan. 1981. Adolescent life stress, work stress, and social support: Psychological, somatic, and behavioral consequences. Unpublished doctoral dissertation, University of California, Irvine.

Vulcan, Beatrice. 1968. American social policy toward youth and youth unemployment. In M. Herman; S. Sadofsky, and B. Rosenberg (Eds.), *Work, Youth, and Unemployment.* New York: Thomas Y. Crowell.

White, Robert. 1959. Motivation reconsidered: The concept of competence. *Psychological Review* 66: 297–333.

Whiting, Beatrice. 1984. Colloquium on Learning and Work. School of Social Sciences, University of California, Irvine.

Williams, Robin. 1970. *American Society: A Sociological Analysis,* 3rd ed. New York: Knopf.

Winn, Marie. 1984. *Children Without Childhood.* New York: Penguin.

Wrigley, J. 1986. Compulsory school laws: A dilemma with a history. In J. Simon and D. Stipek (Eds.), *Reconsidering Compulsory Schooling for Adolescents: Studies in Social Science, Education, and Law.* New York: Academic Press.

Yankelovich, Daniel. 1973. *The Changing Values on Campus.* New York: Washington Square Press.

———. 1974. *The New Morality: A Profile of American Youth in the 70's.* New York: McGraw-Hill.

———. 1981. *New Rules.* New York: Random House.

Yovovich, B. G. 1982, August 2. A game of hide-and-seek. *Advertising Age,* p. 17.

INDEX

Health, impact of job stress on, 136–40

Hedin, Diane, 220, 221

High School and Beyond survey (1981), 16–18, 21, 62, 63, 73, 76, 115, 116, 121, 149, 240–41, 243*n*1, 245*n*11

High school, *see* School

High-school dropouts, 150, 152–53

Higher education, *see* Postsecondary education

Hill, John P., 184

Hirschi, Travis, 125

Hispanics: labor-force participation of, 19, 20

Homework: reduced assignment of, 120, 189, 191, 192; time commitment to, 121–23, 136

Hurried Child, The (Elkind), 174, 187

Identity: Youth and Crisis (Erikson), 166

Identity development, 7, 9, 167–73, 209; autonomy and, 175; in extracurricular activities, 219; social connectedness and, 210

Identity foreclosure, 169, 171, 185, 186

Illich, Ivan, 194

Independence, *see* Autonomy

Industrialization: and disappearance of apprenticeships, 54; and economic change, 69; and role discontinuity, 162; and transition to adulthood, 165; and urbanization, 83–84

Inflation, 16, 28; women in labor force and, 35, 36

Initiative, 91, 93, 95

Inkeles, Alex, 176

Interdependence, experience of, 101–2; *see also* Cooperation

Intergenerational contact, 51, 198–200; activities promoting, 209, 211; decline of, 79–83; lack of, *see* Age segregation; limitations of, 86–88; methods for increasing, 230; in traditional societies, 160–61

Interpersonal aggression, 126

Interpersonal skills, development of, 217–18

"Inward-lookingness," of youth culture, 198

Irregular work hours, 25–26

It's a Wonderful Life (film), 47–50, 67

Jacobi, Maryann, 112

Japan: education in, 23; labor force participation in, 23

Jencks, Christopher, 182

Job-evaluation forms, 232–33, 253*n*1

Job rotation, 228–29

Job skills, on-the-job learning of, 65, 108–9; settings for learning, 44

Job stress, 130, 134, 250*n*15, 251*n*19, *n*20; adult, 183; health and behavioral problems related to, 136–40; occupational deviance and, 146, 147

Johnston, Lloyd, 8, 16, 30, 35, 74, 103, 132, 141, 151*n*18

Juvenile Justice and Delinquency Prevention, U.S. Office of, 126

Kahn, R., 136

Kandel, Denise, 4, 181